EVERYDAY FASHIONS OF
THE FORTIES
As Pictured in Sears Catalogs

Edited and with an Introduction by

JoAnne Olian

Curator, Costume Collection
Museum of the City of New York

Dover Publications, Inc.
New York

Copyright © 1992 by Dover Publications, Inc.
All rights reserved under Pan American and International Copyright Conventions.

Published in Canada by General Publishing Company, Ltd., 30 Lesmill Road, Don Mills, Toronto, Ontario.
Published in the United Kingdom by Constable and Company, Ltd., 3 The Lanchesters, 162–164 Fulham Palace Road, London W6 9ER.

Everyday Fashions of the Forties as Pictured in Sears Catalogs is a new work, first published by Dover Publications, Inc., in 1992.

Manufactured in the United States of America
Dover Publications, Inc., 31 East 2nd Street, Mineola, N.Y. 11501

Library of Congress Cataloging-in-Publication Data

Everyday fashions of the forties as pictured in Sears catalogs / edited and with an introduction by JoAnne Olian.
    p.   cm.
  ISBN 0-486-26918-3 (pbk.)
  1. Costume—United States—History—20th century. 2. Fashion—Company—Catalogs. I. Olian, JoAnne.
GT615.E9 1992
391′.00973′09044—dc20
                                                     91-42700
                                                         CIP

Introduction

The sense of being perfectly well-dressed gives a feeling of
inner tranquility which religion is powerless to bestow.
Ralph Waldo Emerson, *Journal,* 1870

The high quality and spirited style of America's clothing, at
every price level, is one of the hallmarks of our society. Long
before the ready-to-wear industry was introduced in Eu-
rope, it was flourishing on American soil, thanks in large
measure to the genius of nineteenth-century entrepreneurs
who took advantage of rapid improvements in technology
and manufacturing methods to create attractive, well-
made, affordable mass-produced clothing.

"We are a clothes-crazy people—. . . we boast that our
shop-girls look as attractive as our social butterflies, that our
jerk-water towns tilt their hats at the same angle as our big
cities; we're even a little smug about being called, as we
frequently are, the best-dressed women in the world,"
observed *Vogue* in 1938:

> Actually, it isn't so much that we are the best-dressed—it is
> that *more* of us are well dressed. A handful of top-flight
> Frenchwomen easily outstrip us in creating and wearing
> clothes, but collectively, en masse, our 40,000,000 adult
> females are better dressed, more fashion-conscious than
> any others on the face of the earth.
>
> But, you say, these are commonplaces. And so they are,
> the commonplaces of mass production and mass distribu-
> tion; the ordinary week-day tale of great businesses that
> cater to the great mass of American women; of a nation that
> has grown strong because it has believed that commonplace
> needs were important. Perhaps the founding fathers would
> be surprised if they should wake to-day, to see our literal
> interpretation of their theories, to see a democracy of gov-
> ernment achieve also the only democracy of fashion in the
> world. They might be surprised, but we do not believe that
> they would be displeased.

Undoubtedly, the first incarnation of the "democracy of
fashion" was the Gibson Girl, who personified the American ideal of radiantly healthy femininity. Her wardrobe
consisted chiefly of ready-made, mass-produced apparel
worn without apology and with a great deal of panache by
millions of American women of every economic level for an
infinite variety of occasions. Her signature, the shirtwaist
blouse, an important component in the democratization of
fashion, was so popular that in 1905 the Sears catalog featured 150 models, ranging in price from one of lawn at $.39
to a delicate silk taffeta at $6.95. The embodiment of our
national style, the handsome Gibson Girl in her sprightly
shirtwaist and skirt was dressed in the earliest example of

sportswear. Invented in America, this comfortable, casual
way of dressing, unlike Parisian "dressmaker" fashion, addressed the specific requirements of American life. The
Gibson Girl's direct descendants can be found in the pages
of the Sears, Roebuck catalog, whose clean-cut models,
dressed in attractive, well-fitting, uncomplicated clothes,
present a healthy, animated appearance.

The wide range of garments offered in the catalog is a
chronicle of Sears's vast numbers of customers, living in
diverse climates and circumstances from coast to coast. A
picture story in 1941 featured "two good Sears" families.
The Gees were a farm family whose son hoped for a 4-H
club ribbon at the county fair while his sister fed the family
flock of hens and played schoolteacher to her dolls. Mrs.
Gee, pictured modeling a new Sears dress for her husband,
had just put up nearly 400 quarts of fruit and vegetables for
the winter. The Bollingers lived in a small town where Mr.
Bollinger worked the night shift at the mill and his wife
served as treasurer of the P.T.A. For recreation they played
bridge, their daughter was a cheerleader at Calumet High
and their son raced on ball-bearing roller skates. Both
women were the purchasing agents for their families and
planned their expenditures carefully. When admiring
friends wondered how they managed to dress so well, Mrs.
Bollinger, "with frankness born of gratitude," would bring
out the "Big Book" and lay it in their laps.

To today's sophisticated eyes, the Geeses' milking chores,
piano practice and Sunday dinner, and the Bollingers'
church attendance on Sundays, their daughter's double
dates and fudge-making depict a cliché-ridden, Norman
Rockwell America, and it was, even then, an idealized por-
trayal of life on the threshold of World War II. The realities
can be deduced from the 1940 census, which revealed that
only one out of five Americans owned a car, one in seven had
a telephone and a mere 15 percent of the college-age population attended college. One quarter of America's homes
still had neither a refrigerator nor an icebox, 60 percent
lacked central heat and three out of four farmhouses were
lit with kerosene lamps. In a 1941 profile of a typical catalog
customer, Sears recounted the red-letter day when power
lines reached their Minnesota farmhouse: "First on their
list of 'musts,' of course, was a centrifugal pump for running
water. Then came the electric range. And as the months
went by, other conveniences were added: vacuum cleaner,
toaster, iron, radio and clock." In addition, by using a Sears
electric cream separator and a Sears motor to power the
fanning mill and tool grinder, all from the "Nation's Wish
Book," they were able to save precious time and labor.

The merchandise advertised in the catalogs was selected in direct response to Sears customers' actual needs and desires. Hence, their pages provide an unparalleled view of the social and economic changes taking place in the 1940s. Even in the remotest farmhouse the book was avidly perused by women wanting to look their best and aware of the latest styles, choosing from clothes photographed on the same high-fashion models seen in *Vogue* and *Harper's Bazaar*. However, Sears layouts were more straightforward and less glamorous, with an emphasis on clarity and detail. With garment industry copyists capable of turning out versions of current Paris and New York fashion almost instantaneously, Sears customers were able to dress as fashionably as urban women.

Five size ranges were available, from size 9 for juniors to size 57 for "larger women" who could buy garments "scientifically designed to slenderize from neck to knee." The flirtatious young juniors, the darlings of the catalog, whose fashions were selected by a male "jury," set the style for their high-school and grade-school sisters. Clothes were made in sizes for teens, big and little girls and sometimes even in identical styles for mothers and daughters. The 1940s classics—the camel's hair boy coat, the reversible raincoat, twin shetland sweater sets, the shirtwaist dress, saddle shoes and the prized velvet-collared Chesterfield coat that even won a Coty award in 1943—were suitable for women of practically every age and size, starting with toddlers and excluding only the "gracious lady," as the silver-haired, grandmotherly, large-size woman was euphemistically termed.

Steadily increasing numbers of sportswear pages featured slacks. Originating in California, as befitting the informality of the West Coast lifestyle, they enjoyed great popularity for work as well as recreation. Denim, previously confined to men's overalls, appeared in playclothes for women and girls, perhaps through the influence of New York's Best & Company, long renowned for its casual clothes, whose vice president, Mary Lewis, became Sears's fashion director in 1943. Hollywood's influence is apparent in the square-shouldered suits created by Adrian for Joan Crawford, as well as romantic evening gowns and picture hats inspired by *Gone With the Wind*, released in 1939. Girls' hats were modeled by juvenile screen stars Deanna Durbin and Shirley Temple, while the ubiquitous turban owed its exotic appeal to Carmen Miranda and Dorothy Lamour. Even the "larger woman" could choose a Marie Dressler ensemble designed especially for her.

In the 1940s the catalog held a mirror up to life dominated overwhelmingly by the ordeal of World War II. The years immediately preceding America's entry into the war were marked by a turning inward, manifested in a dawning appreciation of native traditions and culture. Aaron Copland and Ferde Grofé interpreted America musically, Agnes deMille and Martha Graham looked to the landscape for inspiration as did an entire generation of painters including Edward Hopper, Thomas Hart Benton, John Steuart Curry and Grant Wood. A strong Latin American craze was evident in the popularity of the rumba and the conga, while an unprecedented Mexican exhibition was held in 1940 at the

Museum of Modern Art, followed by an American Indian show in 1941.

As Kate Smith belted out "God Bless America," Sears captured the prevailing mood in sailor dresses, red, white and blue outfits and captions such as, "It's the American Way . . . to Live in a Dress with Jacket," and the "Miss America" polo coat. A cotton skirt in a tropical print was a "sunny California fashion" and a two-piece playsuit featured "California styling in the Season's most famous print," a "Hawaiian-inspired design." Shoes were huaraches "inspired by Mexico," the Moc-inette, "Frontier Fashion . . . fringed like an Indian's moccasin" and the "cactus country style" tooled leather with "all the tang and dash of the romantic West."

With the fall of France in 1940, American fashion abruptly found itself dependent on its own resources. Not only were there no Paris styles to copy, but, as shipping was diverted to war goods, such items as French perfumes and Swiss watches ceased to be available. In 1941, the government took over all remaining stocks of raw silk, necessitating the substitution of other fibers, chiefly rayon, for dresses. In 1942 Sears offered a domestic rayon raincoat for women to replace the imported silk they could no longer obtain. However, rayon was soon in short supply for civilian use as it, too, was needed in the war effort. Nylon hosiery, introduced in the 1940 catalog, vanished three years later. In 1942, the War Production Board placed severe restrictions on the use of wool, dyestuffs and the amount of yardage that could be used in garments. Sears and *Vogue*, displaying a marked similarity, editorialized regarding the need to buy quality and to dress conservatively, while Stanley Marcus, apparel consultant to the War Production Board, told designers it was their patriotic duty to devise clothing that would remain fashionable for several seasons, since the materials and labor that formerly helped to create obsolescence and consumerism were crucial to the manufacture of war goods. However, this was not meant to discourage buying completely. As *Vogue* explained in February 1942:

Many a woman with the best intentions in the world thinks she is doing her bit, making a noble sacrifice, by refusing to buy any new clothes during the duration. But so complex is our economic life that this very act of self-denial may work injury to the delicately adjusted gears which must continue to mesh if that great machine is to continue to function, if that great machine is to swing into the mightiest armaments production efforts of all time.

Arms and munitions, boats and planes are made by workers, who are paid in the money that comes from defense bonds and taxes. A sizable part of these taxes comes from the clothing industry—in peacetime, the second largest of our country.

The makers of fashionable shoes and hats, gloves and bags, of dresses and coats and suits—all these makers are operating with full government approval. Whatever is on sale in a shop is there to be bought, with the Government's full permission. Refusal to buy only helps to dislocate the public economy.

The operative word was "challenge." Government, press, retailers and Sears called on the American designer to create with ingenuity within the restrictions imposed on textiles, yardage and the lack of rubber and metal. In adherence to regulation L-85 mandated by the War Production Board, resourceful designers made sporty young suits with short, narrow skirts and jackets not exceeding 25 inches in length.

One third of the female population went to work, replacing men in factories or joining the diminished number of male civilians, whose square-shouldered suits were minus vests and pocket flaps, and whose trousers had lost both pleats and cuffs to L-85. Sears praised the American housewife for meeting the challenge on the home front, where, with the help of *McCall's* patterns, she performed feats of magic on her Sears sewing machine, transforming cast-off clothing into usable garments for her children. Lauding her for "keeping her family healthy and all its working members fit and efficient," Sears claimed, "No war job is more important," while saluting the American farmer for the "generalship it takes to run a farm short of hands, of equipment, of everything but grit and the will to do!" (Fall/Winter 1943–44).

In spite of war-imposed shortages and hardships, and "sorry, not available," stamped with increasing frequency over items in Sears wartime catalogs, the smiles of the clean-cut American women modeling in its pages never faltered. Wearing cotton stockings or leg makeup and rationed leather shoes, they took Sears's advice and saved their treasured service-weight rayon stockings for "furlough dates," conserving gasoline by walking in comfortable low heels or wedgies. They wore slacks for comfort and warmth even when pregnant. Wartime weddings and a rising birthrate (averaging a yearly increase of 29.6 percent for the decade) occasioned additional pages of maternity ensembles and baby clothes in the forties' catalogs, in direct contrast to the absence of long formal gowns after 1942. The 1944 jewelry pages even offered a 3½-carat emerald-cut diamond engagement ring for $4,900.

Exhortations to buy good-quality merchandise and to care for it were common to high fashion and mail order. *Vogue*, *Harper's Bazaar* and Sears's Mary Lewis, introducing herself in 1943, all stressed classic clothing as a way to remain in fashion for several seasons, echoed by articles in women's magazines demonstrating the proper way to care for apparel.

This emphasis on conservatism resulted in few perceptible fashion changes between 1941 and 1946. The essential contradiction between "conservative" and "fashion" was addressed by The Fashion Group in 1942:

It is innocent to think that ingenuity on the part of our designers and producers can surmount every shortage and triumph over every curtailment. Fashion will not be "as usual," any more than life, business, transportation, or taxes. They face a two-fold responsibility. This industry has existed upon the very nature of change, and now change is limited . . . not only by Government Orders . . . not only by diminishing supplies . . . but by the need to avoid obsolescence and waste at all costs. Yet in the face of all this it is their job to keep the flame of creative ability bright, and to keep alive a respect for all we mean by quality.

Classic sportswear as it was worn on college campuses was a way of dressing that somehow managed to reconcile "conservative" and "fashion." Sold initially in department-store college shops in the thirties, its popularity inspired the launching of *Mademoiselle*, the first magazine to address the burgeoning market of young college and career women. Heavily indebted to men's British-style sportswear, requisites included the "Brooks Brothers" Shetland sweater, almost anything of menswear flannel, especially slacks and pleated skirts, fly-front mannish gabardine raincoats, double-breasted camel's-hair polo coats, tailored suits and balmacaans in rugged tweeds, brown-and-white spectator pumps and saddle shoes. Instead of watered-down copies of the French couture, style originating on American campuses enabled students and secretaries to look sporty and fashionable. Separates, sportswear components that could be combined in numerous ways to create outfits that totaled more than the sum of the parts, formed the basis for much of the "college" look amounting to 30 percent of the nation's apparel business by 1949, according to *Life* magazine. Photographed on attractive, outdoorsy-looking models, versions of these garments in every size range for all ages were featured throughout the decade.

Not until 1947, when Sears, including many items available for the first time since the war, published its largest spring catalog in 25 years, was there a pronounced difference in silhouette, with "flare," "fullness" and "soft curves" being promoted in outerwear, suits and dresses for women and girls of all sizes and ages. Sears copy read, "The new look is the long look," explaining, "Skirts are longer. Waistlines look longer. Fabrics are used lavishly." Sears "new look" was a direct result of the sensation created by French couturier Christian Dior. Dubbed the "New Look" by the fashion press, Dior's silhouette reestablished the supremacy of Paris and revolutionized the shape of fashion. Shoulders lost their padding and became rounded, as hips, newly rounded, were accentuated with pads, and waistlines were belted and cinched for even further definition, while mid-calf-length skirts swirled over rustling petticoats. A dramatic reaction to the severely man-tailored garb of the war years, the "New Look" was, in its extravagant use of fabric and curves, an expression of luxury and femininity inconceivable during the years of wartime austerity.

The first customers in Sears's catalog to adopt the "New Look" were fashion-conscious juniors, whose up-to-the-minute suits had short, nipped-in jackets, "bustle peplums" and full skirts. While misses' clothes were indeed longer, initially their skirts remained slim, shoulders were still squared, and waistlines and hips were barely emphasized. As Dior's silhouette gained acceptance in small-town America, its popular-priced translation acquired a marked resemblance to the charming shirtwaists and flared skirts of the Gibson Girl in a welcome revival of the romantic look, after years of maintaining an image of competence and assurance.

Nonetheless, as the "New Look" swept across the country, outcries against it reached a fever pitch. Women with good legs saw no reason to hide them in longer dresses, and men, equally anxious not to be deprived of this pleasurable sight, bombarded the press with letters of protest. A Texas housewife founded the "Little Below the Knee Club," which immediately acquired 1300 members in Dallas, while the rallying cry of the San Antonio chapter was, "The Alamo fell, but our hemlines will not." In less than a month the club could boast members in all 48 states, a Georgia legislator announced plans to introduce a bill banning long skirts, and cartoons and vaudeville skits tried to laugh the "New Look" out of existence. Despite all the vocal opposition and hoopla, women were ready for a change and the "New Look" was here to stay.

Clothes once again became dressy. The crisp, efficient angularity of wartime fashion was abandoned in favor of soft drapery and feminine curves. A rayon faille junior dress and jacket with a gold belt featured a 110-inch sweep of skirt and a sophisticated moire trimmed with real ermine tails measured 115 inches at its hem. Sequins, beads and nailheads, of newly available metals, trimmed dresses and soft "ballerina" suits. Tiers of ruffles edged girls' cotton dresses and rows of elastic thread shirred the abbreviated tops of bare-midriff playclothes with flaring skirts. Baby-doll and ballerina flat-heeled shoes complemented the new wide hemlines, with ankle-strap platform shoes worn with seamless nylon stockings the fashionable alternative.

Servicemen returning to civilian life wanted a new look, too. Weary of uniforms and uniformity, they favored suits with generous amounts of fabric in the drape of broad-shouldered jackets. Trousers sported cuffs, generous pleats and deep patch pockets. Sports coats and "loafer" jackets satisfied the desire for casual, comfortable apparel. Boys' knickers finally disappeared in favor of long pants as their clothing became identical to their fathers'.

Western-style ranch clothing and California beachwear enjoyed equal success with both sexes. Denim was firmly established as the sportswear preference for the entire family. By 1949 the cowboy influence prevailed, as Roy Rogers jeans and jackets, suspender dungarees for toddlers and rolled-up pedal pushers—the postwar suburban uniform for teens—dominated the pages of the catalog.

The decade ended on a note very different from that on which it had begun. As GI's returned, eager to get on with their interrupted lives, marriages reached record levels and women who had emerged from their homes retired to domesticity to raise families, surrounded by the latest labor-saving appliances.

Sears stood ready to supply the needs of this new life-style, complete with up-to-the-minute automatic washing machines and television sets, first advertised in 1949. Potential customers were cautioned that "Your distance from the station, your location in respect to hills, tall buildings, etc., are factors that limit the reception of television. This Silvertone Television Set will give you good reception if you live within 15–20 miles of the station."

In 1950 America was well on its way to becoming a country of ardent consumers. A well-dressed, fashion-conscious people, we were about to embark on an era in which technology, prosperity and communications would combine to create yet unimagined products for our comfort and enjoyment. Chemistry would develop synthetic fibers and textile finishes for apparel requiring minimal care. Sportswear in these new fabrics would remain the mainstay of wardrobes. Sears continued to maintain its time-honored tradition of providing Americans with well-made, affordable, attractive attire. A succinct comment by William C. Browning, a clothing manufacturer, a century earlier on the relationship between democracy and dress is a perfect definition of Sears's contribution to American society and might well have served as its credo

And if it be true . . . that the condition of a people is indicated by its clothing, America's place in the scale of civilized lands is a high one. We have provided not alone abundant clothing at a moderate cost for all classes and citizens but we have given them, at the same time the style and character in dress that is essential to the self-respect of a free, democratic people.

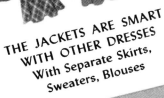

THESE STYLE TEAMS COME IN OTHER COLOR SCHEMES

THE JACKETS ARE SMART WITH OTHER DRESSES
With Separate Skirts, Sweaters, Blouses

It's the American Way . . . to Live in a
DRESS with JACKET

Use Sears Easy Payment Plan to Buy Them at This Low Price—See Page 11

$5.98 Complete

PLAIN JACKET . . . PLAID DRESS

A Good companions . . . the dress and jacket! All-occasion one-piece shirtwaist dress in our best quality Crown Tested Woven Plaid All Spun Rayon fabric. Crown zip placket. The beautifully fitting unlined cardigan jacket is our best quality plain colored All Wool Shetland.

Juniors' Size Range: 11, 13, 15, 17, 19.
Misses' Size Range: 12, 14, 16, 18, 20 only.
State size; see Size Scales on Page 42. Shipping weight, each, 2 pounds.
31 D 7321 M—Red and Green Plaid Dress; Plain Laurel Green Jacket.
31 D 7322 M—Brown and Green Plaid Dress; Plain Brown Jacket.
31 D 7323 M—Navy and Green Plaid Dress; Plain Navy Jacket . . . . Each Outfit, $5.98

The Scotty Cap comes in same color schemes as dress described above. Plain color All Wool Shetland, trimmed with plaid Spun Rayon; grosgrain streamers. **Colors:** Red and Green Plaid on Plain Laurel Green; Brown and Green Plaid on Plain Brown; Navy and Green Plaid on Plain Navy. Measure head; **state size, color.** Shpg. wt., 6 oz.
31 D 7455 M—Fits 21½ to 22½-in. headsize. 98c

PLAID JACKET . . . PLAIN DRESS

B Newest dress-and-jacket team in colors that blend perfectly. One-piece casual dress in our famous Crown Tested *Duo-Spun*, a rich wool-like fabric woven of finest quality Spun Rayon yarns. Crown zip placket. Man-tailored unlined tweed jacket of ⅔ Wool, ⅓ Rayon—correct weight to wear over dress, or as separate jacket.

Juniors' Size Range: 11, 13, 15, 17, 19.
Misses' Size Range: 12, 14, 16, 18, 20 only.
State size; see Size Scales on Page 42. Shipping weight, 2 pounds 4 ounces.
31 D 7318—Gold color Dress; Brown-and-Gold Plaid Jacket.
31 D 7319—Norse Blue Dress; Norse Blue-and-Wine Plaid Jacket.
31 D 7320—Henna Rust Dress; Green-and-Rust Plaid Jacket . . . . Each Outfit, $5.98

Measure Every Time You Order

—at bust, waist, hips, as directed on Page F in back of book. Then find your size in your size range. *Be sure* dress you pick comes in your range. Below are Size Ranges for dresses listed on these two pages.

Juniors' Size Range: 11, 13, 15, 17, 19.
—For Size Scale see Page 42.
Misses' Size Range: 12, 14, 16, 18, 20, 22.
—For Size Scale see Page 42.
Women's Size Range: 34, 36, 38, 40, 42.
—For Size Scale see Page 64.
Shorter Women's Size Range: 16½, 18½, 20½, 22½, 24½—For Size Scale see Page 64.

Send your order to Sears nearest Mail Order House and allow postage from there. Garments on these two pages will be sent from our New York Fashion Headquarters.

SEARS ◇ PAGE 345

NEWS FOR THE U.S.A.

The 1940 Edition of SEARS FAMOUS

Miss America POLO COAT

In Three All Wool Fabrics

Here's the Wonder Coat, *Miss America*, always in fashion, always appropriate, always in good taste. It's the coat that goes everywhere, anytime, becoming to everyone who puts it on! Master tailored to our specifications to stand up under the hardest wear. Winter warm in the stadium or on the campus, battling a blizzard or driving the car. Flattering double-breasted reefer lines, moulded through the body, flaring at the hem. Square shoulders, dashing wide revers, stitched slenderizing panel back. This new *Miss America* is the best yet!

Misses' Size Range: 12, 14, 16, 18, 20 only. See Size Scale, Page 20. Shipping weight, each, 5 lbs. 10 oz.

Our Best Quality Camel's Hair and Wool
50% super warm Camel's Hair, balance All Wool in a smooth soft weave. Earl-Glo Rayon lining guaranteed for life of coat. Warmly interlined. Colors: Polo Tan 604, Black or Henna Rust 645. Sizes above. State size and color.
17 D 5470 .... $12.98

Better Quality All Wool Fleece
All Wool Fleece in extra-warm diagonal weave. Earl-Glo lining guaranteed for the life of the coat. Warmly interlined. Colors: Navy Blue, Henna Rust 645, or Nuberry (Grape) Wine 514. Sizes above. State size and color.
17 D 5465 .... $9.98

Good Quality All Wool Fleece
All Wool diagonal weave, warm and sturdy. Rayon Taffeta lined, warmly interlined. Colors: Henna Rust 645, Skipper Blue 218, or Hockey Green 321. Sizes above. State size, color.
17 D 5460 .... $7.98

Send your order to Sears nearest Mail Order House and allow postage from there. Garments on these two pages will be sent direct from New York.

$12.98 Best Quality 50% Camel's Hair, 50% Wool

$9.98 Better Quality All Wool Fleece

$7.98 Good Quality All Wool Fleece

Own this famous coat—wear and enjoy it—while you're paying for it on Sears Easy Payment Plan. See Page 11 for details.

Young America
O.K.'S THESE

The hat that has won the heart of the co-ed. Soft, fluffy, brushed felt; gay feather, roll brim. **Lively Colors:** Bittersweet (see Page 4), Teal Blue 235, Gold 720, American Beauty 515, Kelly Green 321, Dark Brown 613. **Measure; state color.** Shpg. wt., 14 oz. **$1.00**
78 D 8980—Fits 21¼ to 21¾-in. headsize.
78 D 8981—Fits 22 to 22½-in. headsize.

That little tam you've wanted, made of good wool felt (not cloth) in soft fluffy finish. Stunning tall feather; adjustable headsize; self straps. Fits well. **Colors:** Signal Red 540, Bittersweet (see Page 4), Navy, Dark Brown 613. **Measure; state color.** Shpg. wt., 14 oz. **$1.00**
78 D 9130—Fits up to 22½ in.

Flattering with any hair-do. Wool body felt breton. Smart! **Colors:** Henna Rust 647 with Brown and Green ribbon trim; Burgundy Wine 514 with Wine, Deep Blue; Navy with Royal Blue, Wine; Laurel Green 313 with Green, Bittersweet. **Measure; state color.** Shpg. wt. 12 oz. **$1.00**
78 D 9060—Fits up to 22½ in.

Deanna Durbin's
OWN STYLE!
$1.79

When a young reigning movie star chooses a hat, you know it has style! Wool body felt with gay, multi-color stripes on the draped rayon band and streamers. New high crown; up or down brim. Deanna Durbin tag inside! **Colors:** Bittersweet (see Page 4), Navy, American Beauty 515, Teal Blue 235. **Measure; state color.** Shpg. wt., 14 oz.
78 D 9205 — Fits 21¼ to 21¾ in.
78 D 9206 — Fits 22 to 22½-in. headsize........$1.79

Color numbers refer to Color-Graph.

Good wool felt. Classic roll brim model. Shipping weight, 14 oz. **65¢**
78 D 9065—Fits 21¼ to 21¾-in. headsize.
78 D 9066—Fits 22 to 22½-in. headsize.
Colors: Henna Rust 647, Navy, Burgundy Wine 514, Kelly Green 321, Black. **Measure; state color.**

Fine fur felt. Better quality. A $2.00 value. Shipping weight, 14 oz. **$1.69**
78 D 8860—Fits 21¼ to 21¾-in. headsize.
78 D 8861—Fits 22 to 22½-in. headsize.

Girls love this bonnet with its new brim. Good body felt. **$1.00**
Colors: Royal Blue 218 with Navy grosgrain; Bittersweet (see Page 4) with Dark Green; Burgundy Wine 514, Deep Blue; Brown 613 with Rust. **Measure; state color.** Shpg. wt., 14 oz.
78 D 9025—Fits 21¼ to 22 in.

A veil accents the last minute smartness of this mushroom brim hat. Ribbon binding on brim match band and bow. Good body felt. Shirred elastic head band. **$1.00**
Colors: Burgundy Wine 514 with Deep Blue ribbon, Navy with Royal, Bittersweet (see Page 4) with Brown, Wintergreen 340 with Rust. **Measure; state color.** Shipping weight, 13 oz.
78 D 9170—Fits up to 22½ in.

Imported berets! Famous quality; made in France! What a grand bargain! Brushed all wool, closely knit with a thick felted finish. Nine stunning washable colors. Sizes for women, misses, children. **Colors:** Black, Brown 613, Wine 514, Dark Green 313, Navy, Red 508, Royal Blue 212, Beige 604, White. **Measure; state color.** Shpg. wt., 4 oz.; three, 8 oz. **35¢ Ea.**
78 D 7228—Fits 21¾ to 23 inches.
78 D 7229—Children's Size. Fits smaller heads. Each, 35c.......3 for $1.00

Young Miss America
For Age-Sizes 10 to 16

This coat, by actual count, is the most popular, best-beloved reefer style in the U. S. A. today. So well-liked that we offer it in three fabrics, three prices. So smart that you're one of the nation's best-dressed girls the minute you put it on.

Young Miss America's clean-cut shoulders are lightly padded. Double-breasted closing has eight big smoky-tone ocean pearl buttons. High-wide-and-handsome revers and two deep pockets. Eight-gore flared skirt has knife-edged press on front and back seams. *Age-Sizes:* 10, 12, 14, 16. *State age-size and color;* Size Scale at left. Shpg. wt., each, 3 lbs. 6 oz.

(F) 20% **Camel's Hair,** balance Wool; our best quality. Erl-Glo Rayon lining, guaranteed for the life of the coat.
17 E 7235—Polo Tan 208 or Navy Blue 728.................$8.98

(G) 55% **Wool Tweed,** balance Rayon and Cotton. Rayon Taffeta lined, guaranteed 2 seasons.
17 E 7233—Gray Mixture, Tan Mixture, Navy Blue Mixture.$6.98

(H) All Wool Shetland-type Tweed —good firm, durable quality. Rayon Taffeta lined, guaranteed for two seasons.
17 E 7234—Navy Blue 728 or Rose Wine 612............$5.98

(F) Camel's Hair and Wool $8.98

(G) Novelty Tweed $6.98

(H) Shetland Type Tweed $5.98

Prettiest Hats in Years! Flowers, Feathers, Feminine Frills,

New Brims, New Crowns, New Trims...These New 1940 Hats

Make Your Face a Picture!

Dramatic Fashions by Leading Designers Reproduced for You at Modest Prices

The Deauville "Wing-Clipper"

$2.98 The exact style, the same shape, the same new color schemes and rich effect as in the fabulously expensive original! Designed exclusively for Sears by a milliner so famous and clever she sets styles for all America! Newest postilion crown and curving brim. Fine quality rough straw braid; fine feathers; rayon veiling in snood effect.
Colors: White hat with Royal Blue and Red trim (shown in color on Pg. 8); Navy Blue hat and veil with White and Navy wings; Black hat with Royal Blue veil, Red wings. *Measure* (see Pg. 78); *state color.* Shpg. wt., 1 lb.
78 E 9420—Fits 21½ to 23 in.

The Deauville "Drama"

$3.95 Prettiest picture hat in years! Dips low over the brow, sweeps dramatically skyward in a line that's sheer flattery. Authentic copy of an expensive original designed expressly for Sears. Fine quality straw braid. Daisy cluster, rayon velvet ribbon ornament. Long cloud-drift rayon veiling you may arrange to suit yourself.
Colors: White hat with Fuchsia trim (shown in color on Page 6). Black hat with Pink trim, Navy Blue hat with White trim. *Measure; state color.* Shpg. wt., 1 lb. 8 oz.
78 E 9425—Fits 21¾ to 22¼ inch headsizes.
78 E 9426—Fits 22½ to 23 in.

The Deauville "Parader"

$2.98 Brings out all your best points! We know, because we tried it on 25 different women. New moulded oval shape in smart, rough straw braid—created for Sears by a foremost American milliner. Rayon veiling snood, flowers, and rayon velvet ribbon bow in eye-delighting color combinations.
Colors: Patriot Red with Chartreuse trim and Royal Blue veil (shown in color on Page 8); White with Royal Blue and Red trim; Navy Blue with Rose Coral trim; Black with Blue Violet and Fuchsia trim. *Measure headsize* (see Page 78); *state color.* Shpg. wt., 14 oz.
78 E 9430—Fits 21½ to 23 in.

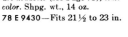

Fashion, always romantic, looks back
to the glamorous past for new designs for today...
This Spring, inspired by Southern Belles
and the Gay Nineties, you'll look your prettiest

Evening Gowns Are Sentimental

Filmy Net (seated)

$5.98 *"Romance."* Hear them murmur "Who is SHE?" as you make a dramatic entrance in this enchanting young gown. It might have stepped right out of a Southern belle's picture. Filmy, lustrous Rayon Net envelops you like a cloud, flaring below a slim waistline. Coquettish rayon velvet bows nestle in the flounces, outlined by frilly self-ruching like the lovely neckline. There's a swishy, matching color Rayon Taffeta slip, and hair-bow to match the bow trim on dress. *Colors:* Aqua Blue 570, Light Blue 616, Pink 550, all with contrasting bows; also White with White bows for weddings and graduations. *Misses' Size Range:* 12, 14, 16, 18, 20, 22. Length, about 59 in. *State size and color;* see Size Scale on Page 15.

31 E 9145—Shpg. wt., 1 lb. 8 oz.......$5.98

Crisp Rayon Taffeta

$2.98 *"Moonglow."* This appealing young dress of fine quality all Rayon Taffeta is shadow patterned in brocade-effect with a lovely flower design. The bodice is shirred to give flattering fullness, and a pointed set-in girdle makes your waistline look tiny. Taffeta pleats emphasize the heart-shaped neckline, the frivolous bows are Rayon Velvet. Full puffed sleeves are very new. Extra flowers to tuck in your hair come with the dress. *Colors:* Aqua 570, Royal Blue 824, Sunset Rose 556, all with contrasting trimming; also White with White trimming. *Misses' Size Range:* 12, 14, 16, 18, 20, 22. Length, about 59 inches. *State size and color;* see Size Scale on Page 15.

31 E 9150—Shpg. wt., 1 lb. 8 oz.......$2.98

Send your order to Sears nearest Mail Order House and allow postage from there. Dresses on these two pages sent direct from New York. Color numbers refer to Color-Graph following last index page in back of book.

NEW YORK-TO-YOU *Styles*

$2⁹⁸

We know what knowing Juniors wear—but definitely! We watch them doing the shag, gathering at luncheon time—these smart young New Yorkers who set fashions—we see them going to business, scurrying across the campus. So naturally we can send you, direct from New York, brisk, bright Junior Fashions.

(C) When the Scottish Queen of England went traveling in America, Fashion went to town on plaids, and here's one of the prettiest results —a darling dress of woven Spun Rayon plaid fabric with sunburst pleats in the skirt to prove swing is here to sway, and a sweet young collar to neatly top it. Tiny buttons down the front, narrow belt, new sleeves—wear it and your friends will say "You're looking smooth"— what more could any one want!
   Colors: Red, Navy or Laurel Green Plaids. Juniors' Size Range: 11, 13, 15, 17, 19. **Misses' Size Range:** 12, 14, 16, 18, 20 only. See Size Scale, Page 47. State size and color.
   31 D 7342—Shpg. wt., 1 lb. 8 oz......**$2.98**

(A) There's a smashing big bow on the plaid Celanese Taffeta blouse top of this gay gad-about, with simulated bolero, and skirt swirling wide from a "hold tight" waistline. Smart Juniors' figures look keen in such frocks, trim enough for school or business, dressy enough for a heavy date. The fabric is our best quality Celanese Rayon Pebble Crepe.
   Colors: Navy with Red Plaid or Black with Red Plaid. Juniors' Size Range: 11, 13, 15, 17, 19. **Misses' Size Range:** 12, 14, 16, 18, 20 only. Size Scale, Page 47. State size, color.
   31 D 7339—Shpg. wt., 1 lb. 6 oz......**$2.98**

(D) Who's got the smartest buttons in town? You have, if you have this dress, which is button trimmed all the way down the front and fastens up to a darling little collar of lace, detachable for keeping spic and span like the cuffs. Deliberately designed to make the most of a pretty slim figure with its nipped-in waistline, long, slim sleeves, square shoulders, swirling hem. Nicely tailored in Celanese Rayon Pebble Crepe.
   Colors: Navy, Nuberry Wine 514, Teal Blue 238, Black. Juniors' Size Range: 11, 13, 15, 17, 19. **Misses' Size Range:** 12, 14, 16, 18, 20 only. Size Scale, Pg. 47. State size, color.
   31 D 7336—Shpg. wt., 1 lb. 4 oz......**$2.98**

(B) Baby cardigan of Rayon and Cotton knit in three colors, sunburst pleated All Wool Flannel skirt. Crown zip placket. Smart two-some for town trotting or twilight twirling and (hooray!) you can wear skirt or sweater separately. Baby cardigan is a new fashion hit—the young crowd calls the costume "Terrific!"
   Colors: Navy, Henna Rust 645, Black, Laurel Green 313, each with sweater in harmonizing tri-colors. Juniors' Size Range: 11, 13, 15, 17, 19. **Misses' Size Range:** 12, 14, 16, 18, 20 only. **State size, color.**
   31 D 7333—Shpg. wt., 1 lb. 10 oz......**$2.98**

Have these new fashions on Sears Easy Payment Plan. See Page 11.

For the First Time in Mail Order History

Marie Dressler RAYON DRESSES...Sizes 36 to 53

$2⁴⁸ Each

EXCLUSIVE WITH SEARS!

Dresses Famous for Fit and Fashion at a Famous Sears Low Price

(A) Becoming in style, becoming in fabric, this nicely fitting dress of Paisley-type print in Crown Tested Spun Rayon Challis is the sort of Marie Dressler frock that a woman can fairly live in. Flared skirt, buttons and ric-rac on bodice.

Women's Size Range: 36, 38, 40, 42, 44. Size Scale, Page 76.

Stout Size Range: 43, 45, 47, 49, 51, 53. Size Scale below. **State size.** Shipping weight, 1 pound 4 ounces.
7 D 6806—Navy Blue Ground
7 D 6807—Medium Brown Ground
7 D 6808—Laurel Green Ground..**$2.48**

(B) Famous Marie Dressler dress of fine Crown Tested *Misti-spun* Rayon that resembles wool. Softly shirred at the shoulders. V neckline is outlined with detachable white.

Women's Size Range: 36, 38, 40, 42, 44. Size Scale, Page 76.

Stout Size Range: 43, 45, 47, 49, 51, 53. Size Scale below. **State size.** Shpg. wt., 1 lb. 2 oz.
7 D 6812—Teal Blue 238.
7 D 6814—Burgundy 514
7 D 6813—Black........**$2.48**

(C) Crown Tested Spun Rayon Challis in a neat tiny two-tone print, ideally suited to this smart shirtwaist dress. Soft, feminine details with the famous Marie Dressler fit and styling.

Women's Size Range: 36, 38, 40, 42, 44. Size Scale, Page 76.

Stout Size Range: 43, 45, 47, 49, 51, 53. Size Scale below. **State size.** Shpg. wt., 1 lb. 2 oz.
7 D 6809—Navy Blue Ground
7 D 6810—Henna Rust Ground. **$2.48**

Check your bust, waist and hip measurements with this scale and order size nearest them. Measure each time you order.

Stout Size Scale

Bust:	43	45	47	49	51	53
Waist:	39	41	43	45	47	49
Hips:	48	50	52	54	56	58
Length:	48	48	49	49	49	49

Build your order to $10—buy on Sears Easy Payment Plan. See Page 11.

MADE TO FIT

1. **Carefully proportioned** through bust and back.
2. **Hips** are cut to slenderize—to fit when you stand and when you sit.
3. **Armholes** are comfortably deep and well fitting.
4. **Waistlines** are designed to fit yours.
5. **Plackets** for smooth and slenderizing fit.
6. **2-Inch hem** on all dresses.

(D) This Marie Dressler dress → of Crown Tested Fine *Misti-spun* Rayon is a quick way to slenderize smartness! Softly draped bodice, shirred shoulders and slimly detailed skirt.

Women's Size Range: 36, 38, 40, 42, 44. Size Scale, Page 76.

Stout Size Range: 43, 45, 47, 49, 51, 53, Size Scale at left. **State size.** Shpg. wt., 1 lb. 2 oz.
7 D 6817—Laurel Green 313
7 D 6815—Navy Blue
7 D 6816—Black... **$2.48**

SEARS ◇ PAGE 77

The "News" in Knicker Suits

Sears Have a Complete Selection...Suits with 1 Knicker...Suits with 2 Knickers ...or Suits with 1 Knicker and 1 Longie...All Are Priced to Save You Money

This suit comes in a complete range of sizes to fit all boys from 8 to 17.

Boyville
Reg. U. S. Pat. Off.

Our Finest

$**7**⁵⁰
2-Pc. Suit

$**9**⁵⁰
3-Pc. Suit

- Choice All Wool fine suiting.
- Latest style diagonal weave with attractive overplaid.
- Available with 1 or 2 pairs of knickers.

Our Finest—For Longer Wear, Better Value

The "Boyville" label in a suit means our best in fabric, style, and tailoring details and choice quality, smooth finish all wool . . . popular diagonal weave with overplaid. Rich shades of Dark Blue or Brown. Double breasted coat has sports back, pleated patch pockets. High luster rayon lined. Full lined, full cut knickers with wool worsted knit bottoms. No vest. For an exceptional value, buy the suit with extra knickers—they practically double the life of this stylish suit.
All Sizes: 8 to 17. *State size.* Shipping weight, 3 pounds 3 ounces; with extra knickers, 4 pounds 3 ounces.

Coat and Knickers	Coat and 2 Pairs Knickers
40 E 2946—Dark Brown.....$7.50	40 E 2947—Dark Brown.....$9.50
40 E 2949—Dark Blue....... 7.50	40 E 2950—Dark Blue....... 9.50

"Hey Fellows!

Look at the swell longies you get with these suits"

Most popular idea in years! Gives you what amounts to two different suits . . . and doubles the wear.

Favorite Style and Fabric

$**7**⁹⁵

Striking Colors! Snappy new styles! Perfect fitting. This handsome double breasted suit is made of long wearing suiting—½ wool, balance cotton and rayon. Diagonal weave with smartly subdued overplaid. Coat is lined with lustrous rayon. Knickers are full lined and have knit bottoms. Drape model longies. No vest. Ideal for those who want to switch from knickers to long pants.
All Sizes: 8 to 17. *State size.* Shipping weight, 4 pounds 2 ounces. Shipped from Chicago or Philadelphia—whichever is nearer. Order and pay postage from your nearest Sears mail order house.
40 E 3093—Medium Brown.................$7.95
40 E 3094—Medium Blue................. 7.95

Diagonal Weave—All Wool

$**9**⁷⁵

Tailored from a smooth finish all wool suiting—fashioned by experts who know what boys want. Double breasted model with pinch back, high luster rayon lining. Knickers full cut and full lined. Knit bottoms. Drape model longies smartly styled with 4 full pleats, dropped belt loops. Choice of rich Green or handsome Gray, diagonal weave with overplaid. No vest.
All Sizes: 8 to 17. *State size.* Shipping weight, 4 pounds 3 ounces. Shipped from Chicago or Philadelphia—whichever is nearer. Order and pay postage from your nearest Sears mail order house.
40 E 3005—Dark Green.................$9.75
40 E 3074—Medium Gray................. 9.75

Ⓐ Double Breasted

$**4**⁹⁵
2-Pc. Suit

$**6**⁹⁵
3-Pc. Suit

Good quality suiting—⅖ wool, bal. cotton, rayon. Ever becoming Herringbone with overplaid. Double breasted coat has sports back, rayon-lining, pleated patch pockets. Full cut, full lined knickers have knit bottoms. No vest. Extra knickers double the life of the suit.
All Sizes: 8 to 17. *State size.* Shipping weight 3 lbs. 5 oz.; with extra knickers, 4 pounds 3 ounces.

Coat and Knickers
40E2911—Med. Gray..$4.95
40E2942—Dark Blue.. 4.95

Coat and 2 Pairs Knickers
40E3011—Med. Gray..$6.95
40E2944—Dark Blue... 6.95

Ⓑ Our Lowest Price

$**4**²⁹
2-Pc. Suit

Despite the rise in fabric prices, this suit is still low priced. Herringbone weave overplaid . . . cassimere (¼-wool, bal. cotton, rayon) or navy blue cheviot (⅖ wool, bal. cotton). Single breasted coat; pinch back. Rayon lined. Full lined knickers; knit bottoms. No vest.
All Sizes: 6 to 16. *State size.* Shpg. wt., 3 lbs. 2 oz.

2-Piece Cassimere Suit
40E3013—Med. Brown.$4.29
40E3014—Med. Gray.. 4.29

2-Piece Cheviot Suit
40E3015—Navy Blue.. $4.29

Complete 5-Pc. Spring Outfit —Coat, Knickers, Shirt, Belt and Tie . . . all included.

Rich Medium Blue

$**5**⁷⁵
5-Pc. Suit

Fine suiting, ⅓ wool, bal. cotton, rayon. Herringbone weave with overplaid. Complete outfit of coat, knickers, shirt, belt and tie priced lower than total cost of individual pieces! Double breasted coat; sports back, rayon lining. Full lined knickers; knit-bottoms. Self belt. White cotton broadcloth shirt. Figured tie.
All Sizes: 4 to 12. *State size.* Shpg. wt., 3 lbs.

40 E 3004
5-Piece Suit........$5.75

HOW TO MEASURE FOR BOYS' KNICKER SUITS Measure **chest** close up under arms, over shirt or blouse. Place tape under arm and over shoulder blades. Measure **waist** around trousers without belt. Refer to chart; order size nearest these measurements.

Size	6	7	8	9	10	11	12	13	14	15	16	17
Chest, In.	24½	25½	26	27	27½	28¼	29	29¾	30½	31½	32	33
Waist, In.	23½	24	24½	25	25½	26	26½	27	27½	28	28½	29½

In-Between-ers Call This Wardrobe "Keen"

(A) 2-Piece Outfit $1.98

(B) Nip-Waist Princess $1.98

(C) Dress and Bag—Cute! $1.98

(E) All Wool Cardigan Jacket $2.98

(H) All Wool Plaid Jacket $2.98

(F) All Wool Skirt $1.98

(G) Chambray Blouse 98c

(J) All Wool Plaid Skirt $2.49

(K) Knit Zip Shirt 79c

For Easy Payments See Page 1038

Detachable Suspenders

(D) Big-and-Little-Sister 2-Piece Dresses

Sizes 12 to 16 $1.59 Each   Sizes 7 to 10

(A) **Classic two-piece** polka-dot dress of better quality Crown Tested Spun Rayon. Wear either piece with other jackets and skirts. Jacket has notched revers, four pocket-effect tabs. Skirt has stitched down pleats in front, detachable button-on suspenders; 2-inch hem. *Colors:* Navy or Rosewine with White Dots. *Age-Sizes:* 12, 14, 16 only. *State age-size, color; see Size Scale on Page 207. Shipping weight, 1 pound 4 ounces.*
7 E 4762—Outfit; 2 Pieces.............$1.98

(C) **Floral-striped** Spun Rayon dress with matching shoulder strap bag. Pleated top pretends to have pockets. White Rayon Pique collar with fagoted edge. Whirling 4-gore skirt. Better quality fabric. Crown Tested for satisfaction. *Age-Sizes:* 10, 12, 14, 16. *State age-size; Size Scale, Page 207. Shipping weight, 1 lb. 8 oz.*
7 E 4754—Copen Blue Floral stripe
7 E 4755—Rose Floral stripe
7 E 4756—Aqua Floral stripe
Dress and Bag; Complete Outfit.......$1.98

Change-about trio gives you keen value. Cardigan jacket has 2 deep pockets and 2 "make-believe" pocket flaps. It's unlined. 4-gore flare skirt has snap and button side closing. Blouse is the new double breasted Fireman's shirt with contrasting colored buttons. Wear all three or *change-about* with other jackets and skirts! *Age-Sizes:* 10, 12, 14, 16. *State age-size and color; see Size Scale on Page 207.*
(E) Jacket—Our fine quality All Wool Flannel. Shipping weight, 1 pound 8 ounces.
7 E 4840 M—Navy Blue 728
7 E 4841 M—Rose 558.................$2.98
(F) Skirt—Our fine quality All Wool Flannel. Shipping weight, 1 pound.
7 E 4872 M—Navy Blue 728
7 E 4873 M—Rose 558.................$1.98
(G) Blouse—Fine quality Chambray. *Colors:* Copen Blue or Dusty Rose. Shpg. wt., 6 oz.
27 E 4595—*Age-Sizes:* 7, 8, 10, 12, 14, 16...98c

(B) **Beautiful Princess** dress with neck-to-hem row of buttons—gored front and back. Contrasting stitching accents lovely lines from shoulder to hem. Graceful swirling, whirling skirt. Matching color zip closing at back of neck. Belt ties back in bow; gives you slim waist. Our better quality Rayon Crepe; Crown Tested. *Colors:* Skipper Blue 824, Sunset Rose 556 or Topaz Gold 106. *Age-Sizes:* 10, 12, 14, 16. *State age-size, color; see Size Scale, Page 207.*
7 E 4758—Shipping wt., 1 lb. 2 oz......$1.98

(D) **Big and Little Sister** two-piece jacket dress. Match-or-mix both pieces. Swing skirt with detachable suspenders. Our good quality printed plaid Cotton Pique; washfast. Wash it in Lux! *Colors:* Navy and Limetint Plaid, or Wine and Copen Blue plaid. *State age-size and color; see Size Scale on Page 207. Shipping weight, each, 10 ounces.*
27 E 4774—*Growing Girl Age-Sizes:* 7, 8, 10
27 E 4778—*Teen Age-Sizes:* 12, 14, 16
Complete Two-Piece Outfit......Each $1.59

More Change-Abouts . . . featuring Plaids, fashion hit of the season! Classic jacket has three patch pockets; high, wide, handsome notched revers. Skirt has stitched down pleats all around; zip placket. Cotton Knit shirt, in plain colors; has zip back-neck closing. *Age-Sizes:* 10, 12, 14, 16. *State age-size; see Size Scale on Page 207.*
(H) Jacket—Our finest quality All Wool Plaid. Shipping weight, 2 pounds 6 ounces.
7 E 4784 M—Copen Blue, Gold and Gray Plaid
7 E 4785 M—Red, Black and Gray Plaid.$2.98
(J) Skirt—Our finest quality All Wool Plaid. Shipping weight, 1 pound.
7 E 4792 M—Copen Blue, Gold and Gray Plaid
7 E 4793 M—Red, Black and Gray Plaid.$2.49
(K) Shirt—Fine quality Cotton Knit; washfast.
27 E 4592—Scarlet Red 508
27 E 4593—Copen Blue 722
27 E 4594—White. Shpg. wt., 8 oz........79c

Numbers after color names refer to Color-Graph following last index page in back of book.

Black Suede

BLACK AS INKY VELVET—SUBTLE
—UTTERLY DEVASTATING ACCENT
FOR AUTUMN FEMININITY!

Ⓙ FEMININE SPAT SHOE $2.98 Pair

Ⓕ DRAPED PUMP OR STRAP $2.98 Pair

The spat shoe takes its cue from the new dressmaker feeling of your Fall coat—dainty—feminine—touched with soft, delicate detail.

Ⓗ SMART SPAT STYLE $1.98 Pair

Ⓖ TAILORED TIE $2.98 Pair

Send your order to Sears nearest Mail Order House and allow postage from there. All items marked with triangle ▲ sent from Philadelphia or Chicago.

Ⓚ EXCITING NEW MODE $1.88 Pair

Ⓕ **Women's Sizes** 5, 5½, 6, 6½, 7, 7½, 8 in AA (extra narrow) and A (very narrow) width. **Sizes** 3½, 4, 4½, 5, 5½, 6, 6½, 7, 7½, 8 in B (narrow) and C (medium) widths. **State size, width.** Sbpg. wt., 1 lb. 2 oz.
2½-In. High Heel Pump, Leather Sole
15 D 8011—Black Suede.
▲ 15 D 8012—Black Patent. Pr.$2.98
2-in. Cuban Heel Strap, Leather Sole
▲ 15 D 8013—Black Suede.
▲ 15 D 8046—Black Patent. Pr.$2.98

PAGE 214₅ ◇ **SEARS**

Ⓖ A smart combination of youth and sophistication. Trimly tailored tie. Rich black suede with mudguard and side inserts of stitched patent leather. 2-inch Cuban heel. Leather sole. **Women's Sizes** 5, 5½, 6, 6½, 7, 7½, 8, 8½, 9 in AA (extra narrow) and A (very narrow) width. **Sizes** 3½, 4, 4½, 5, 5½, 6, 6½, 7, 7½, 8, 8½, 9 in B (narrow) and C (medium) widths. **State size and width.** Shipping weight, 1 lb. 3 oz.
15 D 8010—Pair........$2.98

Ⓗ A spat shoe . . . reflecting the simple elegance of the mode. **Leather sole.** 2½-inch high heel. **Women's Sizes** 5, 5½, 6, 6½, 7, 7½, 8, 8½, 9 in AA (extra narrow) and A (very narrow) width. **Sizes** 3½, 4, 4½, 5, 5½, 6, 6½, 7, 7½, 8, 8½, 9 in B (narrow) and C (medium) widths. **State size and width.** Shipping weight, 1 lb. 3 oz.
15 D 7015—Black Suede with Smooth Leather Trim
15 D 7016—Black Leather with Patent Trim. Pair......$1.98

Ⓙ Quaint suede spat shoe. Button trim. Elastic gores. Leather sole. 2-in. Cuban heel. **Women's Sizes** 5, 5½, 6, 6½, 7, 7½, 8, 8½, 9 in AA (extra narrow) and A (very narrow) widths. **Sizes** 3½, 4, 4½, 5, 5½, 6, 6½, 7, 7½, 8, 8½, 9 in B (narrow) and C (medium) widths. **State size and width.** Shipping weight, 1 lb. 2 oz.
▲ 15 D 8020 — Black, Patent Trim.
▲ 15 D 8021 — Brown, Alligator Grained Trim. Pr..$2.98

Ⓚ Sophisticated tie for street or afternoon wear. It's made of rich, velvety suede with trim of patent leather. Laced from scalloped top to toe through decorative hooks. Fine leather sole. 2-inch Cuban heel. **Women's Sizes** 3½, 4, 4½, 5, 5½, 6, 6½, 7, 7½, 8, 9 in C (medium) width. **State size,** see Page J in back of book. Shipping weight, 1 lb. 3 oz.
15 D 7017—Black Suede
Pair....................$1.88

Bonnets Star in "GONE WITH the WIND"

The bonnet's back—prettiest fashion of the 19th century gets a royal welcome along with Clark Gable, Vivien Leigh and Olivia de Havilland in "Gone with the Wind," Metro-Goldwyn-Mayer's David O. Selznick production.

Ⓐ The Beau-Catcher Bonnet

$1.89 — "Gone With the Wind" demonstrates the charm of the style. Glossy, beautiful rough straw. Double bow of rich rayon moire ribbon.
Colors: Black, Blue Violet 820, Navy Blue, Rose Coral 456, White. *Measure; state color.* Shpg. wt., 14 oz.
78 E 9445—Fits 21½ to 22-inch headsize.
78 E 9446—Fits 22¼ to 22¾-inch headsize.

Ⓑ Scarlett O'Hara Bonnet

$1.89 — Vivien Leigh looks lovely in a style like this; so will you! Brim turns up or down; forehead band may be worn high or low. Fine rough straw braid. Rayon velvet ribbons.
Colors: Black, Burnt Straw 204, Navy Blue, White. *Measure; state color.* Shpg. wt., 1 lb. 4 oz.
78 E 9440—Fits 21¾ to 22¼-inch headsize.
78 E 9441—Fits 22½ to 23-inch headsize.

Two Hats in One!

$1.00 — A charming bonnet! But slip back the brim and it's off-the-face. All wool spring weight felt; laced edge. Fine rayon and cotton grosgrain.
Colors: Emerald Green 376, Navy Blue, Rose Coral 456, White. Tango Rust 408, *Measure* (see below); *state color.* Shpg. wt., 15 oz.
78 E 9530—Fits 21½ to 22¼ in.

The Poke Bonnet

$1.00 — Frames your face in a wide high sweep; the effect is bewitching! Tuscan-like braid; rayon and cotton grosgrain trim. It's a grand value!
Colors: Copen 722, Natural Straw, Navy Blue or White. *Measure* (see below). Shpg. wt., 1 lb.
78 E 9540—Fits 21½ to 22 in.
78 E 9541—Fits 22¼ to 22¾ in.

The "Heartbreaker"

$1.59 — The kind of hat men like…feminine, pretty, gay! Dips low at front; rayon veil ties under chin, if you like. Fine rough straw braid.
Colors: Tea Green 274, Navy Blue, Burnt Straw 204, Patriot Red 510. *Measure* (see below); *state color.* Shpg. wt., ea., 14 oz.
78 E 9450—Fits 21½ to 22¼ in.

Choice—Braid, Felt

$1.19 Ea. — *Colors:* Blue Violet 820, Coral 456, Navy Blue, Tango Rust 408, White.
State color. Shpg. wt., each, 14 oz.
Pedaline Braid—Looks like Milan
78 E 9570—Fits 21¾ to 22¼ in.
78 E 9571—Fits 22½ to 23 in.
Spring Weight All Wool Felt
78 E 9572—Fits 21¾ to 22¼ inch
78 E 9573—Fits 22½ to 23 inch

Smart 2-Way

$1.00 **Shirley Temple's** mandarin pillbox of Pedaline braid. Smart, simple, in good taste. Two-tone rayon and cotton grosgrain ribbon twists over crown, ties under chin. Fruit trim.
Colors: Copen Blue 722, Navy Blue, Pink 552, Patriot Red 510, White. *Measure; state color.* Shipping weight, 12 ounces.
78 E 9815—Fits 20½ to 21¼ in.

79c **Two-way hat.** Daughter can wear it off the face or bonnet style, whichever way becomes her most! Lacy Pedaline braid, with rayon and cotton grosgrain band and chin ties. Dainty flower wreath at tip of crown.
Colors: Copen Blue 722, Navy Blue, Pink 552, White. *Measure; state color.* Shpg. wt., 14 oz.
78 E 9550—Fits 20¾ to 21½ in.

79c **Ripple-brim bonnet** of Tuscan-like braid. A style to delight little girls! Rayon and cotton grosgrain band, chin ties. Rayon plush flower wreath, in gay colors.
Colors: Copen Blue 722, Natural Yellow, Pink 552, White. *Measure* (see above); *state color.* Shipping weight, 13 ounces.
78 E 9555—Fits 20¼ to 20¾ in.
78 E 9556—Fits 21 to 21½ in.

85c **Becoming** to bright young faces! Off-the-face breton with the new high crown and gay two-tone binding. Rayon and cotton grosgrain band, bow, chin ties, and binding. Lacy Pedaline braid.
Colors: Copen Blue 722, Navy Blue, Patriot Red 510, White. *Measure* (see above); *state color.* Shipping weight, 14 ounces.
78 E 9560—Fits 20¾ to 21½ in.

Felt or Braid; up-or-down brim. *State size, color.* Shpg. wt., 14 oz.
69c **Tuscan-like Braid.** *Colors:* Copen 722; Natural Tan, Brown Trim; Pink 552; White.
78 E 9775—Fits 20 to 20½ in.
78 E 9776—Fits 20¾ to 21¼ in.
88c **Good Wool Felt.** *Colors:* Copen Blue 722; Beige 302; Rose 556; Navy Blue.
78 E 9777—Fits 20 to 20½ in.
78 E 9778—Fits 20¾ to 21¼ in.

MARIE EMILIE
YVONNE CECILE
ANNETTE

The Dionne Quints' Favorite Bonnet

$1.00 **Special** — Exactly the same style poke bonnet worn by the famous quintuplets! Makes little girls look their prettiest. Extra-fine Pedaline braid. Brim turns up, off the face, too. Flowers held on by a cunning bow. Rayon and cotton grosgrain ribbon headband and chinstrap.
Colors: Copen Blue 722, Navy Blue, Pink 552, Patriot Red 510, White. *Measure; state color.* Shpg. wt., 12 oz.
78 E 9820—Fits 19½ to 20 inch.
78 E 9821—Fits 20¼ to 20¾ inch.

Daughter's First Hat

79c — A bonnet she will remember all her life, she will look so pretty in it! Lacy Hemp braid daintily trimmed with flowers. Bowband and chinstrap of rayon and cotton grosgrain. Keeps its shape.
Colors: Beige 302, Copen Blue 722, Maize 104, Pink 552. *Measure* (see above); *state color.* Shipping weight, 12 ounces.
78 E 9790—Fits 19½ to 20¼ in. headsizes.

SEARS PAGE 212₂

Swagger Coats .. Keep You Warm and Dry

Rain-o-Shine
DOUBLE PURPOSE COATS

Nothing so unpredictable as the weather—but you're set for it either way with one of Sears fine quality all purpose coats. Utmost protection in stylish good-looking models at money-saving prices. Easy terms, too, on orders of $10.00 or more. See Inside Back Cover!

Lustrous 2-Tone Yoke—Extra Inside Pocket

TREATED WITH
Cravenette
SHEDS SHOWERS

100% Waterproof Coat In Dapper Herringbone

$2.98

Lowest price 100% waterproof dress raincoat we know—equal in quality to coats selling elsewhere for 15% to 20% more. A real bargain leader in Sears array of champions.

Sturdy cotton outer fabric in good-looking nubbed herringbone pattern Vulcanized with pure gum rubber to a rich cotton plaid lining by the special Rain-O-Shine process. All main seams securely strapped and cemented for positive water tightness—not a pin hole left for water to come through.

Good-looking double breasted style with raglan shoulders and an all-around belt. Wide, wind-breaking collar, storm tabs on sleeves, slash pockets that open through to trouser pockets. Average length, 48 inches.

Double purpose—and double value! Here's a big money's worth!

Sizes below: Shpg. wt., 4 lbs. 2 oz.
45 H 7436—Medium Green
45 H 7438—Medium Gray.....$2.98

Reversible Two-in-One All Weather Topcoat

$3.69

A better quality economy special — gives you two-coat usefulness for the price of one. One side of fine twill cotton gabardine in new military tan . . . other side of blue or gray glen plaid cotton. Rubberized together for absolute weather protection. One low price gives you a coat you can wear for any occasion and in any kind of weather—rain or shine. Unbeatable for value!

Cut in roomy proportions for ventilated comfort. Jaunty double-breasted model with all-around belt, and slash pockets with entrances through to trouser pockets. Convertible collar buttons up around neck for storm protection. Average length, 48 inches.

Two stylish coats to keep you well-dressed—a new idea in all-weather protection, and a big idea in saving.

Sizes below. Shpg. wt., 4 lbs. 3 oz.
45 H 7470—Dark Gray Plaid
45 H 7472—Medium Blue Plaid. $3.69

Sold Nationally at $6.00 "DeLuxe Buckskein"

$4.98

Sold by mail only by Sears—this famous nationally advertised 100% waterproof all weather coat at a saving of over $1.00 for you. And look at the "Extras" in service and wear this low price buys!

Outstanding fabric of about 35% wool, rest sturdy cotton in a handsome woven herringbone pattern—rubberized to a colorful plaid cotton lining by the famous duPont process. 100% waterproof and will not wrinkle or crack. Smartly styled double-breasted model with all-around belt, raglan shoulders and slash pockets with inside openings to trouser pockets. 48 inches long.

Take advantage of this actual cash saving on a coat that sparkles with **plus** value. Order now . . . and be set for months of super service!

Sizes below. Shpg. wt., 4 lbs. 6 oz.
45 H 7464—Blue Herringbone
45 H 7466—Gray Herringbone. $4.98

Our Finest Coat—Fine Cravenetted Gabardine in New Oxford Model

$7.45

Sheds Showers!
Repels the Wind!
Authentic Styling!
Money Saver!

As well known for its superb styling as for its dependable all-weather protection. Soft, supple, superb cotton in fine twill gabardine—loose-lined (not vulcanized) to let the cloth keep its natural smoothness and drape. Has the stylish appearance of a deLuxe quality topcoat. Shower-proofed by the famous Cravenette process. Complete protection against ordinary rain—and a real windbeater! We know of nowhere else where you can get a Cravenetted gabardine coat like this at a price so low.

Tailored to Sears highest standards of quality workmanship. Only the finest materials used in every part of the coat. Close, even stitching that adds to the appearance and to the admirable service.

Yoke and sleeves lined with lustrous smooth rayon, easy to slip your arms into. Body lined with durable cotton in a sparkling plaid pattern.

Smart single breasted style with neat fly front, raglan shoulders, and military style collar. Storm tabs on sleeves. Slash pockets with inside openings through to trouser pockets. Handy inside breast pocket. Average length, 48 inches.

Rain or Shine, you'll be dressed for the occasion and looking your best in this—our finest—all weather coat.

Sizes below. Shipping weight, 3 pounds.
45 H 7444—Tan Gabardine Coat........$7.45

SIZES AND HOW TO MEASURE: Sizes 34 to 46-inch chest. Give chest measurement taken over vest; also age, height, and weight. Your measurement is your size. Do not order larger size than your suit size. Perfect fit guaranteed!

FRIENDS IN ANY WEATHER

SEARS *Rain or Shine* **COAT**

Makes You Proud of Yourself in Sun or Rain

$2⁹⁸

In Plaid-Back Cotton Tweed

$1⁹⁸

Ⓐ Ⓒ

$1⁹⁸

Ⓓ

Ⓐ Girls' Rain Cape

$1⁰⁹

An astounding value; this durable cape that can go back and forth to school through many rain storms, and covers you completely. Rainproof, windproof. No sleeves so it slips off and on quick-as-a-wink. Slides over heavy coat, wooly suit or sweaters easily. Four buttons close it snugly. The attached hood in the smart parka-style that's all the rage, covers your hat, or takes the place of one. Head is elastic-shirred to frame your face and keep curls dry! Good quality gay Cotton Plaid with rubberized back.

Age-Sizes: 6, 8, 10, 12, 14. State Size Scale below. Shipping weight, 1 pound 11 ounces.
77 D 3125—Blue-and-Red Plaid only........ **$1.09**

All-Weather Coat and Hat

$1⁹⁸

Girls'-size edition of our "Rain or Shine" coat at far right. Same waterproof and windproof construction. Matching Scotty hat.
Age-Sizes: 6, 8, 10, 12, 14. State size and color; Size Scale below. Shipping weight, 3 pounds.
Ⓑ Checked Cotton Jersey. Sears good quality rubber vulcanized to gay woven Plaid Cotton lining.
17 D 5988—Navy, Wine, Brown or Green Checks............ **$1.98**
Ⓒ Flecked Cotton Tweed with rubberized back.
17 D 5990—Wine-Red, Navy, Brown, each with multi-colored flecks.. **$1.98**
Ⓓ Woven Cotton Plaid with rubberized back.
17 D 5995—Navy-and-Red Plaid only......... **$1.98**

Ⓔ Reversible Coat

$2⁹⁸

Wear either the Woven Cotton plaid or the water-repellent Cotton Gabardine on the outside. This rain-or-shine coat is completely reversible. Single-breasted swagger style, convertible collar, raglan sleeves, slot pockets. Sears price is a bargain price!
Color: Navy-and-Red Plaid, with Tan Gabardine.
Misses' Size Range: 12, 14, 16, 18, 20 only. State size; see Size Scale below. Shpg. wt., 3 lbs. 12 oz.
17 D 5980........... **$2.98**
For Girls 6 to 14
Same style, fabric and coloring as above, in girls' sizes. Scotty hat is included.
Age-Sizes: 6, 8, 10, 12, 14. State age-size; Size Scale below. Shipping weight, 3 pounds 2 ounces.
17 D 5982........ **$2.89**

Size Scale for Girls' Coats

Measure chest over dress, close up under arms. Measure *length* from base of neck in back to bottom of hem. Order size nearest measurements. Make no allowance.

Age-Sizes:	6	8	10	12	14
Chest:	25	27	29	31	32
Lengths:	25½	29	33	37	39

Size Scale for Misses' Coats

Measure yourself! If your measurements come between two sizes, order the larger.

Sizes:	12	14	16	18	20	22
Bust:	30	32	34	36	38	40
Waist:	25	26	27	29	31	33
Hip:	33	35	37	39	41	43
Length:	42½	42½	44	44	45½	45½

See measuring instructions, Page F in back of book.

Send your order to Sears nearest Mail Order House; allow postage from there. These coats sent direct from our New York Fashion Headquarters. Cape sent from Sears Mail Order House nearest you.

Ⓖ **Best Cotton Gabardine** **$5⁹⁸** Ⓗ **Cotton Plaid** **$1⁹⁸** Ⓙ **Good Cotton Gabardine** **$3⁹⁸**

A smart all-weather coat for city or country life, travel, campus or sports events. Especially made and processed to repel wind and rain. Convertible collar; adjustable sleeve straps; double-entry slash pockets. **State size, color.**
Misses' Size Range: 12, 14, 16, 18, 20, 22. Size Scale at left.
Women's Size Range: 42, 44 only. Size Scale on Page 30.

Ⓕ Handsome Herringbone Cotton Jersey Tweed vulcanized to a Cotton Plaid lining. A coat that's both rainproof and windproof.
Colors: Navy Blue, Brown or Medium Gray mixture. **State size and color.** Shipping weight, 3 lbs. 10 oz.
17 D 5970.............. **$2.98**

Ⓗ Woven Cotton Glen Plaid with rubberized back. Windproof; rainproof. Sturdy and good looking.
Colors: Brown, Navy or Gray Plaid.
17 D 5973 Shpg. wt., 3 lbs. **$1.98**

Ⓖ Our best Combed Cotton Gabardine, Cravenetted to make it water and wind repellent. This is an exceptional value! Equal quality coat usually costs at least $7.95.
Colors: Tan, Navy or Brown. **State size, color.** Shipping wt., 3 lbs.
17 D 5978................ **$5.98**

Ⓙ Good quality Cotton Gabardine, rubber vulcanized to Cotton Plaid lining. Wind and water repellent.
Colors: Tan, Navy or Brown.
17 D 5975—Shpg. wt., 3 lbs.. **$3.98**

Hollywood Styles

In All Wool, Tweed-Like
Fabrics . . Only $2.00 Down

Swing Kings

Today's Styles for Tomorrow's Leaders

All Virgin Wool Worsted With Double Breasted Vest

$16.95 3-Pc. Suit

Extreme styling makes this young men's style a smash hit wherever it is worn. The sturdy fabric is all virgin wool worsted. The sturdy tailoring insures excellent wear. And the unusual styling will definitely set you up as a fashion leader among the young bloods!

Look at the features of this brisk two-button single breasted model coat with snappy sports back. Patch pockets — a special, up-to-the-minute feature. Coat half-lined with smooth Earl-Glo rayon, guaranteed to wear the full life of the garment. Smart five-button double breasted vest has modified lapels, four pockets and accentuated points. Campus style trousers have full front pleats, extension waistband and extra wide 22-inch cuffs.

Skillfully tailored to build in all the strength needed for hard everyday wear. We guarantee to fit you perfectly — and we're sure you'll be more than satisfied when you look yourself over in this nifty new style. You can save big money with this low price—and you can pay on easy terms, too. See Inside Back Cover for Terms.

Sizes below. Shipping wt., 5 lbs. 7 oz.
◆55 H 7123—Dark Brown
◆55 H 7125—Dark Blue $16.95

Dapper Swagger Style with Smart Two-Way Vest!

$14.95 Gray 3-Pc. Suit

Here's a mighty thrifty way to dress—in a smartly styled suit that fits comfortably and wears like suits costing twice as much! Alert college leaders are swinging to these low price Cheviot Swing Kings—establishing a new high in debonair dressiness and a new low in clothing costs.

Choice of a good-looking herringbone Oxford Gray that's all wool or a dressy deep blue that's 75% wool (balance cotton). Single-breasted model with accentuated shoulders and a neat, trim looking waist, sports back.

Streamlined reversible vest—regular 6-button front on one side. Contrasting color flannel front with dark-lapels and buckle belt on the other. Full cut trousers in leading swagger style — have six-button wide waistband and extra wide 22-inch cuffs.

Tailored with expert care to insure lasting shape retention and strength enough to resist hard wear. Give yourself the treat you've always wanted — wear the style that really does things for you. We guarantee a perfect fit!

Sizes below. Shpg. wt., 5 lbs. 7 oz.
◆55 H 7157—Oxford Gray, All Wool $14.95
◆55 H 7156—Dark Blue, 75% Wool. 12.95

All Wool Herringbone In Youthful Drape Style

$13.95 3-Pc. Suit

Planned by the leading style centers of the nations film capitol as the style best suited to modern young men. A fabric that's rich—all wool, herringbone weave pepped up with sparkling nubs. Firm and long wearing, in the shades voted most popular for 1941.

Specially designed semi-drape style! Popular three-button single breasted coat with smart plain back. Regular six-button vest. Full cut trousers have modified high rise, full front pleats, set-down belt loops and 20-inch bottoms. Invisible Waldes Kover-zip fly.

Skillful tailoring adds to the long life of this rich fabric. Close, even stitching, fine interlinings and first quality materials throughout insure reserve strength and superb shape retention.

Sizes below. Shipping wt., 5 lbs. 6 oz.
◆55 H 7102—Mist Gray
◆55 H 7104—Teal Blue. $13.95

Tweed-like Herringbone with Subdued Overplaid

$14.95 3-Pc. Suit

For wide-awake young men who know how to be first with the latest. A firmly-woven all wool tweedy suiting in the new season's colors. Blue herringbone with lighter blue nubs or green with lighter green nubs, both complimented by a subdued overplaid pattern. A rough, but firmly woven fabric with plenty of wear.

Dashing double-breasted model with tucks in front and an easy-action sports back. Regular six-button vest. Modified high rise trousers, have front pleats, drop belt-loops, 20-inch bottoms and the invisible Waldes Kover-zip fly.

Well tailored with Earl-Glo rayon half-lining, guaranteed for the life of the suit. Coat front interlined and carefully stitched to hold its shape. Distinctive in appearance—and a favorite for wear. A real buy at this low price!

Sizes below. Shpg. wt., 5 lbs. 6 oz.
◆55 H 7120—Teal Blue
◆55 H 7121—Medium Green. . .$14.95

279A . . SEARS, ROEBUCK AND CO.

SIZES: 33 to 42-inch chest; 27 to 37-inch waist; 28 to 35-inch inseam. Regulars, Shorts, Longs. State all measurements as shown on Order Blank, Page C, Back of Book. All Suits on this page lined with Guaranteed Earl-Glo rayon. ◆ All suits shipped from Chicago. You order and Pay Postage from Sears nearest Mail Order House.

SLACK SUITS Are Smarter Wherever You Go

Enjoy Spring and Summer in Carefree Shoes .. Carefree

Shirts .. Carefree Socks .. Be Comfortable Always!

The Belts . . . hand braided of four soft, folded strands of top grain cowhide. About 1-in. wide. Leather covered buckle. **Colors:** Black and White, Green and White, plain Tan, plain White. Sizes: 30 to 42-in. waist. Shpg. wt., 4 oz. **State size and color.**
33 E 8822—Each.............98c
More Belts on Page 294.

The Shoes . . . walk on air in Spectator Sports oxfords—Fabric and colors same as slack suit on center figure of this page. Kork Krepe soles. **Men's sizes:** 6, 6½, 7, 7½, 8, 8½, 9, 9½, 10, 10½, 11. Wide width. **State size.** Shpg. wt., 2 lbs. 4 oz.
76 E 9638—Green
76 E 9639—Blue
76 E 9640—Brown.........$1.49
More Shoes on Page 344.

The Oxfords . . . Port holes for coolness. Smooth leather uppers. Red cork and rubber sole; wedge heel. Goodyear Welt smooth insoles. **Men's sizes:** 6, 6½, 7, 7½, 8, 8½, 9, 9½, 10, 10½, 11. D (Med. Wide) width. **State size.** Shpg. wt., 2 lbs. 4 oz.
67 E 94139—Brown and White
67 E 94140—Brown....Pair.$2.98
More Shoes on Page 347.

SEARS PAGE 272₂ ✪

Cool Shantung Effect Poplin Sanforized-Shrunk-Vat-Dyed

$2.15 Suit Price

A breezy slack suit in a comfortable shantung effect cool cotton poplin. Attractively styled shirt with matching buttons and button down flaps on pockets. Comfortable sports back with yoke and shirring. Wear it tucked in or out. Full cut slacks with four pleats, drop belt loops and adjustable self belt. 20-inch cuffs. Fabric won't shrink more than 1% or fade because it's Sanforized. Colorfast.
Sizes: Shirt, even chest sizes 34 to 44 in. Pants, even waist sizes 28 to 38 in.; all inseam sizes 29 to 34 in. State chest, waist, inseam sizes. Shpg. wts., shirt, 12 oz.; pants, 1 lb. 4 oz.; outfit, 2 lbs.
41 E 5014M—Brown Shirt.........$0.88
41 E 5015M—Brown Slacks........1.27
41 E 5012M—Green Shirt..........88
41 E 5013M—Green Slacks........1.27
41 E 5016M—Blue Shirt...........88
41 E 5017M—Blue Slacks..........1.27

Long Sleeves, Striped Slacks Sanforized-Shrunk

$2.49 Suit Price

Genuine Match-Tex fabric of crispy cotton and 15% rayon in lustrous deeptones. In-or-outer shirt with choice of long or short sleeves, shirred yoke back. Slacks have 4 pleats, self belt, set-down belt loops. 20-inch cuffs. Try mixing your colors!
Sizes: Shirt, even chest sizes 34 to 44-in.; Pants, even waists 28 to 38-in. All inseam sizes 29 to 34 in. State chest, waist, inseam sizes. Shpg. wt., shirt, 12 oz.; pants, 1 lb. 4 oz.; outfit, 2 lbs.
41E5010 M—Blue Shirt (long sleeves) $1.00
41E5009M—Blue Shirt (short sleeves). 1.00
41E5011 M—Blue Slacks.............1.49
41E5004M—Green Shirt (long sleeves) 1.00
41E5003M—Green Shirt (short sleeves)1.00
41E5005M—Green Slacks............1.49
41E5007M—Brown Shirt (long sleeves) 1.00
41E5006M—Brown Shirt (short sleeves) 1.00
41E5008M—Brown Slacks............1.49

Blazer Shirt, Plain Slacks Sanforized-Shrunk

$2.98 Suit Price

A slack suit made *twice as colorful* by the shirt's bright stripes—*twice as cool* by the 2-ply cotton mesh weave—*twice as zestful* by the new sport features. Worth $5 *at least!* The shirt's worn in-or-out of the trousers. Has a free-fitting yoke back, sports collar that can be buttoned up to neck, inverted pleat pockets with button-down flaps. Slack type trousers with self belt, double pleats and 20-inch cuffs. Superb workmanship throughout, including turned and double stitched pockets. Wash it easily, safely—rich colors are vat dyed, fabric's Sanforized to keep shrinkage not more than 1%.
Sizes: 34 to 44-in. chest; 28 to 40-inch waist; 29 to 34-inch inseam. State sizes; also age, ht., wt. Shpg. wt., 2 lbs. 11 oz.
45E5394—Gray-Blue Complete Suit
45E5396—Gray-Green Suit.......$2.98

Turbans "Certain to Charm"

Cleverly Draped Fabrics...Fit Smooth...Look Trim...Colors to Brighten Any Wardrobe

"How To Measure" on First Hat Page

Nylon Sewn—Zelan Treated

A smart Turban that is made by hand with famous Nylon thread—this gives it elasticity... **$1⁵⁹** and we've Zelan processed the crush-resisting spun rayon to make it drape better...resist water and even ink stains! Wear it anytime without ever a worry about the weather! The casual styling plus Nylon sewing and the Zelan process make it a hat you'll wear and wear all year-around. So flattering you're sure to receive compliments. We've priced it much less—even with all the features—than big city shops!

Colors: Black, Brown 219, Navy Blue, Dark Persian Rose 373, Red 313, Moss Green 825. *Measure; state color wanted.* Shipping weight, each, 14 ounces.

78 F 435—Fits 21¾ to 22¼-inch headsize.
78 F 436—Fits 22½ to 23 -inch headsize.

Rayon Velvet

A beautiful Turban that looks so expensive **$1⁵⁹** you'll never believe it could cost so little at Sears. You'll adore it to wear with your newest frocks. A gold-colored pin in the swirl of soft rayon velvet gives accent to a style that is smart and flattering. Favorite colors.

Colors: Black, Royal 569, Red 313, Mellow Amber 173, Moss Green 825. *Measure; state color.* Shipping weight, 14 ounces.

78 F 230—Fits 21¾ to 22¼-in. head.
78 F 231—Fits 22½ to 23-in. head.

Fan-Front Turban

Fashioned in lovely Rayon Velvet...you'll **$1³⁹** wear it for "dress" and feel as elegant as the smart styling of the Turban. Snugs your head in back...soars high in front in two fan-like bows that give you height and flatter your femininity. Remarkably low priced.

Colors: Black, Dark Brown 219, Navy Blue, Harvest Blue 659, Red Wine 367. *Measure; state color wanted.* Shipping wt., each, 14 oz.

78 F 315—Fits 21¾ to 22¼-in. head.
78 F 316—Fits 22½ to 23-in. head.

Special—Big Value

Softly draped with a flower-like cluster **$1⁰⁰** bunch at front to give you height and add a saucy accent to the styling. It fits superbly, too, because there's an elastic insert that "gives" to fit your head. Made of soft rayon Bagheera cloth. You'll find it practical and pretty for all occasions—for all types! You can have several at this price!

Colors: Black, Royal Blue 569, Rust 265 or Moss Green 825. *Measure; state color.* Shipping wt., 14 oz.

78 F 310—Fits 21¾ to 23-in. head.

2-way Turban

$1¹⁹ Wear the bow-cluster high in front or in a chignon low at the nape of your neck. It's smart either way...and gives you two hats at the price of one! Soft Rayon Bagheera cloth of fine quality.

Colors: Black, Cadet Blue 621, Red 313, Vibrant Green 765, Mellow Amber 173. *Measure, state color.* Shpg. wt., 14 oz.

78 F 330—Fits 21¾ to 23-in. headsizes.

Clever Wrap-around

69c Of course it's becoming because you drape it to suit yourself! Goes round-and-round and tucks in neatly at front or back. In soft suede rayon you'll wear with everything! You'll want more than one—the colors are grand!

Colors: Black, Harvest Blue 659, Dark Persian Rose 373, Brown 219, Gold, Red 313, Navy Blue, Vibrant Green 765. *State color wanted.* Shpg. wt., 4 oz.

78 F 430—Fits all headsizes.

Pert Bustle Back

Lovely rayon velvet turban mode that combines the **$1³⁹** youthfulness of a Scottie style with the sophistication of a Pillbox. Bustle back is gracefully draped to add beauty. In lovely rayon Velvet—perfect for all occasions. Priced very low.

Colors: Black, Dark Brown 219, Navy Blue or Wine Red 367. *Measure; state color.* Shipping weight, 14 ounces.

78 F 320—Fits 21¾ to 22¼-in. headsize.
78 F 321—Fits 22½ to 23-in. headsize.

Veiled Halo Style

A lovely frame for your face. Off-the-face halo style **$1⁰⁰** that women find so young looking...so becoming. Softly draped in wool jersey. The flowing rayon veil makes it dressy enough to wear any place —and is very flattering...as well as inexpensive although so rich-looking.

Colors: Black, Navy Blue, Rust 265. *Measure; state color.* Shpg. wt., ea., 14 oz.

78 F 325—Fits 21¾ to 22¼-in. headsize.
78 F 326—Fits 22½ to 23-in. headsize.

Glamorous *Silver Fox* Collars

The precious fur that makes you so pretty and proud
...and gives your coat a luxury air...Thrilling Values!

Ⓐ Botany All Wool Worsted

$59⁹⁸ Cash
$6.00 Down

Our top quality coat .. for you who love fine things. The side-buttoned style, softly fitted at waistline and flared from hip-to-hem, is collared with a superb full-skin Silver Fox fur. Collar has hidden fullness that pulls up high and warm, when you wish. Coat is equally handsome open or closed, with or without belt. Pocket in lining, inside tie. Superb fabric is our best quality; Botany All Wool Worsted with new fine-nubbed, smoother surface. Lined in our best Rayon Crepe-Back Satin; interlined with Wool (cotton covered).
Misses' Size Range: 12, 14, 16, 18, 20 only; Size Scale, Pg. 20. *Women's Size Range:* 40, 42, 44 only. Size Scale, Pg. 24. *State size.* Shpg. wt., ea., 5 lbs. 8 oz.
17 F 7436—Black only; $6. Down; Cash...**$59.98**

With Fine Silver-dyed Russian Fox Collar
17 F 7438—Black only; $4. Down; Cash...**$39.98**

Ⓑ Rich Beauty ... Real Value

$29⁹⁸ Cash
$3.00 Down

Princess coat with the long-line that is the biggest Fashion news of the Season! It follows the sweeping curve of your body right from bustline to hipline, then ripples away into modified fullness at the hem. A silhouette that is excitingly different, and wonderfully easy to wear. A coat that combines value, glamour and warmth! Its crowning glory is the smart collar of fine quality Silver Fox, shaped the new way with narrow back and two wide crescents of fur in front. In our warm, good quality All Wool coating, with the new smaller, flatter nubs. Warmly interlined with cozy Wool (cotton covered), and luxuriously lined in smooth Rayon Satin that is guaranteed to wear for two years.
Misses' Size Range: 12, 14, 16, 18, 20 only. *State size;* see Size Scale, Page 20. Shpg. wt., 4 lbs. 11 oz.
17F7440—Black only; $3. Down; Cash Price...**$29.98**

18 . . . SEARS, ROEBUCK AND CO. ✪

DO YOU KNOW the Down Payment on our finest fur-trimmed coat is only $4.00 more than the Down Payment on a budget-priced coat? See Inside Back Cover!

For Day or Evening Wear

Smart Separates for All-Around-The-Clock

These Blouses Described on Opposite Page

Rayon Satin $1.98   Rayon Chiffon $1.98

Rayon Satin $2.49   Rayon Crepe $1.98   Rayon Jersey $2.49

© Rayon Chiffon $2.98

Ⓓ Rayon Satin $2.98

Ⓔ Rayon French Type Crepe $1.69

Ⓕ Colorful Stripes $2.98   Plain Colors $1.98

Ⓖ Ⓙ Ⓚ

Be Smart—Mix your Own for Evening!

Choose this basic skirt, in two finer fabrics, and mix it with blouses or evening sweaters from our splendid assortment. Your friends will envy your wardrobe—you'll enjoy knowing you're dressed in top fashion and at such very low prices! A smart idea for daytime, too!

Skirt in Two Lengths. You'll want this very new, full, eight-gored, pointed-front waistband skirt in both lengths. Zip placket. *Misses' Size Range: 12, 14, 16, 18, 20, 22. State size, color.*

Ⓖ **Formal Length Skirt.** About 42 inches long. In two finer fabrics. See Size Scale, Page 60. Shpg. wt., each, 1 lb. 3 oz.
7 F 3470—*All Rayon Jersey-like Weare.* Will not sag. Black, Navy, or Scarlet. **$3.98**
7 F 3471—*All Rayon Pebble Crepe.* Bright Navy or Black **$2.98**

Ⓗ **Street Length Skirt.** About 27 in. long. In two finer fabrics. Size Scale, Page 60. Shipping weight, each, 13 oz.
7 F 3479—*All Rayon Jersey-like Weare.* Will not sag. Navy or Black... **$2.49**
7 F 3480—*All Rayon Pebble Crepe.* Bright Navy or Black **$1.98**

Ⓙ **Dramatic Jacket Blouse** for day or evening. Rich gold color metallic embroidery, fastens down front with gilt buttons. Finer quality Bengaline (half rayon, balance cotton). *Colors:* Scarlet, Black or White. *Bust Sizes:* 30, 32, 34, 36, 38 in. State size, color.
7 F 3165—Shipping weight, 14 ounces.................. **$2.98**

Ⓚ **Gay Glitter Sweater** ... asparkle with gold color sequins! The most dramatic and different of new evening sweaters, worn for dressy daytime, too. Fine Rayon and Cotton Bouclé. Crown zip front. *Even Sizes:* 32 to 38-in. bust. State size. Shpg. wt., 6 oz.
38 F 7331—White.   38 F 7330—Scarlet........ **$2.98**
For Other Sweaters See Pages 70 to 74

◉ > PAGE 63 .... BLOUSES, SKIRTS

The *Junior Jury* says—"More Color"

"Hoods are good . . . bright shiny embroidery is exciting.
We like 2-piece dresses . . . We're happy in pastels"

Ⓓ "Two Timer" $3.98

"Just look at the gilt embroidery flashing on the front of this two-piece Celanese Rayon Pebble Crepe dress! The jacket is snugly fitted with a Crown zip right up the front! The contrasting colored skirt is divinely flared. My dearest date dress! And no wonder!"

Colors: Aqua Blue top or Pastel Rose top, each with Black skirt.

Juniors' Size Range: 11, 13, 15, 17, 19. *State size and color;* Size Scale, Page 38. Shipping weight, 1 pound 6 ounces.

31 F 8600 . . . . $3.98

Ⓔ "Angel Baby" $3.98

"I adore this soft, not too fancy dress! It has the new long waistline, and a dancing skirt! 2 rows of buttons for fun; tie-back sash; Crown zip neck closing and placket. It's made of *Tecasha*—Spun Rayon and 50% fine Teca Rayon, which makes it look and feel like soft Wool." (Story on Page 50.)

Colors: Misty Rose (as shown), Misty Aqua Blue, or Royal Blue 569.

Juniors' Size Range: 11, 13, 15, 17, 19. *State size, color;* Size Scale, Page 38. Shpg. wt., 1 lb. 6 oz.

31 F 8602 . . . . $3.98

Ⓕ "Campus Star" $2.98

"I couldn't resist this softly tailored dress! Just see the neat, bloused top with its pocket-like tabs. The swoopy skirt and set-in belt for smooth waistline — (half sash ties in front or back). Long sleeves for chic, gilt buttons for glitter! Blissful colors in dull Spun Rayon, 20% fine Teca Rayon" (see Page 50.)

Colors: Dark Cadet Blue, Scarlet, or Henna Rust 265.

Juniors' Size Range: 11, 13, 15, 17, 19. *State size, color;* Size Scale, Page 38. Shpg. wt., 1 lb. 4 oz.

31 F 8604 . . . . $2.98

Ⓖ "Hood Winker" $3.98

Ernestine Cline of Little Rock, Arkansas, sponsors a "Bright with Black" dress—like this—the hooded button-front jacket is Spun Rayon, and 20% fine Teca Rayon; the front-fulled skirt is printed Spun Rayon. Unusual contrast —bright color, tiny checks!

Colors: Scarlet or Kelly Green jacket, each with Black and White Check skirt.

Juniors' Size Range: 11, 13, 15, 17, 19. *State size and color;* see Size Scale on Page 38. Shipping weight, each, 1 lb. 4 oz.

31 F 8606 . . . . $3.98

Use a Colorhelm to learn exciting new color combinations. See Page 47.

Garments on these two pages shipped from our Fashion Headquarters. Send your order to nearest Mail Order House, or, for these garments alone, you may send order directly to New York. You pay postage only from nearest Mail Order House. Color numbers refer to Color-Graph in How to Order section at back of book.

✪ PAGE 35 . . . . DRESSES

TWO FOOT-BELITTLING LOW Wedges

Two Young-at-Heart Spectators

For Less Than $2 A Pair

$1.88 PAIR

Classic Pump

A shoe with definite pep-appeal! This spectator has loads of zip. You'll depend on it to take you to school—to work—shopping. Watch what the models wear in your favorite style magazines. You'll see lots of spectators. Leather upper, sole. 1½-inch built-up heel.

Sizes 3½ to 8 in C width
State size. Shpg. wt., 1 lb. 6 oz.
54 H 2300—White Nubuck,
Brown Trim. Pair $1.88

S-T-R-E-T-C-H-A-B-L-E

$1.98 PAIR

Just look at the lines of this spectator! See how the walled toe makes your foot look tiny. Notice that the white suede is elasticized to hug your feet. Good leather sole. 1¼-inch walking heel.

Sizes 3½ to 8 in C width
State size. Shpg. wt., 1 lb. 6 oz.
54 H 2548—White Suede,
Brown Trim. Pair $1.98

Coquetry in Perforated Leather

A beau-bewitcher if there ever was one! Your feet will look simply cunning in this pump. Jaunty bow makes your feet look even smaller. Leather sole. Low wedge heel.

$1.98 PAIR

Sizes 3½ to 8 in C width
State size. Shipping weight, 1 pound 8 ounces.
54 H 2512—White Smooth Leather
54 H 2513—Black Patent Leather
Pair........................$1.98

Wedge Spectator Pump

White Nubuck leather—comfy and easy to clean. Elastic gore under bow for a perfect fit. Leather sole. Low wedge heel. Very smart with all your summer clothes.

$1.98 PAIR

Sizes 3½ to 8 in C width
State size. Shipping weight, 1 pound 8 ounces.
54 H 2496—White Leather, Brown Trim
54 H 2497—White Leather, Black Patent Trim. Pair.........$1.98

All Shoes on This Page in C (Medium) Width . . . See Page 1045

LIKE BLACK? WHITE? OR WILL YOU ANSWER THE Call to the Colors?

WIDTH EXPLANATION
AA . . Extra Narrow
A . . Very Narrow
B . . Narrow
C . . Medium

Check Each Listing for Sizes in Above Widths..If Uncertain of Your Size, See Page 1045

$2.98 Any Pair on This Page

HERE'S THE WEDGEE THAT IS Taking New York by Storm

Yours! . . . In Oxford or Step-in . . . In a Choice of 4 Color Combinations

Dainty Pump

(F) Light as a puff of smoke and looks as delicate. Draped vamp and open toe for more foot freedom. Graceful 2½-inch heel. Durable leather sole. In blue, white, red or black leathers!

Sizes 5 to 9 in AA, A widths
Sizes 4 to 9 in B and C widths
State size, width. Shpg. wt. 1 lb. 2 oz.
◆5 H 8077—Blue Kid
◆5 H 8078—White Kid
◆5 H 8079—Red Kid
◆5 H 8080—Black Patent Leather
Pair..............$2.98

120 . . SEARS, ROEBUCK AND CO.

Constantly Correct

(G) Draped open work vamp. Open toe. Good leather sole, of course. Choice of two heel heights. A cute shoe.

Sizes 5 to 9 in AA, A widths
Sizes 4 to 9 in B, C widths
State size, width. Shipping weight, 1 pound 2 ounces.

2½-inch Heels
◆5 H 8076—Black Patent
◆5 H 8075—Red Kid
◆5 H 8074—White Kid
◆5 H 8156—Blue Kid

2-inch Heels
◆5 H 8111—Black Patent
◆5 H 8157—White Kid
Pair....$2.98

Starred for Success in Patent, Suede, or Crushed Leather

Two of the smartest—most practical shoes you'll see all spring! Both styles come in either suede or crushed leather—soft as marshmallows. Contrasting leather mudguard trim shortens the appearance of your foot. Both have wedge heels. By now you know that wedges are THE thing for restful walking—for proper foot support. Whether you choose the elasticized step-in or the open throat tie, you're getting a smooth-fitting, comfortable shoe—and the last word in clever styling. Fine leather soles.

Sizes 6 to 9 in AA width
Sizes 4 to 9 in B and C widths
State size, width. Shipping weight, 1 lb. 3 oz.

Step-in
◆5 H 8153—Blue Crushed Leather, Smooth Trim
◆5 H 8151—White and Brown Leather
◆5 H 8152—White and Black Patent
◆5 H 8154—Black Crushed Leather, Patent Trim

Oxfords
◆5 H 8149—Blue Crushed Leather, Smooth Trim
◆5 H 8147—White Suede and Brown Leather
◆5 H 8148—White Suede and Black Patent Leather
◆5 H 8150—Black Crushed Leather, Patent Trim
Pair...................$2.98

New Low Price on a Winner!
$1.98
Value $2.98

THE FAMOUS CALIFORNIA
Matletex
REG. U. S. PAT. OFF.

Play Dress with Panties Attached

Sears 4-Star Feature Because:

★ Famous proven-success fashion.. a favorite on the playgrounds of the nation.

★ Exclusive with Sears! No other mail-order house sells it or can sell it.

★ Fits beautifully because the Lastex-shirred *Matletex* adjusts to your figure-size.

★ Perfect all-in-one play dress; complete in itself; eliminates underclothes!

Whirl-skirt play dress with bodice and attached panties of patented *Matletex* Lastex shirring; stretches whichever way you do; is guaranteed to stay shirred. Straps criss-cross in back, or tie halter-style at neck. Fine novelty Cotton; washfast.

Colors: Navy-and-Copen Blue Check with Red-centered daisies; or Wine-and-Rose Check with Green-centered daisies.

Sizes: Extra-small (fits 30 to 31-in. bust); Small (fits 33 to 35-in. bust); Medium (fits 37-in. bust). **State size, color.**

◆ 7 H 3502—Shpg. wt., 14 oz......$1.98

Garments on these two pages marked with diamond ◆ are shipped from our Fashion Headquarters in New York City. Order and pay postage from nearest Mail Order House.

22 ... SEARS-ROEBUCK

Junior Jury Playmates
Colors gay as sunshine ... Action-free cut and a fine figure-fit

Two to Team-up!
69c $1.00
Shirt   Overall

Ⓐ **Classic Shirt.** Convertible collar; yoke front and back. Patch pocket. Cut long. Cotton Slub Broadcloth. **Colors:** Scarlet or White. **Sizes:** 30, 32, 34, 36, 38-in. bust. **State size, color.** Shipping weight, 7 ounces.

77 H 3226...........69c

Ⓑ **Built-up Bodice Overall.** Colorful braid and lacing. Cotton Gabardine Twill. Wear with or without shirt. **Colors:** Navy, Rust 262 or Blue 559. **Juniors' Size** (Not Age) **Range:** 11, 13, 15, 17, 19. **State size, color; Scale, Page 23.** Shpg. wt., 13 oz.

77 H 3629..........$1.00

3-Pc. Sailor Suit
$1.98 Set
Choice of 2 Fabrics

Ⓒ Shipshape in-or-out shirt, waistband slacks, decked out with braid, buttons, stars! Hat, too! **Juniors' Size** (Not Age) **Range:** 11, 13, 15, 17, 19. **State size, color;** Scale, Page 23. Shpg. wt., ea., 1 lb. 9 oz.

Fine Cotton; novelty herringbone Weave.

◆ 7 H 3627—White or Navy.....3 Pcs., $1.98

California Type Yarn-dyed, fine woven Cotton. Sanforized Shrunk. (Max. shrinkage 1%).

◆ 7 H 3631—Ensign Blue, White Trim. 3 Pcs., $1.98

2-Pc. Pinafore
$1.69 Striped $1.49 Plain
White Shorts Included

Ⓓ Ric-rac ruffles on pinafore with shirred waist, wide skirt. Buttons down back! Separate white shorty pants make this a perfect play dress. Washfast.

Juniors' Size (Not Age) **Range:** 11, 13, 15, 17, 19. **State size, color;** Size Scale, Page 23. Shpg. wt., each, 14 oz.

Pin Wale Cotton Pique

77 H 3504 — R e d or Deep Copen, with White Stripes. 2 Pcs....$1.69

Plain Cotton Pique

77 H 3506—White with Red Trim. 2 Pcs..$1.49

Sports Change-arounds
$1.00 Ea.   69c
Blouse or Shorts   2 Halters

State size, color when ordering.

Ⓔ **Rayon Jersey Blouse**—in flying flag colors. Washable. **Color:** Red-White-and-Blue. **Bust Sizes:** 30, 31, 33, 35, 37 in.

77 H 3001—Shpg. wt., 6 oz., $1.00

Ⓕ **Sanforized-Shrunk Shorts**— Cotton Gabardine Twill. (Max. shrinkage 1%). **Colors:** White with Red, or Navy with White Stripes. **Juniors' Size** (Not Age) **Range:** 11, 13, 15, 17, 19. Size Scale, Page 23.

77 H 3507—Shpg. wt., 9 oz., $1.00

Ⓖ **Washfast Cotton Halters;** Figure-moulding bra type. **Colors:** Red-White-and-Blue Stripes, or Colorful Tropical Print. **Sizes** same as Play Dress 7 H 3502, left.

77 H 3512—Shpg. wt., 5 oz., 2 for 69c

Ⓖ Jacket

Ⓕ Shirt

Ⓔ

Ⓓ Skirt

Ⓐ Many-Way Suit

Ⓑ Two-Piece Suit

Ⓒ Shirt and Skirt

Cold-Weather Play Clothes
Professionally correct ... down to the last detail

Ⓐ Hoods On or Off!

$5⁹⁸　This smart 3-piece, fine All Wool Flannel suit has a matching detachable hood fully lined in contrasting color flannel. The shorter length circular skirt (about *two* inches shorter than regular skirt) is faced with Red All Rayon Taffeta. Zip placket. The hip-bone length fitted jacket, gilt-buttoned in a double-breasted effect, slims your waist. Convertible collar. Squared shoulders, pockets. All Rayon Taffeta yoke lining and bound seams. For winter fun.

Colors: Red Jacket with Navy Skirt, as illustrated.

Juniors' Size Range: 11, 13, 15, 17, 19. *State size;* Size Scale, Page 42.
7 F 3860—Shpg. wt., 1 lb. 14 oz...$5.98

Ⓓ All Wool Skirt

$2⁹⁸　Fine Flannel. Eight gores for flare in the new shorter length (about 1 inch shorter than regular skirt). Full Rayon Taffeta lining. Zip placket. *Colors:* Copen, Bright Red 313, or Hockey Green 763, with Scarlet lining.

Misses' Size Range: 12, 14, 16, 18, 20, 22. State size, color; see Size Scale on Page 60.
7 F 3869—Shipping weight, 1 pound 1 ounce......$2.98

Ⓑ With Quilted Jacket

$7⁹⁸
Velveteen

It's the quilting, the silvery buttons and two handy patch pockets that make this 2-pc. suit the big favorite! Comes in two velvety fabrics, both full lined with gay color All Rayon Taffeta. 4-gore skirt (abt. 1-in. shorter than regular skirt) has zip placket. Jacket about 19 in. long. *Misses' Size Range:* 12, 14, 16, 18, 20 only. *State size and color;* see Size Scale, Page 22. Shipping wt., each, 2 lbs. 5 oz.

Fine Quality Velveteen
7 F 3861—Black, Scarlet lining....$7.98

Fine Narrow Wale Corduroy
7 F 3862—Laurel Green 767 with Scarlet lining or Sparkling Burgundy 415 with matching lining..........$6.98

Ⓔ Quilted Jacket

$3⁹⁸　Fine Cotton Poplin, quilted all over. Self lining. Windproof, water repellent, Sanforized-shrunk throughout (max. shrinkage 1%). Metal buttons. Adjustable sleeve tabs. Lgth. abt. 19 in. *Colors:* Scarlet or Natural, with Natural color lining. *Misses' Size Range:* 12, 14, 16, 18, 20 only. *State size, color;* Size Scale, Page 67.
7 F 3866............$3.98

Ⓒ Sold Separately

$2⁹⁸　**Suspender Swing Skirt** (abt. 1 in. shorter than regular skirt). Fine All Wool Flannel full lined with All Rayon Taffeta. Detachable suspenders button to waistband. Zip placket. *Colors:* Bright Navy or Black, Scarlet lining. *Misses' Size Range:* 12, 14, 16, 18, 20 only. *State size, color;* Size Scale, Page 60.
7 F 3868—Shpg. wt., 1 lb. 2 oz...$2.98

$1⁹⁸　**Sport Shirt.** Fine All Wool Jersey, beautiful tailoring! Gathered yoke, front, back. 2-way collar. Fine buttons. *Colors:* Scarlet, Pastel Beige 123, Copen 607. Bust Sizes: 30, 32, 34, 36, 38 inches. *State size, color.*
7 F 3302—Shipping weight, 14 oz...$1.98

Ⓕ Sports Shirt

$2⁹⁸　Fine All Wool Flannel in beautiful Prince Charlie Clan Plaid (matches beanie 7 F 3894M, sold on Page 68 and lining of jacket (G) on this page). Expertly tailored. 2-way collar, beautifully finished cuffs. Double stitched seams. Cut long. *Bust Sizes:* 30, 32, 34, 36, 38, 40 in. *State size.* Shipping weight, 13 ounces.
7 F 3300M—Plaid as illustrated............$2.98

Ⓖ Reversible Jacket

$6⁹⁸　One side water repellent, windproof, Sanforized (max. shrink. 1%) fine Cotton Poplin. The other, fine All Wool Prince Charlie Clan Plaid Flannel (matches shirt [F]). Elastic at sides, zip front. Lgth. abt. 20 in. *Colors:* Ice Blue or Scarlet 311, with Plaid. *Misses' Size Range:* 12, 14, 16, 18, 20, 22. *State size, color.* Size Scale, Page 67. Shipping weight, 1 lb. 9 oz.
7 F 3863M—*Jacket only* ..$6.98
7 F 3864M—Jacket with matching "beanie" $7.98

With Sheepskin or Kasha Lined Jacket

With Reversible Jacket

With Embroidered Jacket

Butterball Jacket

Reversible Jacket

$7.98

Warm . . Water-Repellent . . Windproof

Handsome suits and jackets . . . for work, play or sports

Ⓐ Two Warm Linings!

Warm, water-repellent suit of fine All Wool Snow Cloth. Jacket, about 25 in. long; 4 roomy pockets, convertible collar, adjustable button tabs on sleeves. Expertly cut. Pants have Crown zip side closing, Cotton Kasha lining, and zip knit anklets. The fine quality and excellent workmanship make this an outstanding suit, not to be confused with cheaper types. *Colors:* Green Plaid Jacket, Plain Dark Green 771 Pants; or Navy Plaid Jacket, Plain Navy Pants. *Misses' Size Range:* 12, 14, 16, 18, 20, 22. State size, color; Scale, below.
With Sheepskin Lined Jacket
7 F 3872—Shipping weight, 5 lbs. 5 oz. 2-Pc. Suit $9.98
With Cotton Kasha Lined Jacket
7 F 3873—Shipping weight, 2 lbs. 4 oz. 2-Pc. Suit $7.98

$9.98 Cash $2.00 Down Sheepskin Lined

Ⓑ Two All Wool Fabrics!

From one of America's finest makers! Our best, expertly fitted suit, *full cut,* completely reversible jacket—it's windproof, water-repellent, Sanforized-Shrunk (max. shrinkage 1%). Red Cotton Poplin on one side; Navy Gabardine or Snow Cloth on other side. About 19 in. long. Lastex side-inserts; zip front, welt pockets, button cuffs. Tapered professional-type pants have flap pockets, adjustable waist, zip side closing. Double elastic instep strap. *Misses' Size Range:* 12, 14, 16, 18, 20, 22. *State size;* Size Scale below. Shpg. wt., each, 3 lbs. 11 oz.
Finer All Worsted Gabardine
Windproof, water repellent. Warm, but light in weight. Navy unlined pants.
7 F 3874—2-Piece Suit $14.95
Fine All Wool Snow Cloth. Water repellent. Navy pants, Cotton Kasha lined.
7 F 3876—2-Piece Suit $11.95

$14.95 Cash $2.00 Down Gabardine

Ⓒ A Best Seller!

Gay ski motifs are embroidered all over the jacket of this warm, comfortable, two-piece suit of finer water-repellent All Wool Snow Cloth. Such a popular style—one of our best sellers! The Crown zip front, belted jacket, about 24 in. long, boasts two zip pockets, two flap pockets and a Cotton Kasha lining. The well-cut pants have detachable embroidered suspenders, 2 pockets, adjustable waist, button side closing, zip knit anklets and completely lined with Cotton Kasha. *Misses' Size Range:* 12, 14, 16, 18, 20, 22. *State size;* see Size Scale below. Shipping weight, each, 4 pounds 14 ounces.
7 F 2223—Dark Brown 219
7 F 2225—Dark Green 771
7 F 2224—Navy. 2-Pc. Suit . . $7.98
For Easy Terms See Inside Back Cover

$7.98 All Wool

Ⓔ Slim, Longer Length Jacket

Flattering White Bunny Fur trims the attached hood of this slim waisted, longer length, completely reversible jacket. Superbly tailored by a foremost American maker—of windproof, water-repellent Cotton Poplin—Sanforized-Shrunk (max. shrinkage, 1%). Zip fastening! Button cuffs. Warm but light in weight. Cut full to allow for sweaters underneath, as professionals wear it. Length, about 27 in. *Color:* Cadet Blue 575 with Red 313. *Misses' Size Range:* 12, 14, 16, 18, 20, 22. Scale, left.
7 F 3870—State size; Shpg. wt., 1 lb. 15 oz. $7.98

Ⓓ Hooded Sheepskin Favorite

Your darling "Butterball" now may be had with or without a detachable hood! Deep furred natural color Sheepskin with leather buttons and 2 roomy pockets—full-lined in bright Plaid Cotton Flannel. *Misses' Size Range:* 12, 14, 16, 18, 20 only. Length, about 24 inches. *State size;* Size Scale at left.
7 F 3871—Hooded Jacket. Shpg. wt., 4 lbs. 3 oz. . . $12.98
7 F 3880—Jacket without Hood. Shipping weight, 3 lbs. 13 oz. $2.00 Down . . . . Cash $11.98

$12.98 Cash $2.00 Down With Hood

SIZE SCALE for Misses' Ski Wear and Winter Jackets

Have someone else measure you. Don't guess your size. Take measurements each time you order at *All* figure points in Size Scale. Measure over underwear as explained on Page 44C. Order size that corresponds with your body measurements. Make no allowances: your size is determined by actual body measurements.

Size	12	14	16	18	20	22	
Bust	30	32	34	36	38	40	inches
Waist	24	26	28	30	32	34	inches
Hips	33	35	37	39	41	43	inches
Outseam length of Pants, taken down side of leg, waist to ankle, as illustrated	41	41	41	42	42	42	inches

Garments on these two pages are shipped from our Fashion Headquarters in New York City. Send your order to nearest Mail Order House, or for these garments alone, you may send order directly to New York. You pay postage only from nearest Mail Order House. Color numbers refer to Color-Graph in back of book.

◉ ▶ **PAGE 67 . . . . SPORTSWEAR**

A

LONG, SWEEPING FORMALS

Charmode Successes ..Sizes for Misses, Women, Juniors
Glamorous "After Dark" Styles That Flatter All Figures
In Sleek Rayon Jersey, Marquisette, Taffeta or Velvet

(A) Dramatize yourself . . . $6.98
and the evening, in a
slender classic gown of
Rayon Jersey. The snug side-
zipped bodice is draped and shirred to perfection . . . with a flattering deep V-neck . . .
softly folded sleeves.   A lovely gilt-thread
embroidered girdle hugs your waist . . . to
show off the full sunburst-pleated skirt!
Colors: White, Black, Bright Red 311. Misses'
Sizes: 12, 14, 16, 18, 20. Lengths, 58 to 59
in. State size and color.
◆ 31 NK 4070—Shpg. wt., 1 lb. 8 oz. $6.98

(B) Gay, rustling, embossed $2.98
Rayon Taffeta for parties
and dances! You'll love the
clever draped bodice . . .
high slim waistline with a youthful tie-back
sash . . . wide, wide skirt, and the matching
hair bow that comes with it! Colors: Light
Blue 555, Rose Pink 401, White. State
size and color. Shpg. wt., ea., 1 lb 8 oz.
◆ 31 NK 4072—Misses' Sizes: 12, 14, 16,
18, 20. Lengths, 58 to 59 in....... $2.98
◆ 31 NK 4073—Juniors' Sizes: 11, 13, 15,
17, 19. Lengths, 58 to 59 in........ $2.98

(C) Angelic party dress, in $4.98
floating Rayon. Mar-
quisette and fine Rayon
Taffeta . . . tiny-waisted . . .
exquisitely trimmed! Perfect in white for a
dreamy bride; or delicate pastels for her
maids! Colors: White, or Lt. Aqua 705, Rose
Pink 401. State size, color. Shipping
weight, each, 1 lb. 8 oz.
◆ 31 NK 4074—Misses' Sizes: 12, 14, 16,
18, 20. Lengths, 58 to 59 in........ $4.98
◆ 31 NK 4075—Juniors' Sizes: 11, 13, 15,
17, 19. Lengths, 58 to 59 in........ $4.98

(D) Distinguished Gown. $9.98
In the finest crush resis- Cash
tant (silk-backed) Rayon $2 Down
Velvet. You'll love its soft
figure-flattery, the cameo-like brooch at
the V-neck, the deep sleeve shirring re-
peated at the moulded waistline. Snugly
Crown-zipped bodice and sweeping skirt.
Colors: Black, Wine 417, Royal Blue 567.
Women's Sizes: 34, 36, 38, 40, 42, 44.
Lengths, 58 to 60 in. State size and color.
◆ 31 NK 4522—Shpg. wt., 1 lb. 14 oz.
$2.00 Down on Easy Terms..Cash $9.98

SEARS EASY ORDERING AND NEW, FASTER SERVICE

—*Check Your Size . . .* see size measurements
Page 1254. It's easy to get correct fit
(we guarantee it) by mail, phone or through
Sears Order Offices.
—*To See The Color . . .* whenever a number
follows color name, you will find the shade
illustrated on Color-Graph, Page 1248.

—*Order and pay postage only* from your
nearest Sears Mail Order House. All garments on these two pages are now
shipped from Kansas City or New York,
whichever is nearer you. Faster Service.
—*Available on Sears Easy Payment Plan . . .*
see the Inside Back Cover for Easy Terms.

Charmode dress-up frocks with quality fabric, finish

$7.98

Tucked bodice Charmode in Rayon Crepe Romaine

A solid panel of tucking gives a look of luxury to this soft cross-over bodice. You can catch the neckline back with clips as shown . . . and wear it high or low. Slim-waisted look comes from an interesting midriff yoke that fits low over the hips. Softly shirred fullness adds swing to the skirt. Four decorative fabric loops guide the long tie-front sash. The beautiful quality Rayon fabric dry cleans . . . and takes the deep colors very well. Sizes 12 to 20 will want this dress for important occasions in spring and summer.
Colors: Red 311, Navy or Black. **Misses' Sizes:** 12, 14, 16, 18, 20. State size, color. Shpg. wt., 1 lb. 8 oz.
◆31 NL 4220 . . . . $7.98

$7.98

Young whirl-skirt Frock in fine Rayon Crepe Romaine

Youth and charm translated into whirling pleats for the Charmode version of a smash success! Elongated bodice and the lowered waistline give the new longer look. Figure moulding drapery is released from shoulder shirring and caught into a solid shirred triangle at the waist. The neckline drapes high or low. Contrasting-color corsage points out the interesting new side sweep. Fabric dry cleans. This dress is a marvel in styling and finest quality dressmaking detail. It proves it pays to buy the best in fashion from Sears—you save money, enough to buy all your accessories.
Colors: Cadet Blue 575 or Black. **Misses' Sizes:** 12, 14, 16, 18, 20. State size and color. Shipping weight, 1 pound 6 ounces.
◆31 NL 4222 . . . . $7.98

$7.98

Spaghetti loop Dress in Rayon Crepe Romaine

Double rows of self-fabric "spaghetti" loops sweeping down from the shoulders to the concealed pockets emphasize the long torso line of this Charmode date dress. The neckline is cut high, as a perfect background for your glitter jewelry. The bracelet length, push-up sleeves, the waist-defining front-tie belt, the cleverly flared skirt, all accent its youthful lines. The Rayon fabric dry cleans well.
Colors: Red 311, Cadet Blue 575, Black. **Misses' Sizes:** 12, 14, 16, 18, 20. State size and color. Shipping weight, 1 lb. 6 oz.
◆31 NL 4224 . . . . $7.98

For Hats, Gloves and Bags on these two pages, see index

♡ **PAGE 37** . . . . **DRESSES**

**Blue Fox-dyed
Guanaco Fur**

$52.50 Cash

$6 Down on
Easy Terms

Fur Jackets for Spring

Dressy Charmode-Fashions .. in Quality Furs;
Satisfaction guaranteed or your money back

Silver Fox-tail Jacket

Ⓐ $74.50 Cash $8 Down
on Easy Terms

This 22-inch, Tuxedo-front fur jacket is made
from the natural tails of pedigreed Silver Foxes,
and is especially designed to look like a luxurious cape. Each tail is mounted separately on
a foundation of soft, rich, black Rayon Satin.
Under-side of full-length sleeves, and sides of
jacket are made entirely of same rich satin.
Cardigan neck is finished with rayon satin tie-
strings. Fine workmanship, guaranteed lining
are fully described in panel below.
Color: Silver Fox Tails. **Sizes:** 12, 14, 16, 18,
20. (Fit Juniors, Misses, Women.) Length, 22 in.
State size. Shipping weight, 3 pounds 6 ounces.
◆17CL5266—$8 down.... Cash price, $74.50

See how well these Furs are made

Rich linings of smooth, glistening Rayon
Satin are guaranteed to wear 2 years.

Cardigan necklines are protected and
made prettier by ruching or cording;
ruching encircles all the jacket cuffs.

Three hooks and eyes concealed in the
fur, fasten each jacket front securely.

Armshields of lining fabric prolong
jacket wear . . . and add extra value to
these handsome Charmode fur jackets.

---

100 . . . SEARS, ROEBUCK AND CO.

Mink-dyed Kolinsky Fur

5-Skin Scarf   Single Skins

$47.50 Cash $9.95 Each

$5 Down on $2 Down on
Easy Terms   Easy Terms

Ⓑ 24-inch Blue Fox-dyed Guanaco Fur

The soft smoky taupe color and fluffy texture of this
Blue Fox-dyed Guanaco Fur are becoming to everyone. It looks rich and feels luxurious. Jacket has
Tuxedo revers, ending in hidden pockets. Full-length
sleeves, encircled by swirls of fur. Blue Rayon Crepe
scarf and flower included. Fine workmanship, guaranteed lining, described in panel at left.
Color: Smoky Taupe. **Sizes:** 12, 14, 16, 18, 20. (Fit
Juniors, Misses, Women.) Lgth., 24 in. **State size.**
◆17CL5262—Shpg. wt., 4 lbs. **$6** down; Cash, $52.50

Ⓒ Mink-dyed Kolinsky Fur Scarf

This Mink-dyed Kolinsky Fur Scarf looks right and
feels right in all seasons. Smart with untrimmed coats,
with dresses or suits. (See it with suit on Page 99.)
Has handsome mink-brown tones of a scarf that
would cost many times this moderate price. Can be
worn as shown or in variety of other arrangements;
fastens with matching clasp of plastic material.
◆ 17CL5270—5-Skin Scarf. Brown only. Shpg. wt.,
1 lb. 8 oz. **$5** down on Easy Terms. . . . Cash, $47.50
◆ 17CL5272—Single Skins. Brown only. Shpg. wt.,
each, 5 oz. **$2** down. . . . . Cash, each skin, $9.95
(Each skin, 20 in. long; including tail. If you order 2
or more, we make them into scarf at no extra cost.)

Sears know how to handle fine furs

For 30 years women have trusted Sears word-of-
honor in furs. Our workmanship has won half a million
friends. Now . . . extra value; we service these jackets
for one year if repairs are due to defect in garment.

Easy ordering—fast service

–Check Your Size, see size measurements, page 998.
–All furs shipped from New York. Order and pay
  postage only from nearest Sears Mail Order House.
–Available on Easy Terms; see inside back cover.

All prices on this page include federal tax

In fine
Suiting
$12⁹⁸ Cash

In fine
Flannel
$12⁹⁸ Cash

In best
Suiting
$16⁹⁸ Cash

In best
Gabardine
$18⁹⁸ Cash

Ⓐ Link-button suit fabrics   Ⓑ 3-button suit fabrics

Man-Tailored Suits

Two fine Kerrybrooke versions of this classic American style
Sizes 12 to 20, and Sizes 38 to 44

These truly man-tailored features add to the value, beauty, and wear of each suit..in each quality:

1. Canvas under-collar hand-felled and shrunk for better fit. This is the most important step in good tailoring; we do it right.
2. Lapels interlined with light canvas so they roll softly; hold shape.
3. Buttonholes well made; resist wear.
4. Armholes well strengthened with hand-basted tape and hand-felled.
5. Smooth shoulders, lightly padded.

Fur Scarf
described
on page 100

Ⓐ Link-button classic

Most enduring fashion of all! The simple, beautiful link-button suit .. man-tailored by experts. Smart now and for years to come. Correct for all seasons, all occasions. Becoming to everyone who wears it. This latest edition has lovely low-rolling revers and new longer length 26-inch jacket. Six-gore skirt has a graceful kick-pleat in front; zipped closing. This classic fashion comes in a choice of two splendid fabrics. Each quality with jacket fully lined with rich smooth Earl-Glo Rayon Twill; guaranteed to wear 2 years.

Colors: Navy with White stripe, or Black with White stripe. **Misses' Sizes:** 12, 14, 16, 18, 20. **Women's Sizes:** 38, 40, 42, 44. Skirts in correct lengths. **State size, color.**

Our fine Worsted Suiting (40% Wool, 60% Rayon) Lined as above. Shipping weight, 2 pounds 3 ounces.
♦ 17 NL 6919—$2 down; $2 a month.....Cash, $12.98

Our best Worsted Suiting All New Wool; lined as above. Shpg. wt., 3 lbs.
♦ 17 NL 6918—$2.50 down; $3 a month...Cash, $16.98

Ⓑ Boyish 3-button

Popular last year; more popular now .. and winning new wearers every day. This superbly smart suit, with longer jacket, was inspired by a man's fashion...and is made by men's tailors. Youthful jacket has natural shoulders, slightly fitted waist, three pockets, open vent cuffs and is 26 in. long. Skirt has two kick pleats, front and back; zipped closing. Choice of fine fabrics, each jacket lined in Earl-Glo Rayon Twill; guaranteed to wear 2 years.
Misses' Sizes: 12, 14, 16, 18, 20. Jackets, 26 inches. Skirts in correct fashion lengths.

Our fine All Wool Flannel 70% New Wool, 30% Re-used Wool. Lined as above. **Color:** Menswear Gray only. Sizes as above. **State size.** Shipping weight, 3 pounds.
♦ 17 NL 6921—$2 down; $2 a month.....Cash, $12.98

Our best Wool Gabardine All New Wool. Lined as above. Finest suit we sell. **Colors:** Cavalry Beige or Navy Blue. Sizes as above. **State size, color.** Shipping weight, 3 pounds 4 ounces.
♦ 17 NL6920—$2.50 down; $3 a month...Cash, $18.98

Ⓐ		Ⓑ	
Fine Worsted Suiting	Best Worsted Suiting	All Wool Flannel	Wool Gabardine
$12⁹⁸ Cash	**$16⁹⁸** Cash	**$12⁹⁸** Cash	**$18⁹⁸** Cash
$2.00 Down	$2.50 Down	$2.00 Down	$2.50 Down

These suits styled to the minute .. you can wear them for years. Buy the best quality. For Easy Terms, see inside back cover.

♡ *PAGE 99 .. COATS AND SUITS*

Saddles

Beloved Free 'n' Easy Classics in Quality We're Proud of!

$2.85 PAIR

4-STAR FEATURE
5 WIDTHS .. 50 SIZES

★ Extremely Flexible Because They're Goodyear Welted
★ Smooth Leather Insoles
★ Leather Quarter Linings
★ Fine Quality Leather Uppers

Features Seldom Found Under $4!

Made by a famed maker of $4 shoes—with all their fine features! Authentic saddle last that has slight toe-fullness for extra comfort! White suede-finish rubber soles wear well—and are easy to clean neatly! Wide eyelets and laces. Goodyear welt construction for superb flexibility. Elk-grained leather uppers.
Women's and Girls' Sizes 5½ to 9 in AA (Extra Narrow) width; Sizes 5 to 9 in A (Very Narrow) width; 4 to 9 in B (Narrow) Sizes 3½ to 9 in C (Medium) width; 3½ to 8 in D (Med. Wide) All ½ sizes included. State size, width. Shpg. wt., 1 lb. 12 oz.
15 K 2355—White and Brown Leather. Pair.........$2.85

Our Finest Quality Saddle

$3.85 PAIR

And we doubt if you could find finer quality at **any** price! Entire upper made of fine buck finished white leather—with brown full-grained calf saddle overlay—a more expensive, smarter-looking process! Thick red gum rubber sole and heel. Superior Goodyear welt construction. Unlined for light flexibility.
Women's and Girls' Sizes 5 to 9 in A (very narrow) width; 3½ to 9 in C (Medium) width
All half sizes included. State size, width.   See Page 1255. Shipping weight, 1 pound 12 ounces.

15 K 2069—White and Brown Leather
        Pair.....................$3.85

Quality at a Special Price!

$1.88 PAIR

Finest saddle shoe we know of at this low price! Goodyear welt construction for flexibility. Long-wearing ¼-inch rubber sole, leather welting. Elk grained leather uppers. 4 color combinations. See Page 1255.
Women's and Girls' Sizes 5 to 9 A (Very Narrow) Sizes 3½ to 9 in C (Medium) width
All half sizes included. State size and width. Shipping weight, 2 pounds 2 ounces.
15 K 2190—White and Brown Leather
15 K 2191—Smoke and Brown Leather
15 K 2192—White and Black Leather
15 K 2095—White and Blue Leather
        Pair.....................$1.88

$1.98 PAIR

Walled Toe for Short Look

Finest construction, materials, and workmanship possible in a shoe at this low price! Expensive Goodyear welt construction, for flexibility, comfort, and longer wear. Leather welting. Elk grained leather uppers with smooth leather saddle. And the wall toe is roomy and comfortable to wear—it gives your foot the tiny "little girl" look that's so smart! Here's an excellent buy in both quality and style! See our easy-to-use Scientific 4-Point Foot Measuring Chart, Page 1255.
Women's and Girls' Sizes 5 to 9 in A (Very Narrow) width; 3½ to 9 in C (Med.)
All half sizes included. State size and width. Shipping weight, 2 pounds 2 ounces.
15 K 2097—White and Brown Leather
15 K 2098—Two-Tone Brown Leather
        Pair.................$1.98

EASY PAYMENTS Everything and anything in this Big Book may be purchased on Sears convenient Easy terms. You may buy shoes for the entire family all at once. . . . . See Inside Back Cover.

Kerrybrooke
POLO COAT

THE POLO COAT
that Everybody Wants

SEARS BRING IT TO YOU AT A $5 SAVING

$14.98

Similar Quality Elsewhere $19.98

$2 Down on Easy Terms

- *Shown on the Fashion Magazine Covers*
- *And worn on every street in America*
- *By actual count, favorite coat in U.S.A.*
- *In Misses' and Juniors' Sizes .. at Sears*

Sears BLUE RIBBON Edition of this winning polo coat brings you authentic style and super-value savings. The rich fabric alone is worth many-a-dollar more .. Fine tailoring looks like far costlier polo coats and its accurate fit has a truly custom-made air.

LINING is rich glistening Skinner's Rayon Satin; the fabric that's been famous for two generations and today is unconditionally guaranteed to give you two years' wear.

BUTTONS are beautiful true Ocean Pearl ... smoky white and extra lovely. And the buttonholes have an equal perfection; they're sturdily made and well-finished.

COLLAR is well-cut and fitted as though made for you alone. Then stitched in back to maintain its excellent, neck-hugging shape through a long term of smart service.

REVERS have fabric reinforcement, basted in place by hand and then securely stitched by machine, so they will fit smoothly and smartly for lifetime of your coat.

Kerrybrooke
BLUE RIBBON VALUE

One of the Finest Coat Fabrics Made, and the perfect material for this classic style; it is the famous North Star Woolen Mills' All Wool-and-Camel Hair Fleece (54% Virgin Wool, 12% Reprocessed Wool, 7% Reprocessed Camel Hair, 27% Reused Wool). Tightly textured, long wearing; yet soft and lovely to touch. Lined with long-famous Skinner's Satin, guaranteed as above; and warmly interlined.

Thoroughbred of all Polo Coats; this youthful style is top-favorite from coast to coast. Cherished by campus celebrities, work-a-day career girls, pretty brides and young-in-heart grandmothers. Because it's comfortable, becoming, and light as a cloud. Wonderfully simple .. but beautifully correct in every detail, from the open vent and belted back to the double-breasted wide-revered front. 2 huge flap pockets coddle your hands and also hold all the things you usually put in your pocketbook. Compare this masterpiece of a Kerrybrooke coat with other polo coats costing dollars more elsewhere; see what you save at Sears Roebuck. Count up all the wonderful things you can buy with the difference.

Color: Polo Tan only. **Misses' Sizes:** 12, 14, 16, 18, 20. Length, about 42½ ins.
Juniors' Sizes: 11, 13, 15, 17, 19. Length, about 42 inches. **State size.**
♦ **17 NK 6084**—Shpg. wt., 5 lbs. $2 Down on Easy Terms. Cash....**$14.98**

SEARS EASY ORDERING AND NEW, FASTER SERVICE

—*Check Your Size* . . . see size measurements Page 1254. It's easy to get correct fit by mail, phone or through Sears Order Offices.

—*To See The Color* . . . whenever a number follows color name, you will find the shade illustrated on Color-Graph, Page 1248.

—*Order and pay postage only* from your nearest Sears Mail Order House. All garments on these two pages are now shipped from Kansas City or New York, whichever city is nearer to you.

—*Available on Sears Easy Payment Plan* . . . see Inside Back Cover of Catalog.

○ **PAGE 29** . . . . **POLO COAT**

Surf Blue Denim Play Togs
Sanforized for lasting fit

Especially well cut and well tailored . . . rayon braid trimmed
Strong seams and neat inside finish . . . Sizes from 12 to 18

Ⓓ Jacket and Culotte
$1 98
Each

Well-tailored jacket in double-breasted effect. Two handy big pockets. Inside seams pinked. Length, about 23 inches.
Culotte (divided skirt) Cut to look like a sports skirt; gives trouser freedom as you move. Flap pocket at waist. Popular for bicycling, bowling, all sports.
Both in our sturdy Sanforized-Shrunk Denim, maximum fabric shrinkage 1%. Color: Surf Blue. Sizes: 12, 14, 16, 18 only. Be sure to state size.
7 L 2904—Jacket. Shpg. wt., 15 oz., $1.98
7 L 2906—Culotte (divided skirt). Shpg. wt., 1 lb. 2 oz. $1.98

Ⓔ Popular new Shortall
$1 98

Cross between an overall and shorts . . . so smart and young-looking, it's first choice with the young crowd everywhere. Sears version has all the right details: cuff bottoms, well-fitted, high-cut top so you can wear it without a shirt. Real pocket, rayon braid-trimmed flap. Sanforized-Shrunk Denim; won't shrink over 1%. Strongly made, well-finished. Attractive Knit Cotton Shirt shown is described on our Active Sportswear Page 19.
Color: Surf Blue. Sizes: 12, 14, 16, 18 only. Be sure to state size.
7 L 2907—Shpg. wt., 15 oz. $1.98

Ⓐ Overall   **$1 98**   **Sports Shirt**   **$1 39**

Overall especially cut for good fit . . . note set-in waistband, high-cut top darted snugly so you can wear it without shirt, too. Nicely detailed . . smart-flap pocket has spic-and-span rayon braid trim. Sanforized-Shrunk Denim; won't shrink more than 1%. Strongly made throughout; neat inside finish. Color: Surf Blue. Sizes: 12, 14, 16, 18 only.
7 L 2903—State size. Shpg. wt., 1 lb. 4 oz. $1.98
Chintz-print Sports Shirt. Cut long; yoke back. Fine washfast Percale in sunny yellow for gay contrast or soft blue to harmonize with Denim. Nicely made. Colors: Yellow or Copen Blue Ground; Red Berry Print.
7 L 3067—Sizes: 12, 14, 16, 18, 20. State size, color. Shpg. wt., 8 oz., $1.39

Ⓑ Trim Slacks   **$1 98**

Cut for lasting good fit. Sanforized Denim won't shrink more than 1%. Our own expert cut for trim fit and good hang. Flap pocket, rayon braid trimmed. Well tailored button placket, 2-button waistband. Crotch seams strongly double-stitched. Inside seams pinked. (*Shirt shown is described on Pg. 19.*) Color: Surf Blue. Sizes: 12, 14, 16, 18 only. State size.
7 L 2905—Shpg. wt., 1 lb. 2 oz. . . . $1.98

Ⓒ Handy Halters   **59c**
Each

Snug V front. Two-button back closing cross-over straps. Neat inside finish. Sizes: Small (fits 32-inch bust), Medium (34 to 36-inch bust), Large (38 to 40-inch bust). State size. Shipping weight, each, 5 ounces.
7 L 2970—Sanforized Denim (maximum shrinkage 1%). Color: Surf Blue . . . 59c
7 L 2971—Denim (not Sanforized). Color: Multi-color Mexican Stripes 59c

Why not pay as you wear? Sears offers Easy Terms . . . see inside back cover

Mother and Daughter Dirndl Dresses
Charming for big or little sisters too
A winsome fashion more popular than ever

Ⓐ Percale in Gay Candy Stripes

$3⁹⁸
Mothers' Sizes

$3³⁹
Growing Girls' Sizes

$2⁴⁹
Little Girls' Sizes

Whirl-skirt dirndl dress over separate romper panties. Bodice has *Matletex* "Lastex" yarn shirring, guaranteed to stay shirred. Fits snugly . . stretches. Washable Percale. Colors: Red or Copen Blue, with White Stripes. State color. **7 L 2922—Mothers' Sizes.** Small (fits sizes 10 to 12), Medium (fits sizes 14 to 16), Large (fits sizes 18 to 20). State size. Shipping weight, 1 pound 2 ounces.... **$3.98** **77 L 7588—Growing Girls' Sizes.** Small (fits 7 to 8), Medium (fits 10 to 12), Large (fits 14 to 16). State size. Shipping weight, 1 pound 2 ounces.......... **$3.39** **38 L 5704—Little Girls' Sizes.** Small (fits 1 to 2), Medium (fits 3 to 4), Large (fits 5 to 6). State size. Shipping weight, 7 ounces.......... **$2.49**

Ⓑ Fine Cotton Pique

$2⁹⁸
Mothers' Sizes

$2²⁹
Growing Girls' Sizes

$1⁸⁹
Little Girls' Sizes

Cool, crisp and snowy white .. with ric-rac in contrasting color. Perfect for mother .. for big or little daughters. True dirndl style with beautifully fitted bodice, full skirt. Closes down back with ocean pearl buttons. Two-inch hem. Pinked seams. Washfast. Colors: White with Red ric-rac; or White with Blue ric-rac. Be sure to state color and size. **7 L 2901—Mothers' Sizes:** 12, 14, 16, 18. Shipping weight, 1 pound 3 ounces................... **$2.98** **77 L 7590—Growing Girls' Sizes:** 7, 8, 10, 12, 14, 16. Shipping weight, 14 ounces................. **$2.29** **38 L 5702—Little Girls' Sizes:** 3, 4, 5, 6, 6½. Shipping weight, 7 ounces........................ **$1.89**

Ⓒ Our Front Cover Dirndl Dress . . .

Sweetest of dirndl styles with sprightly flounced skirt— flattering style for Mother, darling on big or little girls. Beautifully made in a lovely calico-patterned print on fine Percale; tested washable. Ric-rac trim. pinked seams. **State size and color.** Colors: Dainty Print on Yellow or Soft Blue.

Mothers' Sizes $2⁹⁸   **Growing Girls' Sizes $2²⁹**   **Little Girls' Sizes $1⁸⁹**

7 L 2900—Mothers' Sizes: 12, 14, 16, 18. Shipping weight, 1 pound 1 ounce.................... **$2.98** **77 L 7594—Growing Girls' Sizes:** 7, 8, 10, 12, 14, 16. Shipping weight, 14 ounces................. **$2.29** **38 L 5700—Little Girls' Sizes:** 3, 4, 5, 6, 6½. Shipping weight, 7 ounces....................... **$1.89**

♡ PAGE 13 . . . . SPORTSWEAR

ⓔ Bright with color
$1 98

Dirndl in calico print on fine Percale . . . excellent value at our thrifty price. Cut full for plenty of swing . . . trim-two-button waistband to nip your waist. Bands in merry colors for gay accent. Washable.
Colors: Yellow or Blue Ground, with Colorful Floral Print. **Sizes:** 10, 12, 14, 16, 18. State size, color. Shipping weight, 13 oz.
7 L 3202—Each . . . $1.19

ⓕ Tie-around Dirndl
$1 98

Clean-cut stripes on fine Cotton Pique . . . launders beautifully. Ties any way you like . . . front, back or at side, with splashy bow. Wide lap-over, deep hem.
Colors: Red-and-White Stripe or Blue-and-White Stripe. **Sizes:** Small (fits 23 to 25-in. waist); Med. (26 to 28-in. waist); Large (29 to 30-in. waist). State size, color. Shipping weight, 15 ounces.
7 L 3201—Each $1.98

ⓖ Fiesta Dirndl
$1 98

Whirls with a wide sweep like a rhumba dancer's skirt. Twin print ruffles . . the under one in gay color. Slim, wide waistband; tie-tight sash. Fine calico-patterned Percale. Washable.
Colors: Gay Print on Red or Blue Ground, both with Yellow Print under-ruffle. **Sizes:** 10, 12, 14, 16, 18. State size and color. Shipping weight, 15 ounces.
7 L 3203—Each . . . $1.98

Buy by mail and save . . everything available on Sears
Easy Payment Plan . . see inside back cover for details

Gay Dirndl Skirts in fine prints and the right Blouses to wear with them

Newest favorites . . . All washable . . . Sizes from 10 to 20

Ⓐ Skirt in tropical print sunny California fashion $1 98

Summer-cool and softly colorful . . a print of real distinction. Makes a dress-up dirndl nice enough to dance or dine in. Cut luxuriously full, made with deep hem. Two-button waistband for neat, nipped look. In better Percale, tested washfast.
Colors: Bright Red or Bright Blue, with Contrasting Print. **Sizes:** 10, 12, 14, 16, 18. State size, color.
7 L 3205—Shipping weight, 12 ounces $1.98

Ⓒ Suspender Dirndl Skirt in lovely rosebud print $1 98

Sweet as Grandma's courting days . . wide-skirted, tiny-waisted dirndl with eyelet embroidery frilled hem, 2 rows of ric-rac. Trim two-button waistband. Good quality Percale in an adorable rosebud print that washes beautifully. Fine fashion value!
Colors: Copen Blue or Yellow Grounds, Rose-and-White Print. **Sizes:** 10, 12, 14, 16, 18. State size, color.
7 L 3204—Shipping weight, 12 ounces $1.98

Ⓑ Dirndl Blouse with low square-cut neck so popular $1 00

Sears version is a splendid value . . crisp-finished, fine Cotton Batiste with eyelet embroidery trim in unusually nice quality. Full cut; well made with fine stitching, pinked inside seams, ample tuck-in.
Color: White only. **Sizes:** 12, 14, 16, 18, 20; see How to Measure on Page 998. State size.
7 L 3008—Shipping weight, 4 ounces $1.00

Ⓓ Button-front Dirndl Blouse with little-girl round neck $1 00

Beautifully made in our dainty, crisp-finish fine Cotton Batiste. Eyelet embroidery is fine quality, rare at this price. Deep front facing; yoke at back and front. Perfect with skirt shown . . any skirt.
Color: White only. **Sizes:** 10, 12, 14, 16, 18; see How to Measure, Page 998. State size.
7 L 3011—Shipping weight, 4 ounces $1.00

Buy by Mail and Save . . . it's easy to order from Sears

All garments on these 2 pages are stocked in your nearest Sears Mail-Order House so we can serve promptly. This means that most shipments will arrive in a few days. Order and pay postage from your nearest Sears Mail-Order House.

—Check your size . . . see size measurements, Page 998. Measurements for fit used in our skirts, blouses and dresses are same as best standards used in America. It's easy to get correct fit at Sears by mail, phone or through our helpful order offices.

Kerrybrooke
PLAY CLOTHES

Buy the Shirt to wear with Playsuit

California styling in the Season's most famous print

Hawaiian-inspired design on luxurious Rayon Crepe .. superbly styled and finely made .. Sizes 12 to 18

Bra-Top Playsuit

2-piece set complete **$3⁹⁸** Set
"Bra" and Shorty Skirt

Ⓐ Fashion a Hollywood star would choose .. the bare-waist playsuit that glorifies a fine figure, sets off your tan. Brief shorty skirt has side zip, fine Rayon jersey underpanties with snug elastic legs. Fitted, lined halter bra. Order Shirt, too .. wear it over Playsuit, the ultra-smart way. Fine Rayon Crepe, tested hand washable. Use gentle Lux to keep it fresh and new-looking longer.
Colors: White Print on Sun Red or Blue. **Sizes:** 12, 14, 16, 18. **State size, color.** Shpg. wt., set, 11 oz.
◆ 7 NL 2921M......2-piece $3.98

Sears easy ordering

—Check your size, see Page 998.
—Easy Terms available, see inside back cover.
—Garments on these 2 pages marked ◆ shipped from Kansas City or New York; others from Sears nearest Mail Order House. Order all from nearest Mail Order House and pay postage from there.

Shirt and Dirndl Skirt

Both sold **$3³⁹** Each
separately

Ⓑ **Softly Tailored Shirt** .. cut long like a man's, slit at sides. Yoke back. Casual style, perfect in soft, cool Rayon Crepe. Finely finished.
Ⓒ **Swirling Dirndl Skirt** shows off superb print proudly; is full-gathered onto wide, two-button waistband for nipped look. Two-inch hem. *Both hand washable;* we recommend Lux for ideal results.
Colors: White Print on Sun Red or Blue. **Sizes:** 12, 14, 16, 18. State size, color. Shipping weight, each, 12 oz.
◆ 7 NL 2919M—Shirt......$3.39
◆ 7 NL 2920M—Skirt......$3.39

4-pc. Set **$10⁰⁰**
Complete Cash .. $2 Down
Save on complete 4-pc. set. Shirt, Skirt and 2-pc. Playsuit. Colors and sizes as above. **State size, color.** Shipping weight, set, 1 lb. 8 oz.
◆ 7NL2924M—4-pc. Set. Cash $10.00
$2 down .. $2 month on Easy Terms

☐ PAGE II.........SPORTSWEAR

Both in Sizes
48 to 52, too

Jacket Slack Suit in Spun Rayon Gabardine

The season's most popular slack suit adapted for larger women . . with all the good style you admire in smaller sizes. Slenderizing long jacket has set-in belt at back, easily adjusted front ties. Slacks have soft front pleats, trim two-button waistband, well-tailored button placket. Fabric is smooth and smart . . a fine quality, beautifully tailored to add to slenderizing effect. Inside seams neatly pinked. Dry cleaning recommended. **Colors: Copen Blue or Navy. Larger Women's Sizes: 38, 40, 42, 44, 46.** State size, color. Shpg. wt., 1 lb. 7 oz.

$4.98 Set

♦ 7 NL 2960—2-Pc. Suit $4.98

Special Playclothes for larger women

Youthful styles in sizes 38 to 46

- Scientifically cut to slenderize . . . to fit comfortably
- Roomy hips and armholes . . . easy fulness you like at bust

2-piece Slack Suit
$2.98 Set

Thrifty slack suit, especially well tailored in durable Cotton Suiting, tested washable. Long in-or-out shirt with double-stitched yoke back. Cuff-bottom slacks have 2-button waistband, buttoned placket. Inside seams pinked. **Color: Lt. Navy with White Stripes. State size.** Shipping weight, each, 1 pound 5 ounces. **7L2956—Larger Women's Sizes: 38, 40, 42, 44, 46. 2-pc. suit** . . . . **$2.98** **7L2957—Larger Women's Sizes: 48, 50, 52** **$2.98**

Denim separates
$1.29 Jacket   **$1.69** Overall

Overall. Wear with or without shirt. Buttons at back. **Color: Surf Blue. State size.** Shipping weight, ea., 13 oz. **7 L 2952—Larger Women's Sizes: 38, 40, 42, 44, 46. Each** . . . . **$1.69** **7 L 2953—Larger Women's Sizes: 48, 50, 52. Ea.** . . **$1.69**

Jacket. Makes a handy all-around separate. Well tailored. **Color: Multi-color stripes. State size.** Shpg. wt., ea., 9 oz. **7 L 2954—Larger Women's Sizes: 38, 40, 42, 44, 46.** **$1.29** **7 L 2955—Larger Women's Sizes: 48, 50, 52** **$1.29**

2-piece Playsuit
$3.29 Set

Neat, slenderizing print in smart fashion fabric (95% durable cotton, 5% Rayon). 1-pc. playsuit has yoke-back shirt, shorts with front pleats. May be worn with or without belt. Well-cut 7-gore skirt buttons down front . . easy on, easy to iron. Washable. **Colors: White Print on Copen Blue or Rose.** **Larger Women's Sizes: 38, 40, 42, 44, 46. State size and color.** Shipping weight, 1 pound 2 ounces. **7 L 2958—2 Pcs.** . . **$3.29**

Culotte Dress
$3.98

Divided skirt in newest most expert cut . . looks just like a dress when you stand, gives trouser freedom when you walk. Undersection has smooth zip closing. Our better washfast Cotton Seersucker in smart narrow stripes. One-piece style; set-in belt. **Colors: Red-and-White or Copen Blue-and-White stripes.** **Larger Women's Sizes: 38, 40, 42, 44, 46. State size and color.** Shipping weight, 1 pound 2 ounces. ♦**7NL2959—1 Pc.** . **$3.98**

Buy by Mail and Save . . . it's easy to order from Sears

—Check Your Size . . . see size measurements, Page 998. It's easy to get correct fit by mail, 'phone or through Sears helpful Order Offices.
—Available on Sears Easy Terms . . . payments may be budgeted over months ahead. See inside back cover.

Garments marked ♦ on these 2 pages are shipped from Kansas City or New York, whichever is nearer you. Others are shipped from your nearest Mail Order House. Order all garments from your nearest Sears Mail Order House and pay postage from there.

You'll want Play Shoes too . . styles shown here are described on pages 136, 137, 138

Charmode Dresses for a Gracious Lady

Specially designed . . . painstakingly styled . . . carefully proportioned for the poised matron. Softly tucked or gathered bodices . . . graceful gored skirts give you the lines you love! Easy to slip-on button-fronts, side plackets, long sleeves, and hems that can be let out make these frocks completely wearable and Sears-guaranteed for correct fit.

Ⓐ CROWN TESTED RAYON
$1⁹⁸

The coat-dress everyone loves. Buttons up the front to white cotton lace bow and becoming round collar. Styled to flatter and cut for comfort and fit with tailored shoulder yoke, long sleeves, and snap cuffs. 1-inch hem.
Women's Sizes: 34, 36, 38, 40, 42, 44, 46. **State size, color.** Lengths, 47 to 49 inches. Shipping weight, each, 1 lb. 6 oz.
31 K 4600–Plain Navy or Black. $1.98
31 K 4601–White Polka Dots on Navy or Black ground..............$1.98

Ⓑ PRINTED OR PLAIN RAYONS
$2⁹⁸

Eyelet organdy and cotton lace for the dickey of this charming dress . . . with V neckline, full sleeves and a lovely six-gore skirt. 2-inch hem.
Women's Sizes: 34, 36, 38, 40, 42, 44, 46. **State size, color.** Lengths, 47 to 49 in. Shpg. wt., each, 1 lb. 6 oz.
Washable Rayon French-type Crepe
◆**31 NK 4604** — White Print on a Navy or Black ground......$2.98
Celanese Rayon Crepe *Serene*
◆**31NK4605**–PlainNavy,Black.$2.98

Ⓒ THE SHIRTWAIST FROCK
$5⁹⁸

57% Spun Rayon; 33% Wool with 10% rabbit hair added . . . a favorite for warmth and beauty! Detachable and washable white cotton eyelet collar, cuffs, hanky. Dress buttons to the waist... there are soft pleats and gores in skirt. . . . 2-inch hem . . . Crown zip Placket.
Colors: Navy, Black, Gray. **State size, color. Women's Sizes:** 34, 36, 38, 40, 42, 44, 46. Lengths, 47 to 49 inches. Shipping weight, 1 pound, 10 ounces.
◆ **31 NK 4606**..............$5.98

SEARS EASY ORDERING . . . SEARS EASY PAYMENT PLAN

–*Check Your Size* . . . see Page 1254. It's easy to get correct fit by Mail, phone or through Sears Order Offices now that our measurements-for-fit are the same as the best standards everywhere. Sears guarantee correct fit or your money refunded:
–*Available on Sears Easy Payment Plan*—see Inside Back Cover.

–*Order and pay postage only* from your nearest Sears Mail Order House. Garments with diamond ◆ before catalog numbers on these two pages are now shipped from Kansas City or New York, whichever is nearer you.* All other garments are shipped from your nearest Sears Mail Order House.

A Gracious Lady Selects a
SUCCESS STYLE
With Convertible Neckline and a Generous 3-inch Adjustable Hem

Very Specially
Priced at
$4⁹⁸

The ever-popular shirtwaist frock tailored to a queen's taste! Fine Celanese Rayon Crepe *Serene* shows up the workmanship of the tucked bodice . . . drapes beautifully for the amply-cut back and front shoulder yoke . . . hangs straight and slim for the smart gored skirt! Note the washable white cotton eyelet over-collar, the dainty buttons on the blouse, the Crown zip placket! 3-inch hem.
Colors: Navy or Black. **Women's Sizes:** 34, 36, 38, 40, 42, 44, 46. **State size, color.** Lgths., 47 to 49 in.
◆ **31 NK 4608**—Shipping weight, 1 lb. 8 oz..$4.98

○ *PAGE 107* . . . . DRESSES

FOR FURLOUGH DATES and all your dress occasions

Cleverly cut, beautifully fitting, easy-to-wear dresses in fine quality rayons
Plains, prints, basic types and 2-pc. dresses: all the 1943 success styles are here

RAYON CREPE Ro- **$5.98**
maine in a jacket dress
you can wear for best or
everyday. Flattering trim of fine white
rayon organdy and lace is detachable.
Composition buttons close the softly
shirred jacket. Front gored skirt has
plain back. Dry cleanable.
Colors: Navy or black. *Misses' sizes:*
12, 14, 16, 18, 20. See size scale on
page 18. *State size and color.*
◆ 31E4042–Shpg. wt., 1 lb. 8 oz. $5.98

RAYON JERSEY . . **$6.98**
sleek, smooth-fitting in
a splashy print . . . a
beautiful wrinkle-resistant fabric
that drapes so gracefully. New, easy
to wear cross over bodice. Modified
peg-top skirt has curved set-in pockets, self belt. Dry cleanable.
Colors: White ground floral print.
Misses' sizes: 12, 14, 16, 18, 20. See
size scale, page 18. *State size, color.*
◆ 31E4043–Shpg. wt., 1 lb. 8 oz. $6.98

RAYON CREPE Ro- **$5.98**
maine coat dress has
dainty lingerie collar
and cuffs of fine rayon marquisette.
Unpressed pleats in front and gored
back skirt for easy fit. A favorite
style becoming to all types.
Colors: Navy or black with pale pink
collar and cuffs. *Misses' sizes:* 12,
14, 16, 18, 20. See size scale on page
18. *State size and color.*
◆ 31E4040–Shpg. wt., 1 lb. 8 oz. $5.98

A BASIC DRESS to **$5.98**
dress up or down, as
you wish. Wear either
the plain self fabric belt or simulated jewel trimmed self belt. Note
the new shoulder treatment on this
basic dress. Good quality rayon crepe
Romaine. Dry cleanable.
Colors: Black or navy. *Misses' sizes:*
12, 14, 16, 18, 20. See size scale on
page 18. *State size and color.*
◆ 31E4041–Shpg. wt., 1 lb. 8 oz. $5.98

14 . . . SEARS, ROEBUCK AND CO₂ □ ◈   Garments on these 2 pages shipped from New York. Order, pay postage from mail order house which sent you this catalog.

Platforms are high fashion for Spring

High soles are high fashion
$3.69

J Exciting version of a favorite South American fashion note. Bow makes your foot look smaller. Fine crushed kid or patent leather. 2½-inch Cuban heel.
• A (very narrow) width in sizes 5 to 9. C (med.) width in women's sizes 4 to 9. All half sizes, too. *State size and width.*
♦5 E 8027—White crushed kid
♦5 E 8026—Black patent leather
Shipping weight, 1 lb. 3 oz......Pair $3.69

Port hole perforations
$3.69

H Fine, sleek patent or soft crushed kid. Neat bow. Cushiony platform. Leather soles, 2½-in. Cuban heels.
• A (very narrow) only in sizes 5 to 9. C (medium) in women's sizes 4 to 9. Half sizes, too. *State size, width.*
♦5 E 8024—Beige crushed kid
♦5 E 8025—White crushed kid
♦5 E 8023—Black patent leather
Shipping weight, 1 lb. 3 oz......Pair $3.69
♦Means sent from Chicago. Order, pay postage from nearest mail order house.

Leg Make-up for that silk stocking glamour

Ann Barton Leg Make-up—Lotion type
Save precious hose—wear liquid make-up in place of stockings. Easily, quickly applied with powder puff, cotton, sponge, or smoothed on with the hands. Gives legs a smooth sheen, stocking-like finish; does not rub off on clothes. May be removed with soap and warm water. **State shade:** Light Suntan or Dark Suntan.
8 E 5774—4-ounce bottle. Postpaid.............**39c**

Harriet Hubbard Ayer Stocking Lotion
Lasting. Easily applied—goes on without streaking—dries rapidly—gives legs a golden sun-tan finish.
8 E 5141—4-ounce bottle. Postpaid...........**$1.10**

Patrick's Leg Art—Liquid Dye type
Use Patrick's Leg Art. Three popular shades: Beige (light), Copper (medium), Rust (dark). **State shade.**
8 E 5986—3-ounce bottle. Shpg. wt., 12 oz......**41c**

Leg Charm—Cream type
For a smooth silk stocking effect. Applies just like cold cream. Run-proof, wrinkle-free "sheer-silk" leg make-up. **State shade:** Nude or Sun Tan.
8 E 3152—3½ ounces. Postpaid.................**52c**

Helena Rubinstein—Leg Stick
Easy to apply. Gives legs a sun tan appearance.
8 E 5963—Postpaid.........................**$1.10**

Ann Barton Cake Make-up (not shown)
Stays on a long time—easily applied with moistened puff or sponge. Convenient to carry in cosmetic bag or purse. Comes in Tulle Mist (light), Ivory Satin (medium), or Heirloom Lace (dark). **State shade.**
8 E 5988—⅞-ounce, Plastic Case. Postpaid....**39c**

Max Factor Pan-Cake make-up
Used by the stars in Hollywood for greater leg appeal. Lends a smooth, silky appearance to your legs. Easy, quick to apply. Natural No. 1, Natural-Rose, Cream No. 1, Tan No. 1. **State shade wanted.**
8 E 4215—1¾ ounces. Postpaid.............**$1.65**

Elmo Photo-Finish Make-up (not shown)
Sponges on in a jiffy—gives a sheer stocking-like appearance . . . lasts for hours. Nude (light), Peach (medium), and Copper (dark). **State shade.**
8 E 5505—1¾ ounces. Postpaid.............**$1.65**

Solitair—by Campana (not shown)
Filmy loveliness for your legs. Contains lanolin. Natural (lgt.), Rachel, Peach Bloom, Brunette, Golden Tan (med.), Bronze (dk.). **State shade.**
8 E 3608—1⅖ ounces. Postpaid.............**66c**

Large Puffs.. for leg or cake make-up (not shown)
Double thick cotton puffs, especially absorbent.
8 E 4174—Shpg. wt., 3 oz.........10 puffs for **10c**

Playsuit in cot-
ton pique to go
with pinafore (A)

Playsuit to go
with suspender
dirndl skirt (B)

Playsuit to go
with classic but-
ton front skirt (C)

Double-duty Playsuits in washable cottons

Two outfits in one . . wear them as go-everywhere dresses,
wear the cool one-piece suits for sports, sun and fun

$3.98

A) PINAFORE playsuit . .
pretty pinafore makes a perfect
separate. Washfast check percale
print, ric-rac trim. Dutch boy
pockets, sash at back. Playsuit
in cotton pique has convenient
drop seat held in place with belt
that ties firmly at front. *Colors:*
Pinafore in red-and-white or blue-
and-white checks; white playsuit. *Sizes:* 12, 14, 16, 18, 20.
Scale, page 18. *State size, color.*
Shipping weight, 1 lb. 8 oz.
◆ 7 E 2858—2 pieces.....$3.98

$2.98

B) SUSPENDER SKIRT over
classic 1-piece playsuit. Both in
better quality chambray that
wears, washes well. Skirt is newest dirndl style with swagger
pockets; opens all the way down
back (with lapover) to slip on
easily over playsuit. *Colors:* Red-
and-white, brown-and-white or
green-and-white stripes. *Sizes:*
12, 14, 16, 18, 20. Scale on page 18.
State size and color. Shipping
weight, 1 pound 2 ounces.
◆ 7 E 2859—2 pieces.....$2.98

$1.98

C) BUTTON FRONT SKIRT
over classic 1-pc. playsuit, Sears
good value in a budget priced
play outfit. Serviceable percale
in colorful stripes stays bright,
colors are tested washfast. Skirt
is well made with dress-up bow
tie at waist and gores to give a
becoming flare. *Color:* Red-white-
and-blue stripes. *Sizes:* 12, 14,
16, 18, 20; measure, see size
scale on page 18. *State size.* Shipping weight, 14 ounces.
◆ 7 E 976—2 pieces......$1.98

COTTON SLACKS . . washables for work or everyday

$1.59

A) SANFORIZED DENIM slacks, with western style pockets. Good fit lasts; fabric shrinks only 1%. Well made; important seams double stitched. Work-or-play slacks that are both smart and serviceable.
Color: Medium blue.
Sizes: 12, 14, 16, 18, 20. Measure, see scale at left. *State size.*
47 E 2842–Shpg. wt., 1 lb. . $1.59

$1.59

B) SEERSUCKER, in woven stripes, menswear weave that takes hard service . . looks smart anywhere. Two deep pockets. Slacks you don't have to iron, ideal for summer.
Colors: Red-and-white, blue-and-white or brown-and-white stripes. *Sizes:* 12, 14, 16, 18, 20. See scale. Shpg. wt., 12 oz.
47 E 2841–*State size, color.* . $1.59

$1.98

C) SANFORIZED COTTON TWILL, shrinks only 1%. Toughies for work; won't soil easily. Side pocket. Navy or brown. *Sizes:* 12, 14, 16, 18, 20. *State size, color.*
♦7 E 2816–Shipping wt., 1 lb. $1.98
STRIPED KNIT COTTON pullover. Washable. Blue-and-white or red-and-white stripes. *Small* (30–32 in. bust), *Medium* (34–36 in.), *Large* (38–40 in.). *State size, color.*
47 E 3168–Shipping wt., 8 oz. 94c

NAVY WITH WHITE for your Spring Suit Dress

You'll wear it now; you'll wear it right through the summer. It's made of fashionable rayon fabrics, splendidly tailored with fine stitched seams, generous hems, and neat shoulder pads.

FLARING PEPLUM jacket dress in alpaca-type rayon crepe. Copy of a higher priced fashion favorite, it's a first choice for furlough dates or service weddings. Dainty lingerie trim is detachable. Note the expensive detailing of self fabric buttons and tie belt. Easy to wear gored skirt. Two wonderful colors for your first spring dress. Dry cleanable.
Colors: Navy or emerald green.
Misses' sizes: 10, 12, 14, 16, 18. To measure, see size scale on page 18. *State size and color.*
◆ 31 E 4001—Shipping weight, 1 lb. 8 oz....$5.98

$5.98

SOFT CARTRIDGE TUCKING joins the pockets of this alpaca-type rayon crepe suit dress. The detachable white over-collar covers notched revers. Belt is bright red patent-like leather. Favorite type skirt has 6-gore front, 3-gore back. A good choice in navy for your first spring costume. Wear it under a coat now and all through summer without one. Dry clean. *Color:* Navy only.
Misses' sizes: 12, 14, 16, 18, 20. To measure. see size scale on page 18. *State size.*
◆ 31 E 4000—Shipping weight, 1 lb. 8 oz...$6.98

$6.98

SNOWY POLKA DOTS on rayon French-type crepe are accented by the popular sailor-type collar and contrast buttons. The shirred jacket waistline gives it a slim fitting line. Popular 3-gore skirt. Come in your favorite navy and popular new shade. Hand wash separately. Use Lux.
Colors: Navy or luggage brown each with white polka dots.
Misses' sizes: 12, 14, 16, 18, 20. *State size and color.* See size scale on page 18.
◆ 31 E 4002—Shipping weight, 1 lb. 8 oz., $4.98

$4.98

20 ... SEARS, ROEBUCK AND CO. ☐ ◆   Add accessories to your dress order. If total amounts to $10 or more, Easy Terms are available; see inside back cover.

MACOMBA CLOTH
CASUALS

Crisp, tailored sportswear in nationally famous Macomba Cloth.. the smooth Rayon-with-Teca fabric that spells summer smartness and coolness. Keeps its freshly-pressed look through hours of active wear because of the care and attention we've given to its making. Buy a whole outfit as the basis of a spring and summer wardrobe.. or order individual items as smart separates.

SOLID COLOR 2-PIECE SUIT. Can be worn with or without a blouse. Skirt pleated front and back. Wear either piece with other outfits too. *Colors:* Sunset red, forest green, navy or pecan beige. Shipping weight, 1 pound 15 oz.
◆ 7 E 2847 . . . . $8.95

CONTRASTING COLOR jacket, slacks, and skirt . . . mix them as you like.

JACKET ONLY. *Colors:* Forest green, sunset red, navy, pecan beige.
◆ 7 E 2848–Shpg. wt., 1 lb. 3 oz. $4.98

SKIRT ONLY. *Colors:* Sunset red, copen or navy blue.
◆ 7 E 3406–Shpg. wt., 12 oz. $3.98

MAN-TAILORED SLACKS, see preceding page for description. *Colors:* Clove brown, pecan beige or navy.
◆ 7 E 2843–Shpg. wt., 1 lb. 4 oz. $3.98

All in Sizes: 12, 14, 16, 18 and 20. *State size, color.* (Dry clean for longest service.) Shipped from New York. Order, pay postage from the Mail Order House from which you received this Catalog.

Work cap 89c

Sturdy, comfortable clothes . . .

Sanforized cotton work cloth . . . guaranteed maximum shrinkage 1%

Utility and safety features . . . factory-tested		Better workmanship insures better wear	
Smooth button closings	Adjustable tabs at ankles	Bar-tacked at strain points	Buttons strongly sewn on
Pockets built into seams	No gapping..no loose ends	Main seams double-stitched	Cleanly finished throughout

Streamlined Coverall

Roomy one-piece suit features cleverly concealed drop seat adjustable by side buttons. Neat fly-front, button closing. Convertible collar, 4 handy work pockets. Button tabs adjust at ankles. Action back; button cuffs on sleeves. Sanforized cotton work cloth—wash separately. **$3.98**
Misses' sizes: 12, 14, 16, 18, 20.
Women's sizes: 40, 42, 44. **State size.**
Shipping weight, 1 pound 8 ounces.
27 D 9702—medium blue. . .**$3.98**

Work Cap—adjustable, fits everyone. Hair can be tucked under it easily. Navy blue cotton gabardine.
78 D 42—Shipping wt., 9 oz. . . .**89c**

Fly-front Coverall

Serviceable one-piece suit with concealed button-front closing. . . easy to slip on and off! Designed for comfort and efficiency . . . notched convertible collar, set-in belt and long button-band sleeves. Well-fitted trousers with adjustable tabs at ankles. Handy breast pocket; two trouser pockets are set in carefully to avoid catching. Back hip pocket, too. Our sturdy Sanforized-Shrunk cotton work cloth . . . wears well. Wash separately. Grand Sears value. **$2.69**
Misses' sizes: 12, 14, 16, 18, 20.
Women's sizes: 40, 42, 44. **State size.**
Shipping weight, 1 pound 8 ounces.
27 D 9690—medium blue. . .**$2.69**

Work cloth or corduroy

Jacket and slack set, specially made for hard work! Easy fitting, button-front jacket has convertible collar, two work pockets. Wear in or out of well tailored slacks which have snug waistband, side-button placket and side pocket. Both fabrics are famous for wear. **$3.69** Work Cloth
Misses' sizes: 12, 14, 16, 18, 20.
Women's sizes: 40, 42, 44. **State size, color.** Shipping wt., ea., 1 lb. 12 oz.
Sanforized-shrunk cotton work cloth . . long wearing, wash separately.
27 D 9697—medium blue. . .**$3.69**
Fine Wale Corduroy-wash separately.
◆**27 ND 9052**—dark green or wine. **$5.98**

Work cloth or corduroy

The perfect all-purpose slacks! Built-up waistband with button placket closing at the side. Trimly tailored with plenty of room in the seat. Handy side pocket. Two popular, long-wearing fabrics! **$1.98** Work Cloth
Misses' sizes: 12, 14, 16, 18, 20.
Women's sizes: 40, 42, 44. **State size, color.** Shipping wt., each, 1 lb.
Sanforized cotton work cloth
Max. shrinkage 1%, wash separately.
27 D 9698—med. blue slacks, **$1.98**
Fine wale corduroy—wash separately.
◆**27 ND 9053**—dark green or wine slacks **$3.98**
27 D 9706—Chambray Shirt shown above at **$1.59** . . . see page 71.

Everything available on Sears easy payment plan; see inside back cover for complete details

Maternity Dresses and Slacks

Easy to put on . . . easy to adjust . . . always smart and trim
Careful study of your needs resulted in these features:

- Pleats or gathers for bust fullness
- Pleats or snaps for waist expansion
- Straight hanging skirts . . . 2-inch hems
- Sleeves allow for full upper arms

$2⁹⁸ Percale   **$4⁹⁸** Rayon

Storkette Slack Suit

Concealing outfit in Spun Rayon or Percale with a pleated back blouse. The roomy slacks have an 8-button waistband for adjustment. Short sleeves, convertible collar. Buy one for everyday, one for best. Sizes: 12, 14, 16, 18, 20. State size, color. Shipping weight, each, 1 lb. 7 oz.
◆7 NL 2949—Fine Spun Rayon in Luggage Brown 212 or Lt. Navy Blue (Dry cleans) $4.98
◆7 NL 2950—Washable Percale in Copen Blue or Wine with White Line Check. $2.98

$2⁹⁸ Spun Rayon   **$4⁴⁹** Rayon Crepe

Popular Smocked Dress

Fresh spring print in two qualities of Rayon, hand washable in Lux. This one-piece maternity frock has fine smocking that releases front fullness, a long belt controls the fullness at waistline.
Colors: Dusty Rose, Navy or Teal with White Print. State size, color. Shpg. wt., ea., 1 lb. 4 oz.
Rayon French-type Crepe
◆31 NL 4800—Sizes: 12 to 20
◆31 NL 4801—Sizes: 34 to 44, Each. . . . $4.49
Buy another in Spun Rayon
◆31 NL 4802—Sizes: 12-20, $2.98
◆31 NL 4803—Sizes: 34-44, $2.98

$4⁴⁹ Rayon Crepe   **$6⁹⁸** Rayon Romaine

Rayon Smock Dress

Boxy jacket with shoulder yoke that releases pleats. Skirt on bodice top has adjustable snaps. Detachable pique trims. Misses' Sizes: 12, 14, 16, 18, 20, 22. State size, color. Shpg. wt., ea., 1 lb. 6 oz.
◆31 NL 4805—Rayon Romaine in Navy or Copen Blue 607 (Dry cleans). . $6.98
◆31 NL 4806—Polka Dot on Rayon in Navy or Copen Blue (Dry cleans). $4.49
◆31 NL 4807—Washable Cotton in Navy or Dusty Rose, each with White Dots. . $2.98

Sears easy ordering . . . Buy by mail and Save

–Check your size . . see Measurements, Page 998. Order your regular size . . make no allowances.
–For explanation of washing terms, see Page 1001.
–Color numbers refer to the Color-Graph facing first green page in the back of the catalog.

–Garments marked ◆ on this page are shipped from Kansas City or New York, whichever is nearer. Order garments and pay postage from your nearest Sears Mail Order House. Your orders usually arrive in a few days.

Redingote Dress in Print or Plain Rayon

$5⁴⁹

Choose printed or Plain Rayon for a redingote-effect dress with tie-front covering the front release snaps. Its features are the panel front to give you long slimming lines and a detachable white rayon bengaline collar.
Misses' Sizes: 12, 14, 16, 18, 20, 22. State size, color. Shpg. wt., ea., 1 lb. 4 oz.
◆31 NL 4810—Washable Print Rayon French-type Crepe with Navy or Teal Ground. $5.49
◆31 NL 4811—Rayon Crepe in Solid Navy or Teal 672 $5.49

Important: Order your regular dress size. Make no allowances.
Slips to wear with these new Maternity Dresses . . . page 179.

☐₂ **PAGE 213B . . MATERNITY WEAR**

Kerrybrooke* is Sears own name for
casual clothes . . styles of the minute
. . . fashions wearable for years

The Seven-button suit

The Cardigan suit

The Three-button suit

Kerrybrooke* is Sears own name for
casual clothes . . styles of the minute
. . . fashions wearable for years

Kerrybrooke

SUITS

♡ **PAGE 33** . . . . **SUITS**

REEFER and BOY COAT in three fine woolens

Cash, each **$9.98** On Easy Terms ½ down

GOOD QUALITY in both styles . . is made of our fine Herringbone tweed, 40% new wool and 60% reprocessed wool. Unusually good colors and nice texture for this moderate price. Lined with Earl-Glo rayon twill; lining guaranteed to wear for two years.

Cash, each **$12.98** On Easy Terms ½ down

BETTER QUALITY in both styles . . is made of our superior Herringbone tweed, 100% new wool. Extra sturdy; with beauty of color and texture that is well worth the difference in price. Earl-Glo rayon crepe lining guaranteed to wear two years.

Cash, each **$16.98** On Easy Terms ½ down

OUR BEST QUALITY in both styles . . features our best Herringbone tweed, 100% new wool . . superbly soft and strong. Lining is of our best rayon crepe; guaranteed to wear two years. Best tailoring; collar and fronts canvas interlined to keep shape.

CLASSIC REEFER with smart London drape; easy fullness through the bust and smooth line at hips. New narrower revers. Back is four-gored; has pleat at back hem. *Colors:* Herringbone in oatmeal tan or powder blue. *Misses' sizes:* 12, 14, 16, 18, 20. See size scale, page 95. *State size, color.* Shpg. wt., 3 lbs. 8 oz.
♦17E6530–Good . .$9.98   ♦17E6529–Better. .$12.98   ♦17E6528–Our best. .$16.98

CLASSIC BOY COAT with roomy shoulders, deep armholes, wide sleeves. Slips on easily over suits. sportswear or dresses. Flap-top pockets are good size. *Colors:* Herringbone in oatmeal tan or powder blue. *Misses' sizes:* 12, 14, 16, 18, 20, 22. See size scale on page 95. *State size and color.* Shpg. wt., 3 lbs. 8 oz.
♦17E6527–Good. .$9.98   ♦17E6526–Better. .$12.98   ♦17E6525–Our best. .$16.98

No ration stamp required for these smart desk-to-date styles

ENDURA-FLEX SOLES . . . featured on Sears non-rationed women's footwear, are guaranteed to wear as long as leather . . . if not perfectly satisfied your money will be returned. They are either synthetic soles of rubber-like compound . . . plastic coated soles . . . or soles of a strong heavy belting-like material, impregnated with compounds to resist moisture and wear. They have been doubly tested. . . . rigidly tested by Sears own laboratory and wear-tested on hundreds of feet. We know you will be more than satisfied with their long wearing qualities.

"Baby doll" ankle strap in a premiere appearance

$2.98

This new little number is a real eye catcher with its provocative, new anklet strap and its rounded little girl vamp. Packed with prettiness, it will be seen all around town—from offices to dance-floors, because it's so much fun to wear. You can have these shoes and your stamp, too, because they're non-rationed. The endura-flex soles are specially treated to give resistance to wear and weather.

● C (medium) width in women's sizes 3½ to 9. All half sizes are included, too.

No ration stamp required for these shoes

54 H 7826—Black gabardine . . . . 2½ inch heels . . . . 54 H 7828—White sail cloth
54 H 7827—Black gabardine . . . . 1½-inch heels . . . . 54 H 7829—White sail cloth
State size. Shipping weight, 1 pound 2 ounces . . . . Pair **$2.98**

D'Orsay pump . . . thrillingly beautiful' . . . truly outstanding

$3.98

Charming salute to a new spring with a flattering version of the inimitable D'Orsay . . . its graceful open back, open toe styling and accordion pleated circle bow give it a height of smartness that puts the world at your feet. Made with endura-flex soles . . . wear tested and specially treated to resist weather.

● A (very narrow) width in all women's sizes 5 to 8. All half sizes are included, too.
C (medium) width in all women's sizes 4 to 8. All half sizes are included, too.

No ration stamp required for these shoes

◆5 H 8212—Black gabardine . . 2½ inch heel . . ◆5 H 8213—Wheat; cotton shantung
◆5 H 8233—Black gabardine . . 2 inch heel . . ◆5 H 8234—Wheat; cotton shantung
State size and width. Shipping weight, 1 pound 2 ounces . . . . Pair **$3.98**

◆ Before catalog numbers on this page means shoes are sent from Chicago. Order and pay postage from your nearest Sears mail order house.

B) Drapes well $1.98
D) Big and beautiful $2.49
F) Glamorous veiled Beret $2.49
A) Flattering style $2.39
C) Wear it many ways $1.98
E) Lovely laced Beret $2.49

Kerrybrooke Berets . . . Fashion's Favorites
REG. U. S. PAT. OFF

A) Hand-stitched Pompadour Beret—combines your favorite beret mode with the beloved pompadour! You can perch it above your curls or wear it tilted forward . . . it's equally as smart either way. Wool felt with expensive hand work on top of crown. Made for Sears by one of the world's best millinery makers.

Colors: black, bright red or navy blue. **Measure; state color wanted.** Shipping weight, 1 pound.
78 F 1558—Fits 21¾ to 22¼-inch heads.
78 F 1559—Fits 22½ to 23 -inch heads. . **$2.39**

B) Popular oblong Beret—wool felt with stitched design on top. Grosgrain bandeau hugs your forehead comfortably; bows at the side. Unusual styling makes it drape more easily and look more distinctive. Wear it in side-tilt or off-the-face fashion. A hat that goes with everything . . . and its fine quality assures long wear. Shipping weight, 1 pound.

Colors: black, bright red, flying (soldier) blue or coffee (med.) brown. **Measure; state color.**
78 F 1561—Fits 21¾ to 22¾-inch heads. . . **$1.98**

C) Hand Crocheted Band Beret—no matter what you do these busy days you'll find our Many-way Kerrybrooke beret the answer to what to wear! It drapes beautifully on your head and is so comfortable. Fine quality wool felt. Hand crocheted yarn band assures that "stay-on" satisfaction. Drape it to suit yourself. A nation-wide favorite.

Colors: dark beige with brown; solid navy blue, bright red or flying (soldier) blue with navy blue. **Measure; state color.** Shipping weight, 1 lb.
78 F 1680—Fits 21½ to 23-inch heads. **$1.98**

D) Large Beret—it's fascinating to wear this big, attractive beret, for you can drape it to make it look new and different. Wool felt cloth with yarn crocheted headband to keep it snugly on your head in spite of winds. The quality and styling have the master-touch of a famous maker—looks much more expensive.

Colors: harvest (rust) tan with brown; solid black, navy blue or dark brown. **Measure; state color wanted.** Shipping weight, each, 1 pound.
78 F 1681—Fits 21¾ to 23-inch heads. **$2.49**

E) Laced and Bow-trimmed Beret—a large beret gone glamorous with self lacing at both sides ending in tiny bows. Fine quality wool felt has narrow self bandeau and adjusting back covered with a small grosgrain bow . . . hugs your head comfortably—won't blow off in the wind. Wear forward or in side-tilt version—you'll like it either way. Made by a famous maker for Sears.

Colors: black, dark brown or navy blue. **Measure; state color.** Shipping weight, 1 pound.
78 F 1560—Fits 21¾ to 23-inch heads. **$2.49**

F) "Dress-Up" Beret . . . your favorite beret style gone sophisticated. Fine wool felt with bandeau to snug your head . . . and extra deep back for stay-on satisfaction. The rayon veil is draped across the top and caught on either side with self bows.

Colors: black, coffee (medium) brown or navy blue. **Measure; state color.** Shipping weight, 1 pound.
78 F 1547—Fits 21¾ to 22¼-inch heads.
78 F 1548—Fits 22½ to 23¼-inch heads. . **$2.49**

✲ **PAGE 145** . . . . **MILLINERY**

All wool tweed Balmacaan; welt-seams, 2 pockets

Shirt-collar neckline buttons up warmly or rolls open. Sleeves are raglan style in front, set-in at the back. Buttoned vent at back hemline. Our warmest, best all-new wool tweed in soft herringbone pattern is faintly blurred, like a fine quality menswear fabric. Skinner's rayon satin lining; tailoring and quality features as described on left side of opposite page. *Colors: Herringbone* in rust brown or medium blue. *Misses' sizes:* 12, 14, 16, 18, 20. Size scale, page 62.
♦I7 F 6027—*State size, color.* Shpg. wt., 5 lbs.........Cash, $27.50

All wool Chesterfield with silk velvet collar

Always a favorite with the men, now a first choice style for the gals. Richest quality, handsomest Chesterfield of all has silk velvet collar; raglan sleeves that slip on easily over suits. Coat is welt-seamed throughout; huge pockets. Warm all-new wool coating with firm weave, fleecy surface. Skinner's rayon satin lining; tailoring and quality features as described on left side of opposite page. *Colors:* Brown or black. *Misses' sizes:* 12, 14, 16, 18, 20. Scale, page 62.
♦I7 F 6025—*State size, color.* Shpg. wt., 4 lbs. 8 oz.....Cash, $27.50

⊖₃PAGE **71** . . . . COATS

Classics . . in three casual styles each in three qualities

BETTER . . 100% **Fine Wool** (64% virgin wool, 36% kid mohair). For you who love all virgin wool sweaters, this is a lovely blend. It combines the warmth and durability of fine wool, with the powder-puff softness of baby kid mohair. Firmer, closer knit . . with finer details and workmanship. Necks are smoothly looped to lie flat . . shaped armholes for freedom. Hand washable in Lux.

OUR BEST . . 100% **Imported Virgin Zephyr Wool.** You have to feel the luxurious softness . . to see the luscious beauty of the colors to appreciate how much finer this imported all wool zephyr is. Lovelier in texture, each sweater is hand washed after finishing, a feature found only in finest sweaters. Has flat-lying hand looped crew necks . . shaped armholes for freedom . . tapered sleeves for better fit. Hand washable in Lux.

Long Sleeve Boxy Pullover in three qualities			Long Boxy Cardigan in three qualities		
GOOD . . $1 20	BETTER . . $2.50	BEST . . $3.45	GOOD . . $1.35	BETTER . . $2.85	BEST . . $3.95
100% *soft spun cotton.* See full description top of opposite page. Longer boxy style. Long sleeves you can wear pushed up or down. *Colors:* Red, yellow, baby blue. *State size and color.* 38 E 7007 . . . . . . $1.20	100% *fine wool* (64% virgin wool, 36% kid mohair) . . . see full description at top of page. Popular longer boxy style. *Colors:* Baby blue, red, yellow, white, baby pink. *State size and color.* 38 E 7020 . . . . . . $2.50	100% *imported virgin zephyr wool* . . see full description at top of page. Sweater girl's favorite longer length pullover. Hand washed yarns. *Colors:* Pink, yellow, ice blue, light green. *State size and color.* 38 E 7023 . . . . . . $3.45	100% *soft spun cotton.* See full description at top of page. Rayon and cotton grosgrain button band. Plastic buttons. *Cardigan only.* *Colors:* Red, yellow, baby blue. *State size and color.* 38 E 7008M $1.35	100% *fine wool* (64% virgin wool, 36% kid mohair); see full description at top of page. Favorite boxy style. *Cardigan only.* *Colors:* Copen, red, yellow, white, lt. green. *State size and color.* 38 E 7021M $2.85	100% *imported virgin zephyr wool* . . . see full description at top of page. Finer rayon and cotton grosgrain button band. Fine ocean pearl buttons. Mix or match your own twin set. *Cardigan only.* *Colors:* Pink, yellow, ice blue. *State size and color.* 38 E 7025M $3.95

Even sizes: 32 to 40-inch bust. *State bust size and color.* Shipping weight, each, 1 lb. 2 oz.

☐ PAGE *67* . . . SWEATERS

The Look-Alike Coat Fashion is bigger than ever this year

Big and little sister can look alike and still have top-fashion coats. Special care has been taken in their sizing and cutting. Care that means good fit, fine making, more for your money in value.

$9.98 Sizes 7 to 9   **$10.98** Sizes 10 to 14

Available on Easy Terms, ⅓ down

The boy coat, a favorite look-alike classic. Has the "overcoat" cut, welt seaming, pleated vent back that means special tailoring. Extra value details like padded shoulders, rayon lining, ocean pearl buttons. Warmly interlined. *State size, color.* Shpg. wt., ea., 4 lbs. Scale, page 249.
Soft furry-napped fleece (37% new wool, 15% reused wool, 48% rayon) in polo tan or red.
◆77 F 7326—*Sizes: 7, 8, 9* $9.98
◆77 F 7336—*Sizes: 10, 12, 14* $10.98
Herringbone tweed (32% reused wool, 60% rayon, 8% Aralac) in blue or brown.
◆77 F 7325—*Sizes: 7, 8, 9* $9.98
◆77 F 7335—*Sizes: 10, 12, 14* $10.98

The wrap coat, special look-alike version of a screen-star favorite in soft, warm part wool fleece (37% new, 15% reused wools, 48% rayon). Double-breasted style with the handsome pearl buttons girls love. Set-in belt in the back unbuttons at the sides for a smart change. Lined with silky rayon, warmly interlined. The tailoring is superb . . . padded shoulders, careful seaming detail make it look more expensive.
Two big hit colors: Red or polo tan. *State size and color.* See size scale on page 249. Shipping weight, each, 4 pounds.
◆77 F 7327—*Sizes: 7, 8, 9* $9.98
◆77 F 7337—*Sizes: 10, 12, 14* $10.98

The Chesterfield coat, newest look-alike to match mother's favorite. Smart fly-front button closing, rich velvet collar. Inverted walking-pleat in back. Rayon twill lining, warm interlining. Two fine fabrics . . both extremely good value. *State size, color.* Scale, pg. 249. Shpg. wt., ea., 4 lbs.
Soft, furry-napped fleece (sturdy 37% new, 15% reused wools, 48% rayon) in red or polo tan.
◆77 F 7330—*Sizes: 7, 8, 9* $9.98
◆77 F 7340—*Sizes: 10, 12, 14* $10.98
Herringbone tweed (sturdy 32% reused wool, 60% rayon, 8% Aralac) in brown or blue.
◆77 F 7329—*Sizes: 7, 8, 9* $9.98
◆77 F 7339—*Sizes: 10, 12, 14* $10.98

Look-Alike Coats are easy to buy and pay for . . . they're available on Sears Easy Terms, see inside back cover.   ⊛ ₂PAGE 251 . . . . . .   GIRLS' WEAR

Aridex-treated

SNOW SUITS

Sizes 7 to 16, fully lined

Keep the cold and wind out—keep the body heat in . . . that's the secret of keeping warm. Sears snowsuits do just that. Aridex-treated means they shed water like a duck. Wind can't get through the sturdy, tightly woven fabrics. Fine features plus plenty of good looks.

A SEARS Super Value

Your best buy because:

Jackets have:

- Fly-front closings doubly reinforced . . . specially sturdy buttons and buttonholes.
- Pockets firmly tacked, strongly lined to resist wear. Deep enough for "gadgets".
- Action armholes, strongly double-seamed.
- Action-shirred waistlines for snug trim fit.
- Knit wristlets are reinforced to sleeve.

Regulation pants have:

- Zip knit anklets are reinforced to pants.
- Side-button plackets are doubly faced.
- Adjustable button waistbands are lined.
- Crotch cut full; double seam reinforcing.
- Back hip pocket, nice and deep, lined.

A **"Snowflower" blossoms on warm all wool**

100% reprocessed wool suit with wonderful figure-fitted jacket. Smart piping and embroidered wool flowers. Slash pockets. Regulation pants. *Colors:* Navy or wine. *Sizes:* 7, 8, 10, 12, 14, 16. Size scale below. *State size and color.*

♦77 F 7350—Cotton plaid lined. Shpg. wt., 4 lbs. 8 oz. . . . ⅓ down Easy Terms—cash **$10.98**

♦77 F 7351—Toast-warm, deeply piled sheepskin lining. Shpg. wt., 5 lbs. 6 oz... **$12.98**

B **"Snow Pixie"—with Lambskin fur-trimmed hood**

Two versions of this knockout snowsuit . . . a gabardine twill jacket suit or one in all wool! Contrasting piping, deep waist shirring. *Sizes:* 7, 8, 10, 12, 14, 16. Scale below. *State size and color.* *Cotton gabardine twill jacket* with special Zelan waterproof finish. Lined with deep furry cotton pile. 100% reprocessed wool pants. *Colors:* Red jacket with navy or red jacket with green pants.

♦77 F 7096—Shpg. wt., 4 lbs. . . ⅓ down on easy terms—cash **$10.98**

Same suit in teal blue with wine in 100% reprocessed wool or gray with green in 30% reprocessed, 70% reused wool. Cotton plaid lined.

♦77 F 7090—Shpg. wt., 4 lbs. 12 oz **$10.98**

Size scale for girls' Snow Wear

She wears size:	7	8	10	12	14	16
If her chest measures:	26	27	29	30½	32	34 in.
Jacket length:	19	20	21	21½	22	22½ in.
Outseam(waist to ankle):	32	33	36	38	40	42 in.

Zippers made previous to regulations restricting their use.

Boyville Jr.
OUR OWN TRADE MARK

Smart Military Uniforms, the delight of every youngster

Your choice of these three fine outfits at right, what all boys want, only

$5.98
Each

Not available until August 1. Please do not order before this date.

Deluxe tailoring

All are fine dressy, part wool flannel, 50% reused wool, 50% cotton. Coats have taped fronts to retain shape; full linings of lustrous, easy-fitting rayon.

Sears finest Junior Military Styles

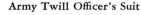

Army Twill Officer's Suit

2-tone Officer's Suit

Like a real officer's. Dark brown coat has brass color buttons; 2 lower flapped pockets; 2 imitation chest pockets; epaulets. Sam Browne belt. Tan, fly-front longies; 2 side pockets. Shpg. wt., 2 lbs. 12 oz.

State size: 4, 5, 6, 7, 8, 9, 10.
40 F 3238—Two-tone....$5.98

Smart, Admiral's Suit

Authentic navy blue color. Coat has 2 set-in lower pockets with flaps; gold color buttons; 3 rows gold color braid and star on cuffs; epaulets. Fly-front longies; 2 side pockets; belt loops. Shpg. wt., 2 lbs. 12 oz.

State size: 4, 5, 6, 7, 8, 9, 10.
40 F 3239—Navy blue...$5.98

Aviator's style

Coat has 2 lower pockets with flaps; welt chest pocket; flyer's emblem; 2 rows braid on cuffs; brass color buttons; epaulets. Sam Browne belt. Fly-front longies; 2 side pockets. Shpg. wt., 2 lbs. 12 oz.

State size: 4, 5, 6, 7, 8, 9, 10.
40 F 3240—Copen blue.$5.98

$4.98
4 Pieces

Outstanding value! Sanforized, washfast tan Army twill of fine combed cotton yarns, max. shrinkage 1%; weighs 8 oz. a sq. yard—a heavyweight for lasting wear. Sam Browne belt. Coat has double stitched seams; 4 pockets; "service ribbon"; metal insignia; epaulets. Fly-front longies. Visored cap. Wt., 2 lbs. 10 oz.

Sizes: 4, 6, 8, 10, 12, 14. State size.
40 F 4510—**Available after Aug. 1.** $4.98

Naval Officer Uniform

$2.98
4 Pieces

Medium weight navy blue cotton twill for active playtime wear. Four pieces include: Coat with gold color braid trim and insignia; epaulets; 4 pockets. Sturdy, all-around white belt. Fly-front longies with braid stripe down legs. Visored officer's type cap. Shipping weight, 2 lbs. 10 oz.
Sizes: 4, 6, 8, 10, 12, 14.
State size wanted.
40 F 4502—4 pieces....$2.98

Jr. "WAAC"

$2.79
4 Pieces

Medium weight olive drab cotton twill. An ideal playtime outfit for little girls. Four pieces include: coat with gold color buttons, braid and gold color insignia; sleeve emblem. Matching all-around belt. Military style, flair skirt; hip pocket. Visored WAAC type cap. Shpg. wt., 2 lbs. 2 oz.
Sizes: 4, 6, 8, 10, 12, 14.
State size wanted.
40 F 4501—4 pieces....$2.79

Army Officer Uniform

$3.40
5 Pieces

Olive drab cotton twill outfit, medium weight and slow to show soil. Five pieces include: coat with 4 pockets; metal lapel pins; shoulder epaulets. Fly-front longies. Visored officer's type cap. Trench helmet of cotton twill with stiff buckram backing. Sam Browne belt. Shipping weight, 2 lbs. 14 oz.
State size: 4, 6, 8, 10, 12, 14.
Available after August 1
40 F 4508—5 pieces....$3.40

Jr. "WAVE"

$2.79
4 Pieces

Navy blue cotton twill in a medium weight for little girls' play-time comfort. 4 pieces include: coat with gold color buttons, braid, and metal insignia; "service ribbon"; lapel pins; realistic emblem on sleeve; 2 rows of braid on cuffs. Matching skirt, all-around belt, and WAVE type hat. Shpg. wt., 2 lbs. 2 oz.
State size: 4, 6, 8, 10, 12, 14.
Available after August 1
40 F 4507—4 pieces......$2.79

4-piece Marine Suit

$2.39
4 Pieces

Lightweight cotton drill and a dandy outfit for his make-believe play. Four pieces: navy blue coat with gold color buttons, insignia; stand-up collar; "service ribbon"; sleeve chevron; braid trimmed cuffs. Copen blue fly-front longies, hip pocket. White all-around belt; navy blue visored cap. Wt., 2 lbs.
State size: 4, 6, 8, 10, 12, 14.
Available after August 1
40 F 4506—4 pieces......$2.39

402 .. SEARS, ROEBUCK AND CO.   *Before ordering any of the Military Outfits listed on this page, see size scale chart on opposite page.*

Jr. Raincoats

Two popular styles for boys
Both of waterproof fabric

Available after Aug. 15

Brown and white striped cotton button-on blouse. Herringbone longies of heavy Sanforized brown cotton suiting, maximum fabric shrinkage 1%; cuffs, 2 pockets; self-belt. Tie. Wash separately. Shipping weight, 1 pound.
Sizes: 3, 4, 5, 6, 7, 8, 9, 10.
State size. See chart B, page 398.
40 F 3213—3 pieces......$1.95

$1 95
3 Pieces

Available after Sept. 1

Navy blue, Sanforized cotton drill longies, fabric shrinkage 1%. Suspenders, 2 pockets, side openings. Blue striped cotton knit, button-on blouse with 3-button neck. Wash separately. Shpg. wt., 1 lb.
Sizes: 3, 4, 5, 6, 7, 8, 9.
State size. See chart B, page 398.
40 F 3306—2 pieces....$1.98

$1 98
2 Pieces

Dressy 4-piece Suit

Dark brown cheviot longies, 40% reused wool, 60% cotton; imitation fly front; 2 pockets. Artificial leather belt. Tan cotton broadcloth button-on blouse, button-down collar. Tie. Shipping wt., 1 lb. 6 oz.
Sizes: 3, 4, 5, 6, 7, 8, 9, 10.
State size. See chart B, page 398.
40 F 3216—4 pieces....$2.64

$2 64
4 Pieces

Available after Sept. 1

He'll be all dressed up and ready to "put to sea" in this inexpensive sailor style suit. Made of strong, Sanforized-Shrunk navy blue cotton drill; fabric won't shrink over 1%, so order exact size. Blouse has white braid trim on collar and cuffs, emblem on sleeve. Button-on sailor longies. "Bosun's" whistle included. Wash separately. Shipping weight, 9 ounces.
Sizes: 3, 4, 5, 6, 7, 8, 9, 10.
Be sure to state size.
40 F 3226—Sailor suit....$1.77

$1 77
Each

Button-on Sailor

Made of smart, navy blue flannel, 15% reprocessed wool, 45% reused wool, 40% cotton. Will give him that wanted nautical appearance, and will keep him warm, too; an ideal chilly weather dress-up suit. Blouse has white braid trim and sleeve emblem; button cuffs; sailor tie. Broad fall front sailor longies. Shipping weight, 1 pound 4 ounces.
State size: 3, 4, 5, 6, 7, 8, 9, 10.
Available after August 1.
40 F 3225—Sailor suit..$3.49

$3 49
Each

Available after Sept. 1

Fabric is long-wearing, warm navy blue flannel consisting of 15% reprocessed wool, 45% reused wool, 40% cotton. It's the realistic middy model that's just about regulation. Blouse has white braid trim on collar; sleeve emblem; braid trimmed button cuffs. Black sailor tie. Broad fall front sailor style longies. Shipping wt., 1 lb. 4 oz.
Sizes: 3, 4, 5, 6, 7, 8, 9, 10.
Be sure to state size.
40 F 3228—Middy suit..$3.49

$3 49
Each

2-piece olive green "Commando" Set

$2 98

This snug raincoat will keep him dry because its made of tightly woven cotton fabric, impregnated with a waterproof plastic substance. Single breasted style. Like a real Commando's raincoat with brass buttons, raglan sleeves and slash pockets. Strongly stitched seams. "Commando" emblem on chest. Officer's cap of same material with visor and military pin. Neck protecting rain cape attached to hat. Shipping weight, 3 pounds.
State size: 4, 6, 8, 10.
Avail-able after August 1.
40 F 7615—2 pieces....$2.98

Artificial leather Junior Raincoat

$2 19
Hat 47c

This sturdy black coat is fine protection for rainy days. Roomy raglan shoulders, 2 slash pockets. Strong double stitched seams. Shipping weight, 2 lbs. 6 oz.
Sizes: 4, 5, 6, 7, 8, 9, 10.
Be sure to state size wanted.
40 F 7609—Raincoat...$2.19

Matching Rain Hat

Black artificial leather with protective cape. Shipping weight, 8 ounces.
State size: Small (4,5), Med. (6,7), Large (8,9,10).
40 F 809—Rain Hat....**47c**

How To Order Jr. Boys' Military Outfits, Overcoats, Overcoat Sets, Outdoor Suits, Mackinaws, Jackets, and Raincoats
Measure height from floor to top of child's head, without shoes. Measure chest over shirt or underwear, well up under the arms.

If boy's height is	And his chest measure is	ORDER THIS SIZE
29 to 33 inches	19 to 21 inches	2
34 to 36 inches	20 to 22 inches	3
37 to 39 inches	21 to 23 inches	4
40 to 41 inches	22 to 24 inches	5
42 to 44 inches	22½ to 24½ inches	6
45 to 46 inches	23½ to 25½ inches	7
47 to 49 inches	24 to 26 inches	8
50 to 51 inches	24½ to 26½ inches	9
52 to 53 inches	25½ to 27½ inches	10
56 to 57 inches	27 to 29 inches	12
58 to 61 inches	29 to 30½ inches	14

☐4 PAGE **403** . . . . . BOYS' CLOTHES

B Collar Box Bag . . . . . **$2.29**   C Vanity Box Bag . . . . . **$3.49**   D Bar Box Bag **$3.49**

F Triangle Flap Bag . . . . **$2.29**   G Fitted Bag **$3.49**

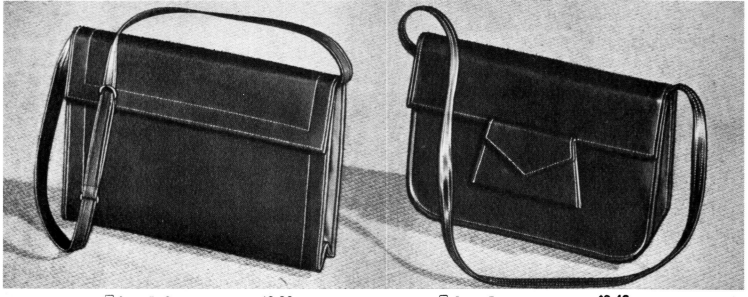

J Long Or Short . . . . **$2.29**   K Quick Change **$3.49**

For descriptions of bags illustrated above, see opposite page

You can buy the latest fashions at Sears. Easy Terms available if order totals $10 or more. See inside back cover

P PAGE 119 . . . ACCESSORIES

Lapel "Pin-ups" in gay hand-painted ceramics

12 styles 85c Each

For your lapel . . . whimsical animals, shy fawns, impish monkeys and many other pets in fun-provoking poses. Bizarre masks, too! They're conversation makers wherever worn, and so low priced you'll want several. Made of ceramic with hand painted colors: luscious reds, vivid greens, soft blues, yellow and white. Trimmed with bits of leather, plastic Lucite, yarn and beads. Make grand gifts. Clever pin-ups for bedroom or kitchen curtains too. Individually gift boxed. Shpg. wt., each, 4 oz.

[A] 4 K 3777E—HOBBY. Prancing thoroughbred with flying green mane and tail. Brown body. 3 inches high...85c

[B] 4 K 3774E—BAMBI. Dear little fawn with soft-blue body and white spots. Pink Lucite ears. 2¾ in. high.....85c

[C] 4 K 3773E—ELIZA. A belle with clear Lucite hat tilted over her eye. Orange color flower trim. 3½ in. high.85c

[D] 4 K 3764E—BUNKY. Mischievous little white monkey with tiny button cap. Purple Lucite tail. 2¾ in. high.85c

[E] 4 K 3772E—WUMPIE. Whimsical giraffe with nodding head. Red Lucite spring neck. Yellow body with green spots. 3½ inches high. Smart on sweaters........85c

[F] 4 K 3763E—SHEIK. Arabian chieftain. Head swathed in yarn turban (variegated colors). 3¼ inches high....85c

[G] 4 K 3779E—MADAME X. Mysterious lady with yellow braid and red yarn pompon hat. Red Lucite bow tied under her chin. 3¼ inches high.................85c

[H] 4 K 3775E—MARY'S LAMB wears pink bonnet tied under her chin, carries purple leather purse. 4 in. high....85c

[J] 4 K 3770E—PEGASUS. Mythical flying horse with wings of clear Lucite. Green body. 3¼ inches high......85c

[K] 4 K 3778E—CAROL ANN. Shy little miss with red felt hat, green dress, yellow pigtails. 2½ in. high..........85c

[L] 4 K 3769E—TEXAS STEER. Outthrust green Lucite horns. Brown leather ears. Brown wood face. 3 in. high...85c

[M] 4 K 3768E—BONNIE. Demure little lamb wears orange pompon bonnet with blue bead trim. 2¾ inches high.85c

Smart, flattering Hair-do fashions

LILLY DACHÉ SNOODS AND NETS. The one great sensation in all style centers . . . created in a rainbow of colors. Designed to flatter your hair-do. Wear them with any costume, any hair style, any hour of the day. Wear them with flowers, with hats or head bands.

[A] DACHÉ FINE MESH RAYON NET. State colors: Chinese green, Chinese red, tiger lily pink, turq. blue, lavender; also lt. brown, med. brown, dk. brown, black, blonde, auburn or gray.
25 K 9073—Postpaid................3 for $1.00   Each 35c.

[B] DACHÉ SNOOD MESH RAYON NET. State colors: Chinese green, Chinese red, tiger lily pink, turquoise blue, lavender, white, black or brown. The smartest style in hair fashions.
25 K 9072—Postpaid.................3 for $2.00   Each 70c

[C] GARDENIAS AND VEILING ON TIARA. Two artificial gardenias with face-flattering black rayon veiling. A glamorous style for day or evening wear. State color: white or pink gardenias.
25 K 9006—Shipping weight, 6 ounces............Each 98c

[D] RAYON VELVET HEAD BAND WITH SNOOD NET. Multi-color chenille-dotted black rayon net attached to head band in a smart fashion. State band color: medium red, black, kelly green.
25 K 9008—Shipping weight, 3 ounces.............Each 59c

[E] SMART CROCHETED SNOOD. Hand-made, of cotton chenille. Extra full. State color: white, yellow, black.
25 K 9095—Shipping weight, 4 ounces.............Each 98c

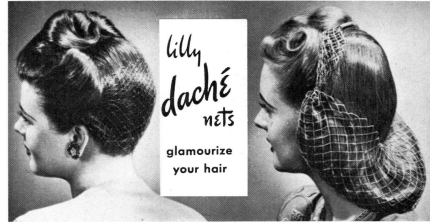

lilly daché nets glamourize your hair

[A] Lilly Daché Fine Mesh Net..Each 35c 3 for $1.00

[B] Lilly Daché Snood Mesh Net. Each 70c 3 for $2.00

[C] Gardenias and Veiling....98c

[D] Head Band with Snood Net. 59c

[E] Crocheted Snood.......98c

Furred Tuxedos on
Botany's All Wool Coats

$49 98
each, cash

⅓ down on Easy Terms

There's nothing like a big splurge of fur on your winter coat. It makes for beauty and warmth as well as good fashion. Popular boxy coats in fine, rich suede-like "Karasham", the famous fabric with a faint diagonal weave...the wear and long-lasting loveliness only a famous mill like Botany can produce.

SKUNK-DYED OPOSSUM, at left, rich glossy fur in a deep glossy black. Set-in sleeves for easy shoulders. Stitched slash pockets; swingy gored back. Hook-and-eye closing. Lovely rayon satin lining; warm interlining. *Sizes:* 10, 12, 14, 16, 18, 20; scale, page 48. *State size.* Shpg. wt., 5 lbs. 3 oz.
♦ 17 K 6179—Evergreen
♦ 17 K 6180—Black.....Cash, $49.98

PERSIAN DYED TINGONA LAMB, at right (processed broadtail), in the silvery gray tones that are so flattering. Full-cut box coat with set-in shoulders, swingy gored back. Slash pockets. Rayon satin lining; interlining. *Sizes:* 10, 12, 14, 16, 18, 20; scale, page 48. *State size.* Shpg. wt., 5 lbs. 3 oz.
♦ 17 K 6181—Cranberry red
♦ 17 K 6182—Slate blue. Cash, $49.98

Actual colors: *Evergreen, Slate blue, Cranberry red* shown on page 43

Shining examples of Sears value-giving in fashion. The glamor-glitter of sequins on costly Mallinson's "Whirlaway" for two charming dine-and-dance dresses. Have you ever bought this fabric by the yard? Then you know finding it in such carefully detailed dresses . . with sequins . . at only $9.98 is truly amazing. It's a rayon crepe with a rich nubby texture that doesn't sag . . that drapes superbly to show off a fine figure. Dry clean. Shipping weight, each, 1 pound 8 ounces.

Sequins on Mallinson's "Whirlaway" Rayon Crepe

$9⁹⁸
each, cash
On Easy Terms, ⅓ down

CLUSTERS OF SEQUINS sparkle on molded bodice of basque dress at left and also outline sweetheart neck. Self bows add softness; skirt full in front, gored in back. *Sizes:* 10, 12, 14, 16, 18, size scale on page 11. *State size.*

♦31 K 5073—Royal blue
♦31 K 5074—Black
♦31 K 5075—Gold. Each, cash . . $9.98

SEQUIN SPRAY gleams on pastel insert of two-piece dress, at right. Button-front top molded to figure; gored skirt has slight ripple; Contour Closure. *Sizes:* 10, 12, 14, 16, 18, 20; size scale on page 11. *State size.*

♦31 K 5070—Brown with pastel blue
♦31 K 5071—Black with pastel rose
Each, cash $9.98

Color *Gold* shown in actual color on page 9

Does your order total $10 or more? Sears Easy Terms available—for complete details, see inside back cover.

ALL *PAGE* 13 . . DRESSES

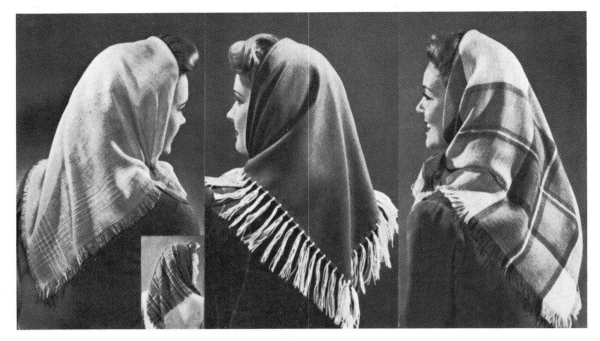

Head Kerchiefs are a warm fashion necessity for fall and winter

Plaid or plain head square 59c

Softer, more exquisitely colored than you'd expect at this low price . . because it's made of spun rayon and Aralac . . science's new, wool-like fiber (made from milk). *Size:* About 26 x 26 inches, including self-fringe. *Plain colors:* White, red, copen blue; or multi-color plaid. *State color.*
88 F 4407—Shpg. wt., 4 oz. 59c

Colorful conga kerchief 79c

Picturesque triangle, darling of the campus crowd. Rayon serge, fringed on two sides with virgin wool . . a gay salute to the "South American Way." *Large size:* 28 x 28 x 44 in. drapes gracefully across shoulders and back. *Colors:* Bright red, white fringe; copen blue, white fringe; or med. green, dark brown fringe.
88 F 4326—*State color.* Shpg. wt., 5 oz. 79c

Larger multi-color square 95c

A huge square to keep head, ears and throat cozy on nippy days. It's soft and wool-like, made of spun rayon and Aralac fiber (made from milk) in a plaid whose colors are as soft as a rainbow-mist. *Size:* Abt. 30 x 30 in. incl. self-fringe. Multi-color plaids on ground of white, copen, yellow. *State ground color.*
88 F 4402—Shpg. wt., 4 oz. 95c

FLUFF-MITTS are tops in comfort, for fashion and fun

Gay angora-like fluff mitts 48c pr.

Fleecy and fluffy . . they feel almost like real angora at a small fraction of angora's cost. The fluffi-knit fabric is 58% rayon, with 42% cotton added for sturdiness . . brushed thick and lustrous . . soft as a kitten's ear. Length, about 9 inches. *Sizes:* Small (6-6½), Medium (7-7½), Large (8-8½ in.). *State size;* see how to measure below. Shipping weight, pair, 5 oz.
88 F 5130—Red
88 F 5131—White
88 F 5132—Royal blue . . . . .Pair, 48c

White bunny fur back mitts $1.00 pr.

Bunny backs and fabric palms, a combination to bring color and coziness down to your fingertips. Snuggly bunny backs are snowy white, soft as a cloud. Cotton palms treated specially to resist wind and water. Fully lined with fleeced cotton for extra warmth. Fits snugly at wrist. Length, abt. 9 in. *Sizes:* Small (6-6½), Med. (7-7½), Large (8-8½ in.). *State size.* Shpg. wt., 7 oz.
88 F 5045—White with royal blue palm
88 F 5046—White with red palm
Federal excise tax included . . . . .Pair, $1.00

Bunny fur, front and back $1.98 pr.

Softest white bunny fur from long wrist top to fingertip . . keep your fingers at the constant glowing warmth of your own hearthfire. They're so lusciously pretty, you'll want to give them as gifts . . to have a pair for yourself. Gift boxed, ready to wrap. Every inch lined with fleeced cotton for extra comfort. Neatly finished at cuff. Length, abt. 9½ in. Shpg. wt., pr., 9 oz. *Sizes:* Small (6-6½ in.), Medium (7-7½ in.) Large (8-8½ in.). *State size.* White only.
88 F 5047—Fed. excise tax incl. . .Pair, $1.98

Top fashion SEA-HO Swim Suits, youthful, dashing
Reg. U. S. Pat. Off.

$2.98	**$3.69**	**$3.69**
Rayon taffeta 2-pc. style	**Satin-like 1-piece, daisy chain trim**	**Print 'n plain half-skirt style**

$2.98

Rayon taffeta 2-pc. style

Stunning floral print rayon taffeta in a suit that's gay, colorful, dramatic. Popular 2-piece open midriff style .. ideal for sunning or swimming. Adorable flare-out skirt buttons in back .. beautifully made up-lift bra is figure molding and flattering. Ties in back for perfect adjustment. Knit cotton lining throughout.
Sizes: 32, 34, 36-inch bust. *State bust size.*
Shipping weight, 10 ounces.
38 L 1731—White ground, floral print
38 L 1732—Med. blue ground, floral print
38 L 1733—Yellow ground, floral print
Each........................ $2.98

$3.69

Satin-like 1-piece, daisy chain trim

A lustrous new fabric to put glamour in your swimming hours. Knit of satin-smooth rayon (with cotton back) in a smart diagonal weave .. that does flattering things for your figure. Pretty princess style .. accented by daisy chain applique at bra top and full flared skirt. Knit cotton lining throughout.
Sizes: 32, 34, 36, 38, 40-inch bust.
State bust size. Shipping weight, 14 oz.
38 L 1700—Royal (bright blue)
38 L 1701—Red
38 L 1702—Black
38 L 1730—Medium blue
Each........................ $3.69

$3.69

Print 'n plain half-skirt style

Beauty of line and color make this a stunning suit. Front is rayon jersey in a ravishing print .. back is Velva-sheen, (velvet-like knit rayon and cotton). One-piece, half skirt style .. it's the glamour suit for active swimming. Softly gathered bra top has adjustable tie. "Lastex" yarn in back of leg for snug, trim fit. Knit cotton lining.
Sizes: 32, 34, 36, 38-inch bust. *State bust size.*
38 L 1734—Black with fuchsia red print
38 L 1735—Black with bright blue print
38 L 1736—black with gold print
Each........................ $3.69

Measure for Bathing Suits this way: Check your weight carefully and order corresponding bust size. Give hip measurement, too, placing tape around fullest part.

Weight—pounds..	80-95	96-115	116-130	131-145	146-160
Order bust size...	32	34	36	38	40

97E . . SEARS, ROEBUCK AND CO. 2 PC

Ⓐ Virgin Wool pullover without sleeves $3.88 Ⓑ Virgin Wool pullover with sleeves....$6.94

Ⓒ Tennis Cap....50c   Ⓓ Tennis Visor...23c   Ⓔ Cotton Socks...20c   Ⓕ Shorts....$1.97

Play a better game in Sears fine Tennis Wear

Designed for action and comfort . ... Styled-to-match accessories

Comfortable cotton tee Shirt

Just the shirt for active sports! **59c**
Knit in a stitch that "gives"
easily, keeps its shape . . . and it
soaks up perspiration like a sponge, dries quickly. Easy to wash, too . . . needs no ironing.
Round neck. Short sleeves. One pocket.
  Sizes: small (34–36 inch chest), medium (38–
40), large (42–44). Shipping wt., each, 6 oz.
83 L 1871—White only. *State size wanted.*

Sanforized white gabardine Slacks

Available after February 15, 1945. **$398**
Just the slacks the summer sports-
man has always wanted . . . ideal
for tennis wear or golf or for any other sport
where good looks and cool comfort are wanted.
High quality, firm textured white cotton and
rayon gabardine woven for coolness and excel-
lently tailored to give you correct style and ease
of action. Sanforized so fabric will shrink a mere
1%. Sturdy trimmings throughout for longer
wear. Four smart pleats in front. Dropped belt loops. Four smart pleats in
front. Neatly tapered cuff bottoms.
  All sizes: 28 to 40-inch waist: 29 to 35-inch
inseam. *State waist, inseam;* tell which is waist.
How-to-measure on page 392. Shipping weight,
1 pound 10 ounces.
45 L 7503—White gabardine slacks.......$3.98

Virgin Wool Pullover without sleeves

Ⓐ Rich-looking cable stitch with hand- **$388**
woven appearance, gives this sweater
its thick, luxurious feel, its smart effect.
Then too, it's actually knit of worsted . . . the finest,
longest strands of virgin wool. Snug fitting bottom.
Wash separately by hand.
  Sizes: small (34–36 inch chest), medium (38–40),
large (42–44). Shipping weight, each, 12 ounces.
83 L 2295—White only. *Be sure to state size wanted.*

Ⓒ **Tennis cap.** White cotton gabardine. Green under
peak; felt sweatband; ventilated crown. *Sizes:*
small 6¾ to 7; med., 7 to 7⅛; large 7¼ to 7⅜.
6 L 1259—*State size.* Shpg. wt., 6 oz 50c

Ⓓ **Tennis visor.** Cotton mesh strap with green cellu-
loid visor and adjustable headband.
6 L 1266—Fits all sizes. Shpg. wt., 6 oz........23c

Ⓔ **Athletic socks.** 100% pure American cotton. Ribbed tops for snug fit. White. *Sizes:* 10, 11, 12.
6 L 2070—*State size.* Shpg. wt., 6 oz. ......Pair 20c

HOW TO MEASURE FOR SWEATERS AND TEE SHIRTS
Measure around chest under arms and over shoulder
blades. Number of inches is your correct size. If
measurement is between sizes, order the larger size.

Virgin Wool Pullover with sleeves

Ⓑ Fine quality virgin wool—the soft, long **$694**
fibered, "worsted" kind—knit in the
twisted cable stitch that has a luxurious
hand knitted look. V-neck style. Close fitting cuffs and
bottom. Wash separately by hand.
  Sizes: small (34–36 inch chest), medium (38–40),
large (42–44). See "How to Measure" below. Shipping
weight, each, 1 pound 3 ounces.
83 L 2292—White only. *Be sure to state size wanted.*

Elastic top cotton twill tennis Shorts

Ⓕ Designed-for-fast-action tennis shorts. **$197**
Washfast and sanforized cotton twill;
elastic top; built in supporter. Button flap
change pocket; larger hip pocket. Maximum shrinkage, 1%.
  Waist sizes: small (32–34); medium (36–38); large
(40–42 inches.) *State size.* Shipping weight, 1 pound.
6 L 1925—White with navy blue side stripes......$1.97
6 L 1926—Navy blue with white side stripes...... 1.97

For Tennis Rackets and Accessories, see page 455

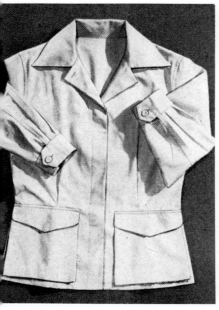

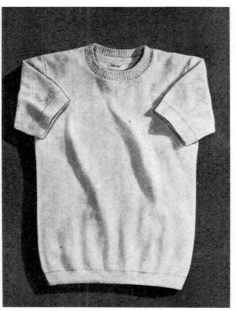

A ACTIVE SPORTS JACKET **$4.98**   C SMART POLO SHIRT **98c**

B CLASSIC PULLOVER **$4.98**   D CLASSIC CARDIGAN **$5.89**

Golf and Tennis Classics ... full cut for freedom of action

Complete ensembles for the sport of your choice ... styled as you like them

A ACTIVE SPORTS JACKETS, in Sanforized (max. shrinkage, 1%), Zelanized cotton. Water, stain resistant (except grease). Deep armholes. Shoulders full-cut for action. Fly front; convertible collar. 2 saddle-type pockets. Adjustable tabs at back. Washfast, sunfast. *Sizes:* 12, 14, 16, 18, 20; scale, page 48. *State size.* Shpg. wt., 1 lb. 4 oz.
♦ 7 L 3919—Light tan..............$4.98

B CLASSIC PULLOVER knit of 100% imported virgin wool worsted yarns. Long and boxy, with quality tailored into every detail. Crew neck and armholes are hand fashioned to lie flat without bulkiness. Washed to enhance its beauty and superb fit. Hand washable. *Colors:* Medium blue, bright red, light green, yellow. *Sizes:* 32, 34, 36, 38, 40-in. bust. *State bust size, color.*
38 L 7056—Shpg. wt., 15 oz.........$4.98

C SMART POLO SHIRT knit of snow white, quality combed cotton yarns . . delightfully soft, smooth and comfortable . . easy to hand wash, never needs ironing. Styled with cool, action-free short sleeves . . fine ribbed knit crew neck that lies flat and snug. Wash in LUX. *Sizes: Small* (32-in. bust). *Medium* (34, 36-in. bust). *Large* (38-in. bust). *State bust size.* Shipping weight, 6 ounces.
38 L 7328—White...................98c

D CLASSIC CARDIGAN in 100% imported virgin wool worsted. Beautifully tailored, with these expensive features . . hand fashioned crew neck and armholes that lie flat and smooth . . washed to insure perfect fit . fresh water pearl buttons . . ribbon lined button band. Hand washable. *Colors:* Red, medium blue, light green. *Sizes:* 32, 34, 36, 38, 40-in. bust. *State bust size and color.*
38 L 7060—Shipping weight, 1 lb......$5.89

MISSES' ACTIVE TENNIS BLOUSE, good quality cotton, cut extra long (about 23 in.) so it won't pull out. Deep armholes, action back. Breast pocket. Hand washable. *Sizes:* 12, 14, 16, 18, 20; scale, page 58. *State size.* Shipping weight, 9 ounces.
♦ 7 L 3257—White................$2.38

MISSES' TENNIS SHORTS in durable, close-woven cotton with 2 knife pleats each side, front and back to permit free action. Pocket on left side. Hand washable in LUX. *Sizes:* 12, 14, 16, 18, 20; see size scale on opposite page. *State size.* Shpg. wt., 9 oz.
♦ 7 L 2947—White................$2.38

TENNIS VISOR with adjustable headband. fits any size head. All white cotton drill cloth; comfortable felt sweatband.
6 L 1258—Shpg. wt., 6 oz.............55c

Catalog numbers marked ♦ shipped from Philadelphia. Order, pay postage from Sears nearest mail order house   P *PAGE 97B ..* **SPORTSWEAR**

JUNIORS

Count on cotton for that spic-span look the summer long . . for noon or moon activities . . brief sleeved to show off a smooth sun tan . . taut waisted to show off your fine figure . . they revive in a jiffy with a Lux sudsing . . a small Sears price to pay for so much flattery

$3.98
Each

Everything about you will look fresh and clean and alive if you wear Cotton—the queen of summer fabrics. Sears has here a prize collection in popular materials, sun-gay patterns and colors. Styled especially for Juniors and featuring 2-piece and full-skirted dresses with no skimping on your pet ruffle, pocket or button decorations. Sears fine sewing insures clean finish inside as well as out, the steady stitching that holds up after countless washings; we recommend Lux suds.

Catalog numbers marked♦ shipped from Philadelphia or Kansas City. Order and pay postage from Sears nearest mail order house. Buy now . . buy the best . . Sears Easy Terms are available if your order totals $10 or more . . see inside back cover for details.

$3.98

The tablecloth check, a new 2-piecer in fine woven cotton gingham ("woven" means pattern is there to stay). Heart-high pockets sprout foamy white cotton pique bands. Button-front cardigan tops a classic kick-pleated skirt. Washfast. *Sizes:* 11, 13, 15, 17; scale, page 28. *State size.* Shpg. wt., 1 lb. 8 oz.
♦27 E 8312—Green-and-white check . . . $3.98
♦27 E 8313—Red-and-white check $3.98
♦27 E 8314—Brown-and-white check . . . $3.98

$3.98

The striped 2-piecer comes in crisp Sanforized cotton pique (max. shrinkage 1%). Its collar is taken from a gob's suit. There is fashion news in its flip-back cuff sleeves and muff pockets . . all touched off with buttons. Skirt has a pleat trio in front. Hand wash; use Lux. *Sizes:* 9, 11, 13, 15; size scale, page 28. *Please state size.* Shpg. wt., 1 lb. 8 oz.
♦27 E 8315—Red-and-white stripe $3.98
♦27 E 8316—Navy blue-and-white stripe $3.98

$3.98

The pinafore dress, a pre-shrunk cotton ging-ham special (max. shrinkage, 3%) in a bright plaid on white ground. See how generous we've been with those flutter-ruffles edged in ric-rac. Gathers below the waist-hugging midriff to give you a dancewide skirt. But-tons to waist in back. Pattern woven to stay. Hand wash. *Sizes:* 9, 11, 13, 15; scale, page 28. *State size.* Shpg. wt., 1 lb.
♦27 E 8318—Red-and-blue plaid $3.98

$3.98

The petticoat-ruffle dress in Sanforized cotton chambray (max. shrink. 1%) is "on the square" with its neckline and pockets. Fitted bodice; gathered skirt billows out from waistline. Perky striped ruffles, finished with ric-rac. Button back closing. Washable. *Sizes:* 9, 11, 13, 15; scale, page 28. *State size.* Shpg. wt., 1 lb.
♦27 E 8320—Med. rose, rose-and-white trim
♦27 E 8321—Med. blue, blue-and-white trim
Each $3.98

$3.98

The window-pane check in crinkly printed seer-sucker has newest shoulder-into-sleeve treat-ment. Wonderful neckline and huge pockets trimmed with bias check and ric-rac. Set-in bias belt with white trim nips waistline. But-ton back closing to waist. Washable. *Sizes:* 9, 11, 13, 15, 17; size scale, page 28. *State size.* Shpg. wt., 1 lb.
♦27 E 8323—Brown-and-white check . . . $3.98
♦27 E 8324—Red-and-white check $3.98
Available after Feb. 1, 1946

ALL **PAGE 33** . . **DRESSES**

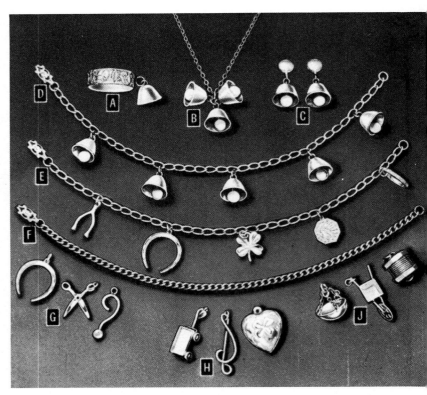

it's Sears for your jewelry

Designed especially for you . . . the prettiest, newest jewelry . . . the kind girls love to wear. There are classic lockets, crosses, and rings . . . jewelry you'll cherish for years and years. Sizes are the right proportion . . . quality and designs as fine as our women's styles. For fun, for loveliness select barrettes, bracelets, pearls, and compacts and you'll have a jewelry wardrobe the envy of the neighborhood. Before selecting these styles Sears buyers asked juniors themselves what styles they preferred: The results . . . a new Junior Miss Shop with just-what-you-like jewelry.

Pearl Choker

It's sweet, swoony, glamorous . . . star of the fashion parade of 1946. Worn high at the neckline on date dresses, sweaters. Simulated pearl choker, 15 inches long. Shpg. wt., 3 oz.
4 E 4631E . . . . for $1.14

Lustrous Pearl Necklace

Take a tip from the smooth dressers. Wear fine quality pearls with everything and be ready to meet your world —coke time, school time, or any time. Gleaming, iridescent simulated pearls, 16 inches long. Sterling filigree clasp.
4 E 4612E—Shpg. wt., 5 oz. $3.25

Happy pickin's for Bracelet and Charm collectors

And who isn't wearing bracelets by the armful these days? Make yours the talk of the town . . . it's easy on the budget when you buy at Sears. For super fun select the new CHARM-BEL set or intriguing charm bracelets. All are sterling silver. In gift box. Shpg. wt., each, 3 oz.

Charm-Bel match-ups. Boost your style rating and wear a set. Each piece has bells that ring out merrily. Made of shining sterling silver.

[A] *Friendship ring* with bell. ¼-inch wide. Sizes 4 to 7.
4 E 4816E—*State size.* $1.14

[B] *Necklace* with three bells.
4 E 4630E—18-in. long. $1.68

[C] *Earrings.* Screw backs.
4 E 4034E—¾-in $1.48

[D] *Charm-Bel bracelet.* 5 bells on a sterling chain.
4 E 4586E—6¾ in.. . . $2.28

[E] *Good Luck bracelet* with four-leaf clover, wishing ring, good luck coin, horse shoe, and wish bone.
4 E 4587E—6¾ in. $1.18

[F] *Sterling starter bracelet.* Inches of room to add many favorite charms.
4 E 4533E—6¾ in $1.10

[G] *Conversation pieces:* horse shoe, ? mark, and scissors.
4 E 4588E—3 charms for . . 78c

[H] *For luck, fun:* heart with 4-leaf clover center, musical clef, and wagon.
4 E 4589E—3 charms for . . $1.14

[J] *Each one works.* Come-to-you concertina moves in and out, barrow wheels go round, hanging dish swings.
4 E 4590E—3 charms for $1.68

Identification Jewelry . . . Barrettes

Identification bracelets in sterling or 1/20 12K yellow gold filled. 6½ inches long. Shpg. wt., 3 oz. *Print engraving.*

[1] With 3 line name, address.
4 ER 5943E—Sterling . . . $1.49
4 ER 5952E—Gold filled . $1.89

[2] Heavy weight links and disc, 1/20 12K yellow gold filled.
4 ER 5956E—3 initials. . . . $2.19
4 ER 5955E—With 3 line name and address. $2.59

[3] *Anklets* in sterling silver. 9 inches long. *Print 2 or 3 initials.* Shpg. wt., ea. 3 oz.
4 ER 4823E $1.10

[4] *Silver plated barrette* for your hair. With 3 initials or first name engraved. 1⅞ in. long. *Print engraving.* Shpg. wt., 4 oz.
4 ER 4805E 59c

Heap on Indian-style Jewelry

Coin silver with Indian good luck symbols, some set with genuine blue green turquoise matrix stones. Rings, bracelet adjustable in size. Shipping weight, each, 4 ounces.

[K] 4 E 4583E — S e t with turquoise stone. $2.68

[L] 4 E 4584E — S e t with turquoise stone. $2.68

[M] 4 E 4582E— All silver. $1.68

[N] 4 E 4033ME—Silver earrings with turquoise ½ inch. Screw backs. Pair $1.68

[P] 4 E 4939ME—Silver ring set with turquoise stone. . . . $1.68

Just for you

[R] *Compact with your name.* Gay red or blue plastic case. Sifter style, 4½ inches. *Print name, state color.*
4 ER 4702—Shpg. wt., 5 oz 85c

[S] *Pouch compact,* plump as a tiny pouch handbag. Jewel-tone red or white top with lacy design. *State color.* Gold color metal case, 2¾ in.
4 E 4706—Shpg. wt., 5 oz. $1.59

[T] *Jitterbug pin,* loose in all her joints. 3-inch. Gold plated metal.
4 E 3626E—Shpg. wt., 3 oz $1.14

A $1.19

B $1.19

C $1.19

D $1.19

E $1.79 set

G $3.29 set

F 87c

H 49c

Your little miss will love a bag with a grown-up look

Eye-catching Accessories for the small set give a lively touch of flattering color

[A] **Glitter is Gay** — small scale version of mother's bag. Nail-heads in front, on grained artificial leather. Snap fastener. Fabric lined, mirror. *Size:* abt. 6 x 4 in. Shpg. wt., 5 oz.
88 E 1845E—Bright red   88 E 1847E—Navy blue
88 E 1846E—Bright green. 20% Fed. Ex. Tax incl. Each $1.19

[B] **Scallops are Smart**—in gleaming white plastic sheeting. Trim, linings are red felt (70% wool, 30% cotton). Plastic chain handle, snap fastener. *Size:* 6¾ x 4 in. Shpg. wt., 4 oz.
88 E 1843E—White with bright red.
88 E 1844E—White with navy. 20% Fed. Ex. Tax incl. ..$1.19

[C] **Fringe is Fun** on a bag — 'specially this zip-topped style in soft sheep leather grained like pigskin. Wide carrying loop. Fabric lined. *Size:* about 7¾ x 4¾ inches. Shipping weight, 4 ounces. 20% Federal Excise Tax included.
88 E 1848E—Bright red   88 E 1849E—Med. Brown .Each $1.19

[D] **Folds add a Flourish** to this frame bag in pique-ribbed artificial leather. Prystal clasp. Fabric lined, mirror. *Size:* about 9½ x 4¾ in. Shpg. wt., 10 oz. 20% Fed. Ex. Tax incl.
88 E 1839E—Bright red   88 E 1840E—Dark brown
88 E 1841E—Navy   88 E 1842E—Bright green.... Each $1.19

[E] **Little Girls Love Match-up Sets** and this one's brightly tricked out with pretty applique and gay stitching. The acorn-shaped 4-section drawstring bag has rayon cords that pull through small loops. *Size:* about 6¾ in. deep. Soft felt (70% wool, 30% cotton) with contrasting trim. Matching Scotch cap in felt (70% wool, 30% cotton) flaunts jaunty back streamers. Adjustable; fits all headsizes. Shpg. wt., 8 oz Price includes 20c Federal Ex. Tax on bag.
88 E 1850—Bright red . . . . Set $1.79
88 E 1851—Navy blue . . . . . . Set $1.79
88 E 1852—Bright green . . . . .Set $1.79

[F] **Bright Suspenders** that add a nice touch of color, worn with a skirt over a sweater or blouse. Bright red felt (70% wool, 30% cotton) with center panel of white cotton tape decorated with contrasting flowers and leaves in a Tyrolean-like design. A nice gift idea. Metal clip-on ends. Adjustable. Shpg. wt., 3 ounces.
88 E 4444—Bright red 87c

[G] **Swiss Miss Vest and Hat Set**, so bright and gay, any little girl will be thrilled to wear it. Darling little vest shows off appliqued flowers, ric-rac effect borders, smart stitching. In soft felt (70% wool, 30% cotton). Fastens with rayon cords laced through four metal eyelets down front. Saucy little cap to match is adjustable; fits all headsizes. Vest comes in *Sizes:* Small (fits chest 25-27½ in.). Large (fits 28-29½ in.). *State size.* Shipping weight, 10 oz.
88 E 4515—Bright red with navy blue . Set $3.29
88 E 4516—Bright green with red.... Set $3.29
88 E 4517—Navy blue with white. ...Set $3.29

[H] **Flowered Rainkerchief** gives pretty protection for rainy or snowy weather. Spun rayon, treated to shed water, resist stains. *Size:* About 27 in. square. Easily kept fresh—just wash by hand; use Lux suds. *Colors:* White, bright red or medium blue background. *Please state color.* Shipping weight, 3 ounces.
88 E 4442—Multi-color floral. 49c

Add your little girl's accessories to your order . . and pay the Easy Terms way. See inside back cover.

Boyville Jr.
SIZES 4 TO 10

Sports Outfits for the little fellow

Rugged longwearing fabrics in smart combinations like Dad's

Dressy cotton gabardine
Available after February 15th

[A] Handsome sturdily woven gabardine is comfortably cool. Perfect for summer—in all white or navy and white. Sanforized—maximum fabric shrinkage 1%. Double breasted coat has sports back, 2 patch pockets. Fly front longies have cuff bottoms, 2 pockets. Self belt. Washable. Shipping weight, 2 pounds. **$4.40**

Sizes: 4, 5, 6, 7, 8, 9, 10. Please state size. See page 385.
40 E 3156—Navy blue coat with white slacks
40 E 3157—All white suit............$4.40

All wool Coat, smart Slacks
Available after February 15th

[D] 100% all wool Casual Coat. Front is Copen blue suede cloth; harmonizing medium blue glen plaid back, sleeves and collar. 2 set-in pockets, full rayon lining, padded shoulders. Inner lined fronts and collar. **$6.73** Coat only

Please state size: 4, 5, 6, 7, 8, 9, 10. See page 385. Shpg. wt., 1 lb. 12 oz.
40 E 3341—Copen (deep) blue coat.$6.73

Gabardine Slacks . . . blend of 68% rayon, 32% cotton. Has fly front, pleats, cuff bottoms, 3 pockets, belt loops. Seam outlet in back. No belt.
Please state size: 4, 5, 6, 7, 8, 9, 10. See page 385. Shipping wt., 1 pound.
40 E 3998—Dark blue slacks.......$3.19

Corduroy and wool outfit
Available after February 15th

[B] Snappy 2-tone sports style he will love. Single breasted coat is fully lined with sateen. Fine pinwale brown corduroy front; back, sleeves and trim of harmonizing brown check suiting (12% new wool, 38% reused wool, 50% rayon). 2 lower set-in pockets, 1 chest pocket. Matching corduroy longies have fly front, 2 side pockets and tabs inside waistband. No belt. **$7.50**

Sizes: 4, 5, 6, 7, 8, 9, 10. Please state size. See page 385. Shpg. wt., 3 lbs.
40 E 3324—Brown 2-tone suit........$7.50

Nifty sport Coat and Slacks
Available after February 15th

[E] All wool cassimere Coat. Goodlooking check weave with overplaid. 47½% new wool, 15% reprocessed wool, 37½% reused wool. Rayon lined. 3 pockets; also inside chest pocket. Padded shoulders, inner lined fronts. **$6.98** Coat only

Please state size: 4, 5, 6, 7, 8, 9, 10. See page 385. Shpg. wt., 1 lb. 12 oz.
40 E 3340—Tan check coat..........$6.98

Gabardine Slacks . . . blend of 68% rayon and 32% cotton. Has belt loops, pleats, fly front, 3 pockets and cuff bottoms. Seam outlet in back. No belt.
Please state size: 4, 5, 6, 7, 8, 9, 10. See page 385. Shipping weight, 1 pound.
40 E 3997—Dark brown slacks.......$3.19

Gabardine and plaid two-tone
Available after February 15th

[C] Casual suit with plenty of style appeal. Coat has plaid front and back (65% reprocessed wool, 35% cotton). Collar and sleeves are of gabardine (68% rayon, 32% cotton). Rayon lining; padded shoulders, inner lined fronts and collar, 2 set-in pockets. Fly front longies in matching gabardine have pleats, cuff bottoms, 3 pockets. Seam outlet in back. No belt. **$9.80**

Sizes: 4, 5, 6, 7, 8, 9, 10. State size. See page 385. Shpg. wt., 2 lbs. 12 oz.
40 E 3334—Brown 2-piece suit.......$9.80

Our Finest all wool Sport Suit
Available after February 15th

[F] Luxurious 100% virgin wool means added wear, better looks. Popular loafer 2-tone style copied after big brother's . . . does double duty for dress or school. The bright check front is in handsome contrast to the solid medium brown sleeves, collar and back. BOYVILLE tailored with shape retaining "Hymo" inner linings in fronts. Better fitting padded shoulders. Full rayon lining. 3 pockets. **$11.00**

Button fly front longies in plain color that matches coat sleeves. Front pleats, 3 pockets, cuff bottoms, seam outlet in back. No belt. Shpg. wt., 2 lbs. 12 oz.
Sizes: 4, 5, 6, 7, 8, 9, 10. Please state size. See page 385.
40 E 3110—Brown 2-tone suit.......$11.00

Budget your needs—pay by the month on Sears Easy Terms. See inside back cover

Boyville Jr.
SIZES 4 TO 10

Dress him up for Spring in a smart 2-pc. Suit

Fully rayon lined coats . . . better tailoring than ever before

Serviceable, navy blue cheviot
Available after February 1

[A] Grown up double breast-ed suit like Dad's. Prac-tical, firmly woven cheviot— **$7⁴⁵** 52% reused wool, 48% cotton. Double breasted coat has full rayon lining; shape retaining inner linings in fronts; good fitting padded shoulders. 2 lower set-in pockets. Fly front longies with pleats, cuff bottoms, 2 side pockets, 1 hip pocket. Seam outlet in back—ad-just as he grows. Shpg. wt., 2 lbs. 12 oz.

Sizes: 4, 5, 6, 7, 8, 9, 10. Please state size. See "How to Order," page 385.
40 E 3335—Navy blue.............. $7.45

Sturdy herringbone cassimere
Available after February 15

[B] Long wearing suit at this low price—popular **$8⁷⁵** herringbone weave cassi-mere, 50% reused wool and 50% rayon. Double breasted coat, full rayon lining, 3 pockets. Inner lined fronts retain shape Smooth padded shoulders. Fly front longies with pleats, cuff bottoms, 2 side pockets, 1 hip pocket. Seam outlet in back. Shpg. wt., 2 lbs 12 oz.

Sizes: 4, 5, 6, 7, 8, 9, 10. Please state size. See "How to Order," page 385.
40 E 3374—Medium brown
40 E 3375—Medium blue...... . ....$8.75

Part wool diagonal weave
Available after January 20

[C] There's a smart diag-onal weave and color-ful overplaid in this sturdy **$9⁹⁵** cassimere suit—27% new wool, 35% reused wool, 38% rayon. Fine quality BOYVILLE tailoring in the rayon lined single breasted coat, padded shoulders and shape retaining canvas lined fronts. Pleated longies have fly front, 3 pockets, cuff bottoms, back seam outlet No belt. Shpg. wt., 2 lbs. 12 oz.

Sizes· 4, 5, 6, 7, 8, 9, 10. Please state size See chart on page 385.
40 E 3371—Medium blue.... ....$9.95

[D][E] Virgin wool Longie Suits, our finest BOYVILLE Jr. quality
Available after February 15th   **$11⁹⁵**
Choice of two colors

• Rich 100% virgin wool in a choice of two popular Spring colors
• Coats fully lined with easy fitting, lustrous, long wearing rayon
• Longies have seam outlets in back . . . easy to adjust as he grows

[D] Firmly woven all wool cassimere with attractive brown herringbone weave and subdued overplaid. Parents will appreciate this suit's fine fabric, its care-ful BOYVILLE tailoring. Single breasted style with manly broad padded shoul-ders and canvas inner lined fronts. Has 3 pockets, also a handy inside chest pocket. Button fly front longies with pleats, 4 pockets, neat cuff pockets. No belt. Shpg. wt., 2 lbs. 12 oz.

Sizes: 4, 5, 6, 7, 8, 9, 10. Please state size. See "How to Order," page 385.
40 E 3122—Medium brown $11.95

[E] Smooth finish, all wool cassimere suiting in rich blue herringbone weave with overplaid—remarkable for long wear and lasting fine appearance. Finest quality BOYVILLE tailoring in-cluding shape retaining, canvas inner lined fronts . . padded shoulders that fit well. Single breasted with 3 pockets plus an inside chest pocket. Fly front longies have pleats, 4 pockets, cuff bot-toms No belt. Shpg. wt., 2 lbs. 12 oz.

Sizes· 4, 5, 6, 7, 8, 9 10. Please state size. See "How to Order," page 385.
40 E 3121—Medium blue........ ...$11.95

Rich all wool herringbone
Available after February 1st

[F] Fine quality smooth finish cassimere—60% **$10⁶⁰** new wool, 40% reused wool. In an attractive herringbone pattern all boys like. Manly double breasted coat is fully lined with lus-trous rayon. Expert BOYVILLE tailoring—padded shoulders for better fit; firm, shape-retaining inner lined fronts. Welt chest pocket, 2 lower set-in pockets Longies have button fly front, pleats, 3 pockets, cuff bottoms. Seam outlet in seat that can be let out as he grows Shpg wt., 2 lbs.12 oz.

Sizes· 4, 5, 6, 7, 8, 9, 10. Please state size. See "How to Order," page 385.
40 E 3370—Medium brown........$10.60

Shop the easy, economical way—buy all your needs from the large selection in Sears big General Catalog.

100% virgin wool worsted Suits
Keep you well dressed...at Sears low prices

A well tailored suit with quality interlinings assures permanently smooth form and good fit. Latest styles will flatter you and give you that well tailored look. A suit that will provide satisfactory service

Attractive subdued stripe

Handsome, well tailored 2-button model with dignified alternating stripe. Semi-conservative style. Good quality interlinings assure good fit. Hard finished fabric will resist wrinkles, give longer wear. Coat lined with Earl-Glo rayon. Full cut, well styled trousers have neat cuff bottoms. 6-button vest. _Sizes below._ Shpg. wt., 5 lbs. 8 oz.
♦55 E 5119—Medium brown
♦55 E 5121—Medium gray
♦55 E 5123—Medium blue.................$23.95

Double-breasted chalk stripe

100% virgin wool worsted fabric . . . richly patterned, well tailored with stylish lines that will flatter most men—give a dressy, distinctive appearance. Hard finished fabric will give longer wear. Good quality interlinings. Coat lined with Earl-Glo rayon. Well tailored trousers, cuff bottoms. No vest. _Sizes below._ Shpg. wt., 5 lbs. 8 ozs.
♦55 E 5125—Medium gray
♦55 E 5127—Medium blue
♦55 E 5129—Medium brown.............$23.95

Popular Hollywood model

Plenty of zip, dash and dressy smartness in this Hollywood styled young men's 2-button model. 100% virgin wool worsted fabric has bold cluster stripe. FASHION TAILORED with full chest, broad shoulders, rolling peak lapels, piped lower pockets. Quality interlinings. Earl-Glo rayon lining in coat. Pleated trousers. Cuffed bottoms. 6-button vest. _Sizes below._ Shpg. wt., 5 lbs, 8 ozs.
♦55 E 5131—Medium blue
♦55 E 5133—Medium brown.............$23.95

SIZES: All sizes 34 to 44-inch chest; 28 to 41-inch waist; 28 to 35-inch inseam. Regulars, shorts and longs. _State chest, waist, inseam, sleeve length; also age, height, weight._
Use Order Blank, page E, back of book. ♦Suits shipped from Chicago. Order, pay postage from Sears nearest mail order house. Easy Terms on inside back cover

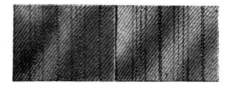
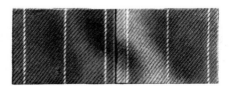
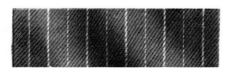

Loafer Coat . . . 2-tone 100% virgin wool

Tailored for casual comfort. Fine quality rich virgin wool worsted gabardine front, **$14.95** novelty weave virgin wool back, sleeves and collar. Body and sleeves lined with Earl-Glo rayon.

Even Sizes: 32 to 46-inch chest. *State chest measure taken over vest.* Shipping weight, 1 pound 15 ounces.

◆55 D 8268—Tan 2-tone Loafer Coat $14.95
◆55 D 8270—Blue 2-tone Loafer Coat 14.95

All merchandise marked (◆) shipped from Chicago. Order and pay postage from your nearest Sears mail order house.

Plaid 'n' Plain Sports Coats and Slacks

Solid color Coat, Glen Plaid Slacks

Available after August 1

Sports Coat . . 100% virgin wool in smooth, solid colors you'll like. **$18.95** Single breasted, three-button style *Coat and Slacks* tailored with firm interlinings, sporty patch pockets, Earl-Glo rayon lining.

Slacks . . . 50% wool, 50% rayon in a colorful glen plaid pattern. Youthfully styled with dropped belt loops, 4 front pleats, zip fly, cuff bottoms.

Sizes below. Colors: medium blue; medium brown. *State size, color.* Shipping wt., 5 lbs. 7 oz.
◆55 D 8296—Coat and Slacks $18.95

Sports Coat only (described above). *Sizes below. State size.* Shipping weight, 3 pounds 8 ounces.
◆55 D 8208—Med. blue Sports Coat only . . $13.95
◆55 D 8210—Med. brown Sports Coat only. 13.95

Glen Plaid Coat, solid color Slacks

Available after August 1

Sports Coat . . 100% virgin wool in a "big yarn," bold glen plaid that's **$21.50** youthfully smart. Three-button *Coat and Slacks* style with three welt pockets, smooth, lustrous Earl-Glo rayon lining.

Slacks . . . 100% virgin wool in rich solid colors. Youthful dropped belt loops, 4 front pleats, zipper fly, neat cuff bottoms. Shpg. wt., 5 lbs. 7 oz.

Sizes below. Colors: med. blue coat and slacks, or tan coat and med. brown slacks. *State size, color.*
◆55 D 8294—Coat and Slacks $21.50

Sports Coat only (described above). *Sizes below. State size.* Shipping weight, 3 pounds 8 ounces.
◆55 D 8204—Tan Sports Coat only $14.95
◆55 D 8206—Med. blue Sports Coat only. 14.95

2-button Sports Coat . . . 100% virgin wool

Broad-shouldered, trim-waisted . . . a youthful drape style that's handsome and **$13.95** comfortable. Long-wearing, tweedy, herringbone weave 100% virgin wool with good quality interlining to hold it in shape for lasting fit; smooth rolling notched lapels and patch pockets for sporty good looks. Earl-Glo rayon lined.

Sizes below. Shipping weight, 3 pounds 8 ounces.
◆55 D 8200—Medium blue $13.95
◆55 D 8202—Medium brown 13.95

SPORTS COATS: all sizes 33 to 44-inch chest; regulars, shorts and longs.   **SLACKS:** all sizes 28 to 40-inch waist; 29 to 35-inch inseam.
State chest, waist and inseam, sleeve length; also height, weight and age. Measure carefully; use Order Blank page E in back of book.

$26.98 cash, $5 monthly, Easy Terms

GRAY FLANNEL, a smooth-textured pure wool, for the exciting new suit with buttons marching two by two. Rayon lined jacket is superbly fitted with flap pockets placed just-so at hips. Skirt is newly slim, has fashionable fly front detail. *Sizes* 10, 12, 14, 16, 18, 20; scale on opposite page. *Please state size.* Shipping wt. 3 lbs. 2 oz.
◆17 G 5158—Gray flannel............26.98

$19.98 cash, $5 monthly, Easy Terms

THE YOKED SUIT in all wool crepe has wonderful shoulders, belts its gathered waistline for the new look. Rayon lined jacket. Slimming fly front skirt. *Sizes* 10, 12, 14, 16, 18, 20; scale, opposite page. *State size.* Shipping weight 3 pounds.
◆17G5160—Gold   ◆17G5162—Med. blue
◆17G5161—Med. brown   ◆17G5163—Black
Each.................................19.98

$19.98 cash, $5 monthly, Easy Terms

TIED-IN-TIGHT SUIT in fine-textured all wool crepe yokes its shoulders in clever scallops. Rayon lined jacket. Pleats to the side on a slim-hipped skirt. *Sizes* 10, 12, 14, 16, 18, 20; scale, opposite page. *State size.* Shpg. wt. 3 lbs. 4 oz.
◆17G5165—Royal (bright blue)
◆17G5166—Rosy red   ◆17G5168—Med. brown
◆17G5167—Med. green Each..........19.98

$89.00 plus $17.80 tax . . total cash price $106.80
$37.00 down; $7.00 monthly on Sears convenient Easy Terms

DARK OCELOT MARKINGS distinguish this sheared ALPINE LAMB
with the rich velvety finish. Swingy tuxedo style with cardigan
neckline, well-set flange shoulders. Exciting new pouch
sleeves caught tight at your wrists. Grand toss-over-everything
coat. 36 inches long. Rayon lining. Sizes 12, 14, 16, 18, 20;
see size scale, page 48. Please state size. Shpg. wt. 7 lbs.
♦ 74 G 0422E—Black and gold ocelot markings......89.00
Plus 20% Federal Excise Tax.....................17.80
Total cash price 106.80

$125.00 plus $25.00 tax . . total cash price $150.00
$51.50 down; $10.00 monthly on Sears convenient Easy Terms

RED FOX GREATCOAT, with fur worked vertically to make it
full-blown and beautiful, mounted on narrow tapes to give
it easy fluid lines. New set-in cape collar, deep suit-accom-
modating armholes. Rayon lined. Underarm of sleeves rayon
lined to conform to smart silhouette. 36 inches long. Sizes
12, 14, 16, 18, 20; see scale, page 48. Please state size.
♦ 74 G 0423E—Red fox. Shpg. wt. 7 lbs.........125.00
Plus 20% Federal Excise Tax.....................25.00
Total cash price 150.00

Kerrybrooke
FASHIONS

THE RIGHT WAY TO SAY
FUR FASHIONS

Catalog numbers marked ♦ shipped from Philadelphia. Order, pay postage from Sears nearest mail order house. Buy
now . . buy the best . . Sears. Easy Terms are available. See inside back cover for complete details on Easy Payment Plan.

cMNKABP ₃ PAGE 53 . . FUR COATS

Flare for 1947

Our little black gabardine suit is so smart from every angle that we show you two views. It's so new and exciting it's the talk of the town. It goes everywhere .. stands out in every crowd.

Misses sizes 12 to 20

$12.98

BEAUTIFUL RAYON GABARDINE . . . rich black, superior quality . . . dramatizes a suit that does wonders for your figure . . . makes you feel equal to any occasion. It has a slim little curved-in waist, big billowing push-up sleeves and a wonderful jacket that flares at the sides, ripples in back. You can wear it with a pretty blouse or as a dress . . . you'll probably do both because it's as useful as it is smart . . . perfect for every important event from Easter to Fall. The expert cut and fine tailoring are in the best Kerrybrooke tradition. Dry clean. *Sizes 12, 14, 16, 18, 20; scale, page 7. State size.* Shpg. wt. 1 lb. 8 oz.
♦31 H 9245—Black $12.98

THE HAT . . . lacy, straw-like braid with a rayon velvet band. *Colors* Black, white, navy blue; toast (golden tan) with brown. Fits 21¾–22½ inch headsize. *Measure, state size, color.* Shipped from Chicago or Philadelphia.
78 H 2000 — Shipping wt. 1 lb. . . $4.98

Catalog numbers marked ♦ are shipped from Philadelphia or Kansas City. Please order and pay postage from Sears nearest mail order house. Sears Easy Terms are available on orders of $10 or more. See inside back cover.

Kerrybrooke
FASHIONS

Junior Coats and Suits shape up smartly

A
$22.98 cash
All wool crepe

B
$22.98 cash
Suede-soft wool

C
$19.98 cash
Shetland-type wool

Buy your Coat or Suit now . . $5.00 monthly on Sears Easy Terms.
See inside back cover of this catalog for complete details.

Teens' Style Parade of wonderful, wearable all wool coats

B $13.98
All Wool Shetland-type

C $13.98
All Wool Check

A $10.98
All Wool Shetland-type

D $14.98
All Wool Shetland-type

Descriptions of coats shown above, on opposite page

200 .. SEARS-ROEBUCK PBC

They're news . . shortcoats over suits . .

A $16.98 each, cash
Checked Wool Coat or Suit
$5.00 monthly on Easy Terms

B $16.98 each, cash
Striped Menswear Flannel Coat or Suit
$5.00 monthly on Easy Terms

Nailhead-studded Kerrybrooke Platforms

Fashion swings to platforms; you'll see these Kerrybrookes everywhere

F $5.50 Without Bow
Black Gabardine

G $5.50 Without Bow
Black Gabardine

H $5.50
Black Plastic

J $6.45

K $6.45

Please do not order shoes on this page before August 15

F SLING SIREN . . . triple rows of nailheads twinkle from the high platform. Made the flexible California way. Leather sole, 2¾-in. heel.
• C (medium) sizes 4 to 8. Half sizes, too. *Please state size.* Shpg. wt. 1 lb. 2 oz.
♦5 G 8036—Black plastic $6.45
♦5 G 8037—Black cotton gabardine (without bow). Pair $5.50
♦5 G 8012—Black rayon faille bow, nailhead trim. Pair 69c

G BLACK BEAUTY . . . high platform a-glitter with nailheads in constrasting patterns. Easy-flex California construction. Leather sole. 2⅛-inch heel.
• C (medium) sizes 4 to 9. Half sizes, too. *Please state size.* Shpg. wt. 1 lb. 2 oz.
♦5 G 8032—Black plastic $6.45
♦5 G 8033—Black cotton gabardine (without bowl. Pair $5.50
♦5 G 8013—Black rayon faille bow nailhead trim. Pair 69c

H DRAMATIC CHARM; for gay evenings ahead. Vivid contrast of gleaming nailheads on rich black high platform. California-type construction. Leather sole, 2¾-inch heel.
• C (medium) sizes 4 to 8. Half sizes, too. *Please state size.* Shpg. wt. 1 lb. 2 oz.
♦5 G 8034—Sparkling bright black plastic . . . . . Pair $5.50
♦5 G 8035—Black cotton gabardine . . . . Pair $5.35

J BEAUTIFUL CHERRY COKE . . . new color sensation, or transparent Vinylite sandal. High platform with green, red and gold color nailheads. Leather sole. 2¾-in. heel.
• C (medium) sizes 4 to 9. Half sizes, too. *Please state size.* Shpg. wt. 1 lb. 2 oz.
♦5 G 8085—Cherry coke (brownish red shiny plastic)
♦5 G 8086—Transparent Vinylite plastic . . . . Pair $6.45

K YOUR FAVORITE SHANKS MARE . . . boasts a new high platform with rows of gleaming nailheads, a new squared vamp. Alligator-grained leather shines up to your dressiest clothes. Easy-flex California-type construction.
• C (medium) sizes 4 to 9. Half sizes, too. *Please state size.* Shpg. wt. 1 lb. 2 oz.
♦5 G 8039—Brown
♦5 G 8038—Black . . Pair $6.45

METAL NAILHEADS in gleaming gold-color
are the favorite trimming for Fall

A $8.88
Tax included

B $3.49
Tax included

C $3.49
Tax included

D $2.34
Tax included

E $2.34
Tax included

F $5.89
Tax included

A POLISHED SADDLE LEATHER, in a fine, rugged zip-top with gold color metal nailheads in front. Fabric lined, coin case, mirror. *Size* about 12¾ x 6½. Shpg. wt. 15 oz
88 G 1907E–Rust brown..8.88
88 G 1908E–Black......8.88

B LEATHER-LIKE PLASTIC—zip-top with gold color nailheads for front interest. Roomy, rounded gussets. Fabric lined, coin case, mirror. *Size* about 14½ x 7¼ in. Shpg. wt. 14 oz.
88 G 1918E–Black......3.49
88 G 1919E–Dk. brown ..3.49

C DURABLE PLASTIC, looks like leather. Gold color nailheads at front. Zip-top. Fabric lined, coin case, mirror. *Size* abt. 7 x 6½ in. Shpg. wt. 14 oz.
88 G 1909E–Black......3.49
88 G 1910E–Dk. brown..3.49
88 G 1911E–Rust tan....3.49

D FINE RAYON FAILLE, even prettier set off with gold color nailheads at front of this gay flower-pot drawstring. Fabric lined, mirror. *Size* about 6¾ x 6¼ in. Shpg. wt. 10 oz
88 G 1912E–Black......2.34
88 G 1913E–Dk. brown..2.34

E SOFT FELT, with gold color nailheads. Felt is 70% wool, 30% cotton. Abt. 10 x 10½ in. Fabric lined. Shpg. wt. 8 oz.
88 G 1914E–Red........2.34
88 G 1915E–Bright green.2.34
88 G 1916E–Black.......2.34
88 G 1917E–Dk. brown ..2.34

F PATENT-LIKE PLASTIC, has four rows of gold color nailheads, down the sides. New cushiony square zip-top with adjustable shoulder strap. Fabric lined, mirror. *Size* about 9¼ x 8½ in. Shpg. wt. 13 oz.
88 G 1904E–Black......5.89

Prices of all bags illustrated include 20% Federal Excise Tax. Why not use Sears Easy Payment Plan . . see inside back cover.

ALL 3 PAGE 187 . . ACCESSORIES

Bemberg **rayon sheer . . lovely and cool . . perfect for Spring and Summer**

pretty new dresses with slim waists and full skirts . . hand wash separately

$6.98
Each

Sizes 12 to 20

A THE CAPE COLLAR is cool and flattering. The print is charming . . . little sailor hats with bright-colored streamers and white scatter dots. Hand wash separately. *Sizes 12, 14, 16, 18, 20; see size scale, page 7. State size. Shpg. wt. 1 lb. 8 oz.*

♦ 31 H 9295—Light gray ground. . . .$6.98
♦ 31 H 9296—Light coral red ground . 6.98
♦ 31 H 9297—Light lime green ground 6.98

B STRIPED BUTTON-FRONT CASUAL with a smart new look . . . perfect to wear right now because it has long sleeves, comes in dark colors. The collar can be worn open. Hand wash separately. *Sizes 12, 14, 16, 18, 20; see size scale on page 7. State size. Shipping weight 1 lb. 8 oz.*

♦ 31 H 9290—Navy blue and white. $6.98
♦ 31 H 9291—Brown and white. 6.98

C DOLL PRINT, button-front style, with expensive loop trimming and the new deep neckline that's so becoming. A perfect dress for warm days. Hand wash separately. *Sizes 12, 14, 16, 18, 20; see scale, page 7. State size. Shpg. wt. 1 lb. 8 oz.*

♦ 31 H 9300—Med. green and white . $6.98
♦ 31 H 9301—Light gray and white . . 6.98
♦ 31 H 9302—Navy blue and white . . 6.98

Numbers marked ♦ shipped from Philadelphia or Kansas City. Order and pay postage from Sears nearest mail order house. Easy Terms, see inside back cover.

Kerrybrooke
FASHIONS

Crown Tested French-type rayon crepe . . soft, flattering, colorful

Smart new fashions to dress up or wear casually . . hand wash separately

[A] LITTLE CHECKS and frilly ruffles . . . a pretty little dress you'll love because it always looks so fresh and neat. You'll look very slim and smart in it too . . . the smooth fitting bodice and big peg pockets see to that. Hand wash separately. *Sizes 12, 14, 16, 18, 20; see size scale, page 7. State size.* Shipping weight 1 lb. 8 oz.
  Please do not order before Feb. 1, 1947.
  ♦ 31 H 9305—Black and white checks $5.49

[B] "SUNDAY IN THE PARK" PRINT . . . tiny trees and people . . pretty bright colors . . a charming new design. The dress is very feminine with its full bodice, slim midriff and front peplum. Hand wash separately. *Sizes 12, 14, 16, 18, 20; scale, page 7. State size.* Shpg. wt. 1 lb. 8 oz.
  Please do not order before Feb. 1, 1947.
  ♦ 31 H 9310—Light pink ground.... $5.49
  ♦ 31 H 9311—Aqua blue ground.... 5.49

[C] CHAIN-LINK PRINT . . . alternating lines of black and bright green make a very smart new design for this button-front casual with its smooth fitting bodice, full skirt and pretty peg pockets. Hand wash separately. *Sizes 12, 14, 16, 18, 20; see size scale on page 7. Please state size.* Shipping weight 1 pound 8 ounces.
  Please do not order before Feb. 1, 1947.
  ♦ 31 H 9315—White ground print... $5.49

$5.49
Each
Sizes 12 to 20

Catalog numbers marked ♦ shipped from Philadelphia or Kansas City. Order and pay postage from Sears nearest mail order house.

Newest "Shut-Eye" Fashions are Charmode Sleep Sets briefed for comfort

$2.98

SLUMBER COAT. Here's a glamorous version of grandfather's nightshirt in floral printed rayon flat crepe. Wonderful wardrobe idea . . . sleeps cool and comfortable, looks so smart ensembled with matching pajamas at right. Man-tailored notched collar style with short sleeves, pocket, plastic buttons. Hand wash. Length about 32 in. *Sizes 32, 34, 36, 38-inch bust. Please state bust size.* Shipping weight 6 ounces.

38 H 1640M—Dusty rose ground
38 H 1641M—Aqua blue ground
38 H 1642M—Pale yellow ground..... Each $2.98

$3.98

SHORTIE PAJAMA. Lovely floral printed rayon flat crepe fashions this clever team-up of tie top bra and shorts. A perfect companion to our slumber coat and long pajama. All major seams are double stitched, ripproof. Tailored shorts have 2 front pleats, 2 back gores. Button closing waistband and placket. Short sleeves. Hand washable. *Sizes 32, 34, 36, 38-inch bust. Please state bust size.* Shipping weight 6 ounces.

38 H 1638M—Dusty rose ground
38 H 1639M—Aqua blue ground
38 H 1654M—Pale yellow ground...... Each $3.98

$3.98

MIDRIFF PAJAMA. Sleeping's easy in this bare midriff pajama that's ensemble-minded too. Top it with the trim slumber coat and you have a style-right set. All major seams are double stitched, rip-proof. The floral printed rayon flat crepe is hand washable. Adjustable tie front. Short sleeves. Trousers have 2 front pleats, 2 back gores. Button waistband and placket. Shipping weight 8 ounces. *Sizes 32, 34, 36, 38-inch. Please state bust size.*

38 H 1635M—Dusty rose ground
38 H 1636M—Aqua blue ground
38 H 1637M—Pale yellow ground..... Each $3.98

Why not add Charmode Sleep Sets to your Easy Terms Order. See inside back cover for details

rugged, and washable . . Erwin Mills *Blue Denims*

•SANFORIZED•
(Max. Fabric Shrink. 1%)

Slacks $2.79   Shirt $1.98

DENIM SLACKS with front pleats, darts in back. All leg seams double needle stitched. 1 pocket. Buttoned side closing. Washable. *Sizes 12, 14, 16, 18, 20; size scale, page 65. State size.* Shpg. wt. 14 oz.
♦ 7 H 938—Light blue $2.79
♦ 7 H 939—Navy blue 2.79

DENIM SHIRT with patch pocket. *Sizes 12, 14, 16, 18, 20; scale, page 72. State size.* Shpg. wt. 11 oz.
♦ 7 H 1589—Light blue $1.98
♦ 7 H 1599—Navy blue 1.98

Overalls $3.79

LIGHT BLUE OR NAVY one-piece overalls with wide contrasting color band at square neck, down to a deep V in back, and on pockets. Buttons in back. Set-in belt. Skillfully cut and smartly tailored, fun to wear at home, at work or for all kinds of sports. Washable.
Sizes 12, 14, 16, 18, 20; see size scale, page 60. Please state size. Shipping weight 1 pound.
♦ 7H726—Lt. blue, navy trim . $3.79
♦ 7H727–Navy blue, red trim 3.79

Dungarees $2.98   Jacket $3.89

DENIM DUNGAREES, red double stitching, copper rivets. 2 pockets, back yoke. Metal riveted buttons at side. *Sizes 10, 12, 14, 16, 18; scale, page 65. State size.* Shipping weight 1 lb. 1 oz.
♦ 7 H 942—Light blue $2.98
♦ 7 H 937—Navy blue 2.98

DENIM JACKET, red double needle stitched. 2 pockets. Back yoke. *Sizes 10, 12, 14, 16, 18; size scale, page 64. Please state size.* Shipping wt. 14 oz.
♦ 7 H 1146—Light blue $3.89
♦ 7 H 1169—Navy blue 3.89

Catalog numbers marked ♦ shipped from Kansas City or Philadelphia. Order and pay postage from Sears nearest mail order house.

PCSLA *PAGE 63 . . . SPORTSWEAR*

Charmode
REG. U.S. PAT. OFF.

THE RIGHT WAY
TO SAY

**WOMEN'S
INTIMATE
APPAREL**

The Girdle . . . $5.88   The Brief . . . . $5.88   The Panty $5.88

It's easy to order Charmode Corsetry — or anything else at Sears — on Easy Terms. See inside back cover   ALL PAGE 179 . . CORSETRY

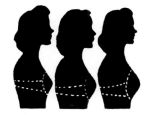

Charmode Wired Bras .. the daring new fashion sensation!

Give you wonderful uplift with comfort and fine fit

Wired Bras—now out of the luxury class—are not "just another fad." The revolutionary use of wire has very definite advantage . . .

- Takes the weight off shoulders .. leaves you free, unrestrained
- Gives you youthful lines plus comfortable uplift.
- Gives smart separation demanded by today's fashion world

Both styles—with and without straps—are smooth fitting and comfortable. Order yours today.

CHARMODE STRAPLESS WIRED BRA. You, too, can join the fashion parade in this lovely, budget-priced bra. Feel perfectly secure in bare shoulder formals, daytime dresses, play clothes, etc. Stitched lower bust-cups; lace edged top. Covered stainless steel wire around entire bust-cups gives wonderful uplift support. Elastic inserts between cups and at adjustable back closing give comfortable release.

For the Medium bust-cup type
Bust sizes 32, 34, 36, 38 inches. Please state bust size. Shpg. wt. 5 oz.
18 H 822—Nude rayon satin **$3.39**
18 H 823—White nylon marquisette . **$3.39**
18 H 824—Black nylon marquisette . **$3.39**

For the Small bust-cup type
Bust sizes 32, 34, 36 inches. Please state bust sizes. Shipping weight 5 ounces.
18 H 815—White nylon marquisette **$3.39**

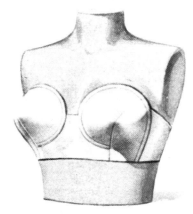

Charmode
REG. U.S. PAT. OFF.
THE RIGHT WAY
TO SAY
WOMEN'S
INTIMATE
APPAREL

OUR BEST STRAPLESS WIRED BRA. Nationally advertised *Quest-shon Mark* patented design. Made of shimmering rayon satin. Two softly padded wires are cleverly curved like question marks in each bust-cup to give smart separation and uplift *without* pressure. Give you wonderful freedom . . . plus smooth, comfortable fit. Double elastic adjustment at back closing for fine fit.
For the Medium bust-cup type
Bust sizes 32, 34, 36, 38 inches. Please state bust size. Postpaid.
18 H 748—White. **$6.79**   18 H 803—Black. **$6.79**

WIRED BRA WITH SHOULDER STRAPS. Plush covered removable wiring gives firm uplift. Stitched lower bust-cups. Adjustable elastic back closing.
For the Medium bust-cup type
Bust sizes 32, 34, 36, 38 inches. Please state bust size. Shipping weight 5 ounces.
Rayon satin; matching adjustable straps.
18 H 826—Nude. . **$3.50**   18 H 827—White. . **$3.39**
For the Large bust-cup type
Bust sizes 34, 36, 38, 40 inches. State bust size. Fine quality rayon and cotton twill; straps.
18 H 866—Nude. Shipping weight 5 oz. . . . **$3.39**

SPIRAL WIRED BRA. Lovely "princess-style" that gives a smooth, rounded contour. Proportioned to give a wonderful, youthful uplift to the average bust. Comfortably boned throughout. Wiring is very flexible—bends easily with your body. Made of fine nylon fabric with dainty lace edging. Darted for smart accentuation. Adjustable back hook closing.
For the Medium bust-cup type
Bust sizes 32, 34, 36, 38, 40 inches. Please state bust size. Shipping weight 5 ounces.
18 H 853—Nude. **$5.79**   18 H 855—White **$5.79**

SEARS HONEYLANES are the most popular slacks in America for Teens

Man-tailored for the young figure . . made to Sears own specifications

- Stitched-in trouser creases to keep their crisp, well-tailored good looks.
- Concealed placket zipper for sleek fit.
- Two roomy pockets, sturdily lined.

- Waistband firmly stitched . . lined to hug waist; has concealed gripper snap.
- Back vent for adjustable trim fit.
- Spaced belt loops, firmly stitched.

- Double stitched leg seams for wear.
- Bar-tacked at points of strain.
- All seams firmly, neatly overcast.
- Two-inch trouser hems for adjustment.

$4.19

[A] MENSWEAR GRAY SLACKS in 27% new wool, 20% reprocessed wool, 15% reused wool, 23% rayon, 10% nylon, 5% cotton. Tailored with specifications above. Dry clean. Sizes 10, 12, 14, 16. *Please state size.* Shipping weight 1 pound 4 ounces.
◆ 77 G 6310–Gray 4.19

[B] PART WOOL BUFFALO CHECK SHIRT in 25% new wool, 20% reused wool, 55% rayon. Convertible collar; button cuffs. Pocket. Dry clean. Sizes 10, 12, 14, 16. *Please state size.* Shipping weight 1 pound.
◆ 77 G 5911–Red and black 3.98
◆ 77 G 5912–Black and white 3.98

$4.98

[C] OUR FINEST FLANNEL SLACKS are all virgin wool and number one favorite. Tailored with all the fine specifications listed above. Dry clean. *Sizes* 10, 12, 14, 16. *State size.* Shpg. wt. 1 lb. 4 oz.
◆ 77 G 6313–Dark brown 4.98
◆ 77 G 6314–Navy blue 4.98

[D] 100% VIRGIN WOOL SWEATER (pictured in color on page 269). Hand washable; use Lux. *Sizes* 10, 12, 14, 16. *State size.* Shipping weight 11 ounces.
98 G 4643–Yellow 2.66   98 G 4641–Med. blue 2.66
98 G 4644–White 2.66   98 G 4650–Bright red 2.66
98 G 4651–Gray . 2.66   98 G 4652–Dk. brown 2.66

$4.19

[E] CHECKED SLACKS in 25% new wool, 20% reused wool, 55% rayon. Made with specifications above. Dry clean. *Sizes* 10, 12, 14, 16. *Please state size.* Shipping weight 1 pound 4 ounces.
◆ 77 G 6311–Brown and white check 4.19
◆ 77 G 6312–Black and white check 4.19

[F] COTTON STRIPED CLASSIC SHIRT has action back yoke. Patch pocket. Cuffs on long sleeves. Wash separately. *Sizes* 10, 12, 14, 16. *Please state size.* Shipping weight 8 ounces.
98 G 5758–Red and white stripe 1.40
98 G 5759–Blue and white stripe 1.40

SIZE SCALE for Teen Slacks, Skirts, Blouses, Sizes 10 to 16	Order size : 10	12	14	16	
	If bust is : 30	31½	33	34	in.
	If waist is : 24	25	26	27	in.
	If hips are : 33	34½	36	37	in.
	Skirt length: (including band) 22	23	24	24½	in.
	Slack length: (including band) 38½	39½	40½	41½	in.

Catalog numbers marked ◆ shipped from Philadelphia or Kansas City. Order, pay postage from Sears nearest mail order house. Easy Terms are available, see inside back cover.

Kerrybrooke Teenright Smoothies . . . styles
to "go steady" with season-in, season-out
Low-down comfort, high-rating fashion . . .
Use Easy Terms . . . see inside back cover

[N] EVERYONE'S "THAT WAY" ABOUT THIS TEENWISE SLIP-ON . . . its
as casual 'n' carefree as a coke session, as smooth as your pet
date dress . . . simply "out of this world" with your tailored sports
togs or sweater 'n' skirt outfits. Upper is of super-soft vegetable
tanned leather . . . antique finished to give it that mellow, worn look
you'd expect from any well-behaved slip-on. Genuine Goodyear
welt construction . . . no nails come through to irritate the feet,
greater flexibility and inner smoothness. Room for good luck penny
in vamp saddle. Firm binding around the collar helps shoe retain its
shape. Easy-bending leather sole, heel. Order your pair today.
• A (very narrow) girls', women's sizes 5, 5½, 6, 6½, 7, 7½, 8, 8½, 9.
C (medium) girls', women's sizes 3½,4,4½,5,5½,6,6½,7,7½,8,8½,9.
Please state size and width. Shipping weight 1 pound 8 ounces.

15 H 2836—Brown leather . . . . Pair $5.45

[P] HARD-TO-DO-WITHOUT SLIP-ON . . . strictly "on the beam" for
Teen-time funtime. As fashion-right with your sportiest casuals
as with your most glamour-wise dresses . . . on the solid side for
classes, for picnics, for sports events, for dates. Supple brown leather
upper accented by "Kitten whiskers" and center seam smartly
stitched in white for the "something new and different." High-peaked
vamp . . . gives you a snugger, smoother fit over the instep. Wall toe
last . . . more room-to-move-around-in for your toes. Comfortable
genuine Goodyear welt construction . . . one of the finest, most flexible ways of making shoes. Durable leather sole, heel.
• A (very narrow) girls', women's sizes 5, 5½, 6,6½,7,7½,8,8½,9.
C (medium) girls', women's sizes 4,4½,5,5½,6,6½,7,7½,8,8½,9.
Please state size and width. Shipping weight 1 pound 8 ounces.

15 H 2842—Brown leather . . . . Pair $5.45

the Long look

Skirts are longer. Waistlines look longer. Fabrics are used lavishly. Trimmings are brilliant. Sears price is less than you'd expect for such elegance. Misses' sizes

$12.98 each

OUR BEST QUALITY rayon crepe is used in these three dresses. It's Mallinson's Whirlaway . . a fine, moss-textured fabric that drapes beautifully, holds pleats, wears wonderfully.

[A] SIDE DRAPERY and front peplum for the long look that makes you seem taller, thinner, more graceful. Glittering sequins for brilliance. A dress you'll love and everyone will admire. Dry clean. *Sizes* 12, 14, 16, 18, 20; size scale, page 228. *Please state size.* Shpg. wt. 1 lb. 8 oz.
♦ 31 K 8300—Black with green, gold color sequins. . . $12.98
Bow CLOCHE, wool felt. *Colors* Black, brown. Dark green with brown; winter white with black. *State color.* Shpg. wt. 1 lb. Shipped from Chicago or Philadelphia.
78 K 6130—Fits sizes 21¾-23¼ in. *Measure*. $3.98

[B] LONG TORSO TOP to give you a new streamlined silhouette. Pleats all around to flutter when you walk, swirl when you dance. Gold-color ornaments to accent your smooth, slim waistline. A handsome dress that will look smart and new for several seasons. Dry clean. *Sizes* 12, 14, 16, 18, 20; size scale, page 228. State size. Shpg. wt. 1 lb. 8 oz.
♦ 31 K 8305—Black.   ♦ 31 K 8307—Pine (dark) green
♦ 31 K 8306—Bright rose   Each. $12.98

[C] THE TUNIC DRESS is bound to bring you compliments. Nailheads sparkle on the front of the bodice. The long peplum ripples and dips in back . . a wonderful style for slender or full figures. Dry clean. *Sizes* 12, 14, 16, 18, 20; scale, page 228. *Please state size.* Shpg. wt. 1 lb. 8 oz.
♦ 31 K 8310–Black with silver-color nailheads. $12.98
♦ 31 K 8311–Moss (med.) green; silver-color nailheads. 12.98
♦ 31 K 8312–Dark brown with gold-color nailheads. . . . 12.98

Kerrybrooke
THE RIGHT WAY TO SAY
FASHIONS

What's in a label?

This label is your assurance of smart fashion, good taste and real value. It means good quality pre-tested fabric, good fit, expert tailoring and finishing: fine, firm stitching . . zipper side closing . . smart shoulder pads . . ⅞ in. side seams . . 2 in. hem . . taped or double-stitched waistline, yoke and shoulders . . blind-stitched sleeve and skirt hem.

Catalog numbers marked ♦ shipped from Philadelphia or Kansas City. Order and pay postage from Sears nearest mail order house. Use Sears Easy Terms, see inside back cover

ALL PAGE 227

THE NEW LOOK is the long look in wool suits

Sears dressy suits own it .. are beautifully tailored in wonderful fabrics .. money-saving prices

[A] IN WOMEN'S SIZES, TOO . . . soft, feminine version of the mannish suit, exquisitely tailored in rich, lustrous all wool broadcloth, neatly bound in shimmery rayon satin. New longer jacket tapers wide lapels to trim, link-button waist, is rayon lined. Front-pleated skirt with TALON zipper. *State size. Misses' sizes 12, 14, 16, 18, 20; scale below.*
♦ 17 K 5466—Black. Shpg. wt. 3 lbs. 8 oz.....$22.98
Women's sizes 34, 36, 38, 40, 42, 44; scale, page 214.
♦ 17 K 5581—Black. Shpg. wt. 3 lbs. 10 oz....$24.98

[B] IN WOMEN'S SIZES, TOO . . . the virgin wool worsted suit, tailored in the mannish manner, is faintly, slimly striped. A rayon lined jacket turns a lapel-collar neatly, links its waistline sleekly. Well-cut skirt with freedom front-pleat, TALON zipper. *State size. Misses' sizes 12, 14, 16, 18, 20; scale below.*
♦ 17 K 5464—Navy blue. Shpg. wt. 3 lbs. 8 oz. $19.98
♦ 17 K 5465—Black. Shpg. wt. 3 lbs. 8 oz..... 19.98
Women's sizes 34, 36, 38, 40, 42, 44; scale, page 214.
♦ 17 K 5579—Navy blue. Shpg. wt. 3 lbs. 10 oz.$21.98
♦ 17 K 5580—Black. Shpg. wt. 3 lbs. 10 oz.... 21.98
Pages 210 and 211 show more women's suits

[C] THE TRIPLE-TIERED SUIT in fine-textured all wool crepe is full of fashion excitement. Rayon lined jacket ripples its peplum below a new rounded hipline, an indented waistline. Beautiful buttons close it. Tape-slim skirt is smartly slit at sides, closes in a wink with TALON zipper. Super tailored throughout. *Sizes 12, 14, 16, 18, 20. State size. Shpg. wt. 3 lbs. 6 oz.*
♦ 17 K 5468 Medium gray | ♦ 17 K 5469–Medium blue
♦ 17 K 5470–Black | Each.............$24.98

[D] BIG-HEARTED LAPELS sprout smartly on a cardigan-necked suit of dressy all wool crepe. Rayon lined jacket is softened with gentle flare below a nipped waistline. Slender skirt is gored for good line, smoothly closed with a TALON zipper. *Sizes 12, 14, 16, 18, 20. State size. Shpg. wt. 3 lbs. 2 oz.*
♦ 17 K 5472–Medium gray | ♦ 17 K 5473–Medium brown
♦ 17 K 5474–Black | Each.............$16.98

[E] SOFT-DRAPING ALL WOOL tailors richly into the exciting new cuff-sleeved suit. Wonderful jacket is rayon lined. Its gentle cutaway turns back into stunning muff-effect. Well-cut skirt is hip-slim, has new short-stop pleat in front. TALON zipper. *Sizes 12, 14, 16, 18, 20. State size. Shpg. wt. 3 lbs. 6 oz.*
♦ 17 K 5476–Medium green | ♦ 17 K 5477–Medium gray
♦ 17 K 5478–Black | Each.............$24.98

Size Scale for Misses' Suits and Coats

Order size	10	12	14	16	18	20
If hips are:	34	35	36½	38	39½	41 in.
If waist is:	24	25½	27	28½	30	32 in.
If bust is:	31	32½	34	35½	37	39 in.
Skirt length (below band at center back)	26¾	27	27¼	27½	27¾	28 in.
Coat length	42	42½	43	43½	44	44½ in.

Catalog numbers marked ♦ shipped from Philadelphia or Kansas City. Order, pay postage from Sears nearest mail order house. For Easy Terms, see inside back cover.

[A] **Sizes 12 to 20 $22.98** cash
$2.50 down, $5 monthly on Sears Easy Terms

Sizes 34 to 44 $24.98 cash
$2.50 down, $5 monthly on Sears Easy Terms

[B] **Sizes 12 to 20 $19.98** cash
$2 down, $5 monthly on Sears Easy Terms

Sizes 34 to 44 $21.98 cash
$2.50 down, $5 monthly on Sears Easy Terms

HOODS ARE NEWEST FASHION ADDITIONS TO ANY-WEATHER COATS

Hooded Coats Ⓒ *and* Ⓓ *illustrated above, in 3 fine fabrics*

Ⓔ **The Cloak Coat**

Rayon Gabardine $19.98 Cash
$2 down, $5 monthly, Easy Terms

Woven Twill $14.98

Cotton Gabardine $9.98

$19.98 Cash
$2 down, $5 monthly, Easy Terms

ALL₂ PAGE 199 .. COATS

JUNIORS'

Sizes 9 to 17

$11.98 Black Rayon Faille

this little suit goes everywhere . .

it's worn with or without a blouse

$9.98 Plaid Rayon Taffeta,

puffed out to belittle your waist . .

slim black skirt of rayon alpaca

[A] When you find a suit that's as smart and versatile and sensibly priced as this one, you've really found something. The broad lapel collar is so flattering, the snug little jacket makes your waist look so small, the skirt is the kind you dream about. It's very full in front and subtly flared in back to give you the new forward-swept silhouette. It's wonderful with Gibson Girl or any dressy blouses. Gold-color metal buttons on the jacket. Tissue rayon faille; dry clean. *Sizes 9, 11, 13, 15, 17; scale, page 143.* Shpg. wt. 1 lb. 8 oz.
♦31 L 9045—Black. *State size* $11.98

[B] Never underestimate the power of these new hip-accenting puffs. They make a not-so-slim waist look little, and a little waist look like a mere wisp . . . especially when they're done in crisp taffeta like this with a soft, slim skirt for contrast. The taffeta top is a beautiful plaid with cross-bars of silvery white and tiny checks of brilliant green, yellow, blue and red against a black background. Sparkling mirror-like buttons. Dry clean. *Sizes 9, 11, 13, 15, 17; size scale, page 143. Please state size.* Shipping weight 1 pound 8 ounces.
♦31 L 9050—Plaid top, black skirt. . . $9.98

[C] The ballerina dress . . . very little waist, very big skirt . . . graceful and glamorous as a dancer's costume. Add flowers or jewelry to make it a wonderful semi-formal party dress. Wear it with the jacket to make a smart little suit. The dress has a deep neckline in front and back. The skirt is the new longer length . . . full all around, about 130 inches wide with a one-inch taped hem. The jacket has tiny mirror-like buttons. Rayon faille; dry clean. *Sizes 9, 11, 13, 15; see size scale, page 143. State size.* Shipping weight 1 lb. 8 oz.
♦31 L 9055—Black   ♦31 L 9056—Dark green
♦31 L 9057—Aqua blue   Each $13.49

$13.49 The Ballerina Dress and Jacket . .

two smart new outfits for the price of one . . rayon

faille in black, dark green or aqua blue

Catalog numbers marked ♦ shipped from Philadelphia or Kansas City. Order, pay postage from Sears nearest mail order house. Use Sears Easy Terms . . . see inside back cover

Ballerina Silhouettes

NIPPED WAISTS . . ROUNDED HIPLINES

All Wool
Crepe Suit **$16.50**

Double-stripe
All Wool Flannel **$16.50**

[A] **SOFT ROUNDED COLLAR SUIT** sweepingly styled in beautiful all wool crepe. Smart new length jacket with dainty cutaway front, simulated pockets, little waist and rounded hipline, rayon lined. Full skirt with TALON zipper. *Sizes 10, 12, 14, 16. Please state size.* Shipping weight 3 pounds.
♦17 L 5758—Bright red......$16.50
♦17 L 5759—Medium gray..... 16.50
♦17 L 5760—Medium blue..... 16.50
♦17 L 5761—Black............ 16.50

[B] **THE DOUBLE STRIPE SUIT** in luscious all wool flannel, brim full of new ballerina swing. Wear it everywhere. Short rayon lined jacket has wide spread lapels, nipped in waist. Swirling skirt has TALON zipper closing. *Sizes 10, 12, 14, 16. State size.* Shipping weight 3 pounds 2 ounces.
♦17 L 5762—Gray ground, red and white stripes................$16.50
♦17 L 5763—Beige ground, brown and white stripes................$16.50

[C] **THE COACHMAN,** beautifully carved along new ballerina lines, is part wool gabardine, (60% rayon, 40% worsted). New length jacket allows skirt to swing in wide circles, nipped in waist, rayon lined. Longer skirt has TALON zipper. *Sizes 10,12,14,16. Please state size.*
♦17 L 5754—Jade bright green.$22.50
♦17 L 5755—Medium blue..... 22.50
♦17 L 5756—Navy blue....... 22.50
♦17 L 5757—Black............ 22.50

[D] **THE NEW CAPE-COLLAR SUIT** will swirl itself right to your heart. Fine textured all wool crepe. Dramatic short jacket with tiny waist, rounded cut away front, rayon lined. Swinging new look skirt has TALON zipper closing. *Sizes 10, 12, 14, 16. Please state size.* Shipping weight 3 pounds.
♦17 L 5750—Jade bright green.$22.50
♦17 L 5751—Medium gray..... 22.50
♦17 L 5752—Bright red....... 22.50
♦17 L 5753—Navy blue....... 22.50

Part Wool Gabardine
$22.50 Cash
$2.50 down $5 monthly

All Wool Crepe **$22.50** Cash
$2.50 down $5 monthly

SWIRLING SKIRTS in new longer lengths

Numbers marked ♦ shipped from Philadelphia or Kansas City. Order, pay postage from Sears nearest mail order house. For Sears Easy Terms, see inside back cover.

Size Scale for Misses' Suits

Order size..	10	12	14	16	18	20	
If hips are..	34	35	36½	38	39½	41	in.
If waist is...	24	25½	27	28½	30	32	in.
If bust is....	31	32½	34	35½	37	39	in.
Skirt length (below band at center back)	29½	29½	29½	30	30	30½	in.

Huge purchase makes possible Tremendous Bargains!

Blue Jeans

SPECIALLY CUT FOR THE FEMININE FIGURE

$1.98 A PAIR

★ Sturdy Sanforized cottons.. long wearing and washable

★ Shiny copper riveted and stitched with bright orange thread

★ Comfortable side opening style .. four big patch pockets

★ And, at Sears low price— A GRAND VALUE

Blue Jeans . . . the casual style, sturdy Sanforized washability (won't shrink over 1%) that have made *Blue Jeans* so popular, plus special styling for the feminine figure. That means no bunching at the waist, no binding at the hips. Wear them to work or to school, at home or in the garden. Side opening at left side fastens with buttons. Two front and two hip patch pockets. Belt loops. Strongly stitched and copper riveted. At Sears low price, a Big, Big Bargain. Belts not included.

Waist sizes 22, 24, 26, 28, 30, 32 and 34 inches in one average length. *Please state waist size and give catalog number of fabric.* Choice of four Sanforized cottons. Shipping weight each 1 pound 9 ounces.

41 K 5—Dark blue denim.
41 K 1—Medium blue herringbone drill
41 K 2—Medium blue twill
41 K 3—Medium blue covert........$1.98

Smart new Shirts

Colorful Plaids. Man-styled to Hercules exacting specifications of one of the finest cotton flannels **$2.79** **Plaid** we've ever seen. Sanforized (won't shrink over 1%), sunfast and washfast. Action-back yoke, sports collar, chest pocket. Long sleeves with 2-button adjustable cuffs. Long shirt tail. *Please state bust size* 30, 32, 34, 36, 38, 40, 42 and 44 inches. Shipping weight each 12 ounces.
41 K 9036A—Red and black
41 K 9037A—Green and black.....$2.79

Chambray Shirt. Same style as above in Sanforized washable cotton chambray. *Sizes above. State size.* Shpg. wt. 12 oz.
41 K 9020A—Blue chambray........$1.49

SIZES 6 TO 18

SEE OUR LOW PRICED
TEE SHIRTS ON PAGE 107

YIPPEE!

Cowboy-style
Blue denim
SADDLE PANTS

• copper riveted
• orange stitched

8-oz. denim—Western style $1⁹⁵

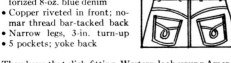

• Sears famous sunfast—San-forized 8-oz. blue denim
• Copper riveted in front; no-mar thread bar-tacked back
• Narrow legs, 3-in. turn-up
• 5 pockets; yoke back

They have that slick-fitting, Western look young Americans want! Copper riveted in front; thread bar-tacked in back; double stitched with strong orange thread. 2 front swing pockets of heavy drill; 2 back patch pockets; watch pocket. Snap fastener waist. Western-style yoke back. Rustproof buttons riveted on to stay. Sanforized, fabric shrinkage 1%. Wash separately.

State size 6, 8, 10, 12, 14, 16. See Chart A at right, below. Shipping weight 1 lb. 7 oz. Belt not included.
50 L 9140—Deep tone blue Saddle Pants........$1.95

112 . . SEARS, ROEBUCK AND CO. ₂PB

Sears sunfast-Sanforized 8-oz. blue denim

Full-cut Bib Overalls **$1.88**

• Full size bib compartment
• Special full-cut, roomy sizes
• 4 pockets (2 front swing type)

Save your boy's dress-up clothes . . . let these super-tough bib overalls take the hard knocks. Same heavy quality, same strong construction as men's. Sunfast—Sanforized, fabric won't shrink over 1%. Bib compartment has watch pocket, pencil slot and utility pocket. 2 front, 2 back pockets. Rustproof riveted buttons. Double stitched Bar-tacked. Sears full cut sizes allow greater crotch-to-shoulder length. Wash separately.
State size 6, 8, 10, 12, 14, 16. See chart B. Shpg. wt. 1 lb. 10 oz.
50 L 9119...............$1.88

Copper riveted Jeans **$1.77**

• Copper riveted strain points
• Double-needle orange stitching
• 5 handy pockets (2 swing type)

Our best sellers! Extra heavy for extra wear. Sunfast—Sanforized, fabric won't shrink over 1%. All points of strain reinforced with tough copper rivets or heavy thread bar-tacks. Western-style front swing pockets; 2 back patch pockets; watch pocket. Rustproof buttons riveted on. Comfortable yoke back. Well turned double stitched seams—no raw edges. Wash separately. Belt not included. Order 2 pairs—then you'll have a spare.
State size 6, 8, 10, 12, 14, 16. See chart B. Shpg. wt. 1 lb. 6 oz.
50 L 9120...............$1.77

Gabardine Outfit

Shirt	Pants
$1.98	**$2.69**

• Washfast—Sanforized for fit
• Buy shirt and pants as outfit

Army-type cotton gabardine twill in washfast tan color. Sanforized, fabric won't shrink over 1%. Comfortable shirt in 6-oz. cloth has dress collar, 2 handy pockets. Pants in heavier 8.2-oz. fabric; 5 pockets. Easy-to-alter outlet seam in back. Double stitched; bar-tack reinforcements at strain points.
State size 8, 10, 12, 14, 16, 18. See size charts on opposite page. Belt not included.
40 L 307M—Shirt. Shipping weight 14 ounces........$1.98
40 L 507M—Pants. Shipping weight 1 pound 8 ounces..$2.69

CHART A—HOW TO ORDER SADDLE PANTS
(50L9140) Measure waist around body over trousers without belt. Extra long inseam lengths allow for cowboy style turn-up. Order nearest size.

SIZE	6	8	10	12	14	16
Waist, inches	23½	24½	25½	26½	27½	28½
Actual inseam, inches	21½	24½	27	29½	32	34

CHART B—HOW TO ORDER BLUE DENIMS
(50L9119 and 50L9120) Measure waist over trousers without belt. Measure leg inseam from crotch to heel. Order nearest size from chart below.

SIZE	6	8	10	12	14	16
Waist, inches	23½	24½	25½	26½	27½	28½
Inseam, inches	19	22	25	27	29	30

Add boys' clothing to your easy terms order—see inside back cover

GRADE SCHOOL CROWD

SIZES 7 TO 14

COOL-OFF COTTONS look pretty .. play-hard Playsuits

and a smart Jumper in gay prints and plain .. some have snug-hug

elastic shirred waistbands .. all washable .. all Sears low priced

SEARS VALUE
Sanforized Chambray
1-Piece Playsuit

$189

- Rich-looking multicolor stripes
- Neat adjustable shoulder straps
- Plenty of spicy red ric-rac trimming
- Shorts deeply pleated for action
- Has sleek-fitting, set-in waistband

This playsuit has everything, including a Sears easy-to-buy low price. The sturdy fabric is crisp, Sanforized chambray (max. fabric shrinkage 1%), in a gay, multicolor stripe. The stripes are wisely used to show off its good lines. Cute bow sash in back. Washable. *Sizes 7, 8, 10, 12, 14. Please state size.* Shipping weight 14 ounces.
98 L 5534—Yellow and green stripes
Each.........................$1.89

58 .. SEARS, ROEBUCK AND CO. ALL

$2.49

Midriff Set

A Midriff two-piecer in a colorful cotton print. Fashionable big bertha collar, trimmed with ric-rac and snowy white eyelet embroidery. Elastic shirring hugs full-gathered skirt to waistline. Buttons down back. Washable. A wonderful value. *Sizes 7, 8, 10, 12, 14. Please state size.* Shpg. wt. 1 lb.
98 L 5537—Yellow print
98 L 5538—Rose pink print
98 L 5539—Blue print
Each, set.........$2.49

$1.98

2-Pc. Playsuit

B Bra and short print playsuit is made for cool comfort as well as flattery. Bra has wonderful elastic shirring on top and bottom for snug fit. Can be worn with or without the neck ties. Shorts have elastic shirred waistband. Washable cotton, wears beautifully. *Sizes 7, 8, 10, 12, 14. Please state size.* Shpg. wt. 14 oz.
98 L 5535—Yellow print
98 L 5536—Blue print
2-piece playsuit.... $1.98

$2.98

2-Pc. Playsuit

C Sanforized chambray classic two-piecer (max. fabric shrink. 1%). Trim, all-in-one playsuit has notched collar, patch pocket, button front to below waistline. Shorts are front-pleated for action. Full gathered skirt with wide elastic-shirred waistband. Washable. A grand buy. *Sizes 7, 8, 10, 12, 14. State size.*
98 L 5540—Medium blue
98 L 5541—Light green
2-piece playsuit.....$2.98

$2.29

Cotton Jumper

D Cotton poplin jumper will team beautifully with blouses and polo-shirts. Deep V-neckline, smart cap sleeves edged with gay contrasting looped braid. More braid on full-gathered dirndl skirt, 2 patch pockets. Washable. (Blouse sold on page 61.) *Sizes 7, 8, 10, 12, 14. State size.* Shpg. wt. 6 oz.
98 L 5452—Medium blue
98 L 5453—Pink
98 L 5454—Light green
Each..............$2.29

Size Scale for Sizes 7 to 14				
Order size.....	7	8	10	12	14
If chest is........	26	27	29	30½	32 in.
If waist is......	23	23½	24½	25½	26½ in.
If hips are......	27½	28½	31	33	35 in.
Slack length....	31	32½	35½	37	38½ in.
(incl. waistband)				

Sears Easy Terms Are Available

Time to select your daughter's summer wardrobe. Add all her new things to your Easy Terms order... available on amount of $10.00 or more. Once you have an open account on our books, you'll find it a real convenience. As you need new things, add them to your present account. See inside back cover of this catalog for complete details.

HONEYLANE
THE RIGHT WAY
TO SAY
GIRLS' WEAR

A $2.29

B $1.98 $1.79
Pedal Jeans   Shirt

C $2.29

D $1.98

E
$2.98
Suit

F $1.69

G $1.39

- PCBKMN 59 .. GIRLS' WEAR

"BLU SURF SPORT DENIM" .. a famous Joshua L. Baily fabric .. Sanforized*(maximum fabric shrinkage 1%) .. extra sturdy, made into a sun-fun wardrobe for sizes 7 to 14

A **RIC-RAC PLAYSUIT**, is smartly cuffed, neatly nipped at waist by a set-in band. Back-buttoning, darts for good line, good fit. 2 patch pockets, built up bib top, sun back. Full cut for action, well stitched for wear. Wash separately. Sizes 7, 8, 10, 12, 14; scale on opposite page. *Please state size.* Shpg. weight 1 pound.
98 L 5532—Light blue . . $2.29
98 L 5533—Barn red . . . 2.29

D **BRONCO-BUSTERS**, newest thing in dungaree slacks, have colorful printing of the "Wild West" all over front. Red buttons at side, red stitching finish, handy back patch pocket. They are cut for action, made for hard wear. Wash separately. (Shirt sold on page 66.) Sizes 7, 8, 10, 12, 14; see size scale, opposite page. *State size.* Shipping weight 11 ounces.
98 L 5332—Navy blue $1.98

F **RED-STITCHED CUFF SHORTS** take tailoring touches from the boys'. Waistband loops. 2 pockets, button placket. Wash separately. (For Polo shirt, see page 66. For belt, see page 252.) Sizes 7, 8, 10, 12, 14, scale, opposite page. *State size.* Shpg. wt. 6 oz.
98 L 5626—Light blue $1.69
98 L 5627—Barn red 1.69

B **PEDAL JEANS** with colorful "boy-meets-girl" printing on pockets. Red-button side placket. Wash separately. Sizes 7, 8, 10, 12, 14; scale, opposite page. *State size.* Shpg. wt. 8 oz.
98 L 5318—Light blue . . $1.98
98 L 5319—Barn red . . . 1.98
Woven Cotton Gingham check shirt. Washable. Sizes above. *State size.* Shpg. wt. 8 oz.
98 L 5780—Blue, white . . $1.79
98 L 5781—Red, white . . 1.79

E **SUPER SLACK SUIT** has a classic tailored shirt of striped chambray. Teamed with slacks of sturdy denim, front-pleated, side buttoned, with pocket in back. Wash separately. Sizes 7, 8, 10, 12, 14; size scale, opposite page. *State size.* Shpg. wt. 1 lb. 4 oz.
98 L 5408—Light blue slacks, multi-striped shirt $2.98
98 L 5409—Barn red slacks, multi-striped shirt $2.98

C **BUILT-UP OVERALLS** you wear with or without shirt, has easy-adjusting suspenders, button back closing. Nicely fitted with pointy set-in waistband, tucked back for smooth fit. Two patch pockets. Wash separately. Sturdy-stitched for long wear. Sizes 7, 8, 10, 12, 14; scale, opposite page. *State size.* Shpg. wt. 13 oz.
98 L 5205—Lt. blue $2.29
98 L 5206—Barn red 2.29

G **ACTION-CUT SHORTS** with stitched-to-stay pleats in front. Side-button placket-closing, darts in back for smooth fit. Wash separately. Wonderful with all your shirts and halters. Sizes 7, 8, 10, 12, 14; size scale, opposite page. *State size.* Shpg. wt. 6 oz.
98 L 5624—Light blue $1.39
98 L 5625—Barn red 1.39

SIZES 10 TO 16

FOR THE HIGH SCHOOL CROWD

Sears has a
reputation for knowing
the kind of fashions
Teens like to wear

It's a date . . and you want to look smooth and dreamy . .

Sears has the kind of dresses that turn Teens into glamour-queens . .

at prices that are unbelievably modest for such out-of-this-world smartness

Teens love to dance in pleats

$7.98

Swingy sunburst dress, pretty when you walk, heavenly when you dance. Sweet high neck with embroidered motif; leather-like belt to make your waistline slender. Just the dress for dating. Zipper. Spun rayon; dry clean. *Sizes* 10, 12, 14, 16; see page 1363. *State size.* Shpg. wt. 12 oz.

◆77 K 2730—Rose pink   ◆77K2731—Med. blue
◆77 K 2732—Kelly green Each $7.98

$5.98

COKE-DATER in two colors. Wide leather-like belt. Gored skirt. Spun rayon dress; dry clean. *Sizes* 10, 12, 14, 16; see page 1363. *Please state size.* Shipping weight 12 ounces.

◆77 K 2727—Rose pink and navy blue $5.98
◆77K2728—Medium blue and navy blue $5.98
◆77 K 2729—Aqua green and navy blue $5.98

$5.98

GLITTER DRESS for a glamour girl, with gold color metal nailheads at neckline; gold color metal belt buckle. Collar ties in back. Spun rayon; dry clean. *Sizes* 10, 12, 14, 16; see page 1363. *Please state size.* Shpg. wt. 12 oz.

◆77 K 2724—Kelly green
◆77 K 2725—Royal blue
◆77 K 2726—Bright red Each $5.98

$5.98

PLAID CUTIE, 50% wool, 50% rayon. White collar detachable for washing; push-up sleeves, silver color metal buttons down the front. Wide leather-like belt. Full skirt; dry clean. *Sizes* 10, 12, 14, 16; see page 1363. *State size.* Shpg. wt. 12 oz.

◆77 K 2718—Red plaid
◆77 K 2719—Brown and green plaid . . Each $5.98

$4.98

STRIPED SWEETIE to make you look slim and willowy. Definitely a dress to dazzle your date. Back of skirt has diagonal stripes too. Spun rayon; dry clean. *Sizes* 10, 12, 14, 16; see page 1363. *Please state size.* Shipping weight 12 oz.

◆77 K 2720—Navy blue and coral rose $4.98
◆77 K 2721—Navy blue and aqua green $4.98

Numbers marked ◆ shipped from Chicago, Philadelphia, Kansas City or Atlanta, whichever is nearer. Order, pay postage from Sears nearest mail order house.

MISSES'
Sizes 12 to 20

[A] **$3.34**   [B] **$3.44**   [C] **$4.14**

[D]
$4.84

[E]
$3.34

Kerrybrooke

THE RIGHT WAY
TO SAY

FASHIONS

[F]
$2.94

BLOUSES PRICED FOR THRIFT
and completely charming with spring skirts
190 . . SEARS, ROEBUCK AND CO. ₂ALL

THE GIBSON GIRL was a famous charmer . .

you'll be one, too, in a Kerrybrooke a la Gibson Girl

[A] GIBSON GIRL SHIRTWAIST has a big fluffy bow of black rayon chiffon. White rayon crepe with unusually deep points on collar. Yoke front with gathers. It's a gem at this Sears low price. Hand washable (remove bow). *Sizes* 12, 14, 16, 18; size scale on page 193. *Please state size.* Shipping weight 10 ounces.
⧫7 L 1872—White $3.34

[B] WOVEN RAYON TAFFETA right out of a Gibson Girl drawing with its rustle, its tiny checks, its puffy ruffled sleeves and narrow black bows. At a price that'll make you hurry to get it. Dry clean. Sizes 12, 14, 16, 18; size scale on page 193. *Please state size.* Shipping weight 10 ounces.
⧫7 L1875–Red and white checks . . $3.44
⧫7 L1876–Black and white checks 3.44

[C] DEEP ROUND YOKE follows the flattering line of the bertha that the Gibson Girl wore. Rayon crepe with wide tucks and scalloped stitching from shoulder to shoulder in front. Pointed collar with black ribbon bow. Buttons in back. Hand wash. *Sizes* 12, 14, 16, 18, 20; scale, page 193. Shpg. wt. 10 oz.
⧫7 L 1877—White. *State size* . . . $4.14   ⧫7 L 1878—Pink. *State size* $4.14

[D] BIG SLEEVES, BIG BOW for the 1948 Gibson Girl. Especially fine rayon with deep rounded collar, detachable bow of black rayon. Full sleeves, buttoned cuffs. Self covered shoulder pads. Hand wash (remove bow). *Sizes* 12, 14, 16, 18, 20; scale, page 193. *State size.* Shpg. wt. 13 oz.
⧫7 L 1880—Pink with black bow . $4.84
⧫7 L 1881—White with black bow 4.84

[E] POINTED BERTHA effect is adapted from a charming Gibson Girl fashion. The cotton lace looks like Irish crochet, but Sears price is down to earth. Rayon crepe blouse has round neckline and small bow. Buttons in back. Hand wash. *Sizes* 12, 14, 16, 18; scale page 193. Shpg. wt. 9 oz.
⧫7 L 1882—White. *State size* $3.34
⧫7 L 1883—Pink. *State size* 3.34

[F] MULTICOLOR STRIPES will go with everything. Lovely shades . . aqua blue, and white . . combine in the stunning pattern. Excellent rayon crepe. Cap sleeves, deep shirring at shoulders, bow tie. Hand wash. *Sizes* 12, 14, 16, 18, 20; see size scale on page 193. *Please state size.* Shipping weight 8 ounces.
⧫7 L 1879—Multicolor stripes $2.94

Catalog numbers marked ⧫ are shipped from Philadelphia or Kansas City. Order and pay postage from Sears nearest mail order house

MISSES' SIZES

[A] $6.94

[B] $6.94

Kerrybrooke
THE RIGHT WAY
TO SAY
FASHIONS

[C] $6.34

[D] $4.94 $4.64
Wool   Rayon

[E]
$6.94

EVERYTHING IS NEWS in these stunning Kerrybrooke costume skirts

Hiplines, waistlines, hemlines so new you'll want them all

[A] THREE-TONE PLAID WITH UNPRESSED PLEATS made in one of the new lightweight woolens that drapes with soft flattery. Unpressed pleats across the front give the smart hipline interest so important now in costume skirts. Zipper side placket and taped hem. An outstanding Kerrybrooke fashion in quality and good looks. Dry clean. *Sizes* 10, 12, 14, 16, 18. *Please state size.* Shipping weight 1 lb. 4 oz.
07 D 2875—Brown, aqua blue and beige plaid.... $6.94
07 D 2876—Navy blue, red and white plaid..... 6.94

[C] HEMLINE TUCKS ON DRESSY BLACK, a skirt with new interest from waist to hem. Made of Romaine-type rayon crepe, a heavy sheer that drapes softly. Unpressed pleats on each side start at front and continue around the sides. Zipper placket and neatly taped two-inch hem. Add one of our lovely new dressy Kerrybrooke blouses and you're ready for a special date. Dry clean. *Sizes* 12, 14, 16, 18. *Please state size.* Shipping weight 1 pound 7 ounces.
07 D 2880—Black.........................$6.34

[E] THE WASP WAIST WITH BONED GIRDLE and a skirt so wide it seems to spin even when you stand still. Rayon faille gives it crispness. The diamond shaped girdle rises high in front, a single bone underneath to hold it there. This, with the great fullness of the skirt, gives you a wasp-waisted look. Add a Kerrybrooke blouse and wear it everywhere. Zipper at center back. Dry clean. *Sizes* 10, 12, 14, 16, 18. *Please state size.* Shipping weight 1 lb. 5 oz.
07 D 2874—Black...........................$6.94

[B] THE CUMMERBUND SKIRT in lightweight all wool flannel with the wide draped girdle you've admired in the fashion magazines. Cummerbund is shirred at left side only, so you can pull it high or crush it low as you please. Four gores give a graceful swing. Side placket zips to top of shirring. Taped hem. Dry clean. *Sizes* 12, 14, 16, 18. *Please state size.*
07 D 2877—Menswear gray   07 D 2879—Spice brown
07 D 2878—Black   Each............$6.94

[D] SLIM WITH SCALLOPED TIERS, so wearable we've had it made in two fabrics. Scalloped tiers in front with a deep slit at center hemline. Hipline darts at back for fit. Zipper placket, two-inch taped hem. Dry clean. *Sizes* 12, 14, 16, 18, 20. *State size. In All Wool Flannel.* Shipping weight 1 lb. 3 oz.
07 D 2881—Light gray   07 D 2883—Black
07 D 2882—Dark brown   Each...............$4.94
Firm Black Rayon. Shipping weight 1 pound 3 ounces.
07 D 2884—Black...........................$4.64

Sears Measurements for Misses' Skirts . . Order the same size whether you buy one of our low priced skirts or our best quality . . check your measurements below.

Order size	10	12	14	16	18	20
If hips are	34	35	36½	38	39½	41 in.
If waist is	24	25½	27	28½	30	32 in.
Length (below band)	29½	30	30	30	30½	30½

Catalog Numbers beginning with "0" shipped from Philadelphia or Kansas City. Please order and pay postage only from your nearest Sears mail order house.

JUNIORS' SIZES

$12.98

$12.98

$13.98

$12.98

DRESS AND BOLERO . . rayon faille
two smart outfits for the price of one

For very special dates . . an adorable dress with a big 110-inch skirt and a little nipped waist accented by a gold-color belt. For afternoons and street wear . . a wonderful bolero ensemble. Scallops all around the bolero and the neckline of the dress. 1-inch taped skirt hem. Rayon faille; dry clean. *Sizes* 9, 11, 13, 15, 17; scale, page 189. *State size.* Shpg. wt. 1 lb. 12 oz.
031 D8000—Black   031 D8001—Dark green
031 D8002—Turquoise blue   Each. $12.98

REAL ERMINE TAILS on rayon moire
. . regal elegance for sophisticates

A dress that makes you feel decidedly glamorous . . one you'll always remember. Big 115-inch skirt . . slim, smooth-fitting waist . . pretty neckline set off by genuine white ermine tails with black tips. Crisp, handsomely self-patterned rayon moire with the fine details and tailoring described below. One-inch taped skirt hem. Dry clean. *Sizes* 9, 11, 13, 15, 17; size scale, page 189. *State size.* Shpg. wt. 1 lb. 8 oz.
031 D 8003—Black with ermine tails. $12.98
031 D 8004—Dark brown with ermine tails. 12.98

Catalog numbers beginning with "0" are shipped from Philadelphia or Kansas City. Order, pay postage from Sears nearest mail order house. Use Sears Easy Terms . . see inside of back cover

THE 6 KERRYBROOKES
shown on these 2 pages are expertly cut and tailored, carefully and evenly stitched,
MADE BETTER 8 WAYS. . . . .

TWINKLING SEQUINS and the new
back-swept silhouette . . rayon crepe

A dress of great charm, skillfully designed to flatter you from every angle. Turquoise and gold-color sequins sparkle on the front. The scalloped peplum dips and flares to give you one of the most exciting new silhouettes in many seasons. Expensive looking mossy-textured rayon crepe. Back bow-tie belt and zipper closing. Dry clean. *Sizes* 9, 11, 13, 15, 17; scale, page 189. *State size.* Shpg. wt. 1 lb. 8 oz.
031 D 8005—Black with sequins. $13.98
031 D 8006—Dark brown with sequins. . . 13.98

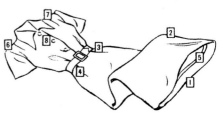

**JUNIORS' SIZES
9 TO 15**

A casual cardigan suit
with its own smart cape
that ties on . . or slips off

$21.50 cash
$2.50 down, $5 monthly

STUNNING TWO-WAY SUIT

Caped or capeless . . it flatters

A dream of a suit that leads a double life . . . the cape with its softly rolled collar makes it headline news . . . and it's only tied on. Whip it off and you have a cardigan suit. Makes Juniors look glamorous because it's new and smart. Expertly tailored in all wool crepe. Novelty buttons down the front and at the hips. The jacket is tucked at the waist to make it curvy . . . has a good quality rayon lining. The longer flared gored skirt has a side zipper. *Sizes* 9, 11, 13, 15. See size scale on page 179. *Please state size.* Shipping weight 3 pounds 2 ounces.
017 D 5120—Medium gray...........................$21.50
017 D 5121—Emerald green...........................21.50
017 D 5122—Black...................................21.50

180 . . SEARS, ROEBUCK AND CO. ALL

ALL WOOL CREPE . . has worsted warp for quality . .

curves and flares worth a whistle . . prices are low

$19.50

THE TIERED HIPLINE makes your waist look small . . . shows that you know what's smart for Juniors. The pert shorter jacket is the perfect partner for the longer flared skirt. Softly rolled collar with small lapels; four attractive buttons. Tucks at the waist make the jacket fit as neat as a glove. Good quality rayon lining. Rippling skirt has a side zipper. *Sizes* 9, 11, 13, 15. See size scale on page 179. *Please state size.* Shipping weight 3 pounds.
017 D 5124—Medium blue......$19.50
017 D 5125—Medium gray...... 19.50
017 D 5126—Cocoa brown...... 19.50

$18.50

THE EMBROIDERED SUIT has shiny black jet-like buttons set in two's all the way down to give it a date-time sparkle. Whittled waistline sets off a Junior's figure. Especially pretty in this soft draping all wool crepe that curves and flares in the new lines. Neat club collar is embroidered with black rayon braid. Good quality rayon lining. Longer swingy skirt, side zipper. *Sizes* 9, 11, 13, 15. See size scale on page 179. *State size.* Shpg. wt. 3 lbs.
017 D 5128—Medium gray......$18.50
017 D 5129—Emerald green..... 18.50
017 D 5130—All black.......... 18.50

Important Customer Information

Catalog numbers beginning with "0" are shipped from Philadelphia or Kansas City. Order and pay postage only from your nearest Sears mail order house. Everything at Sears is available on Easy Terms . . . see inside back cover for complete information.

FOR JUNIORS AND MISSES

$11.98

$10.98

$10.98
Juniors'
Sizes only

NEW BUSTLE BACK SUIT

in our best rayon faille

Simply wonderful, any way you look at it. Straight, slim front . . . rippling, bustle back . . . marvelous profile. One-piece skirt, seamed and zipped in back, smooth as can be over the hips. Unlined jacket with back-dipping peplum, gold-color metal buttons. Dry clean. *Juniors' sizes 9, 11, 13, 15; see size chart, page 130. Please state correct size.* Shpg. wt. 1 lb. 12 oz.
031 E 8200—Black...........$10.98
031 E 8201—Taupe gray....... 10.98
031 E 8202—Dark brown...... 10.98

THE "BACK LOOK" IS THE NEWEST LOOK, dramatic and different .. accented

with lace and scallops . . . both dresses in our best rayon romaine crepe

New butterfly peplum to inspire a backward glance . . . flattering front yoke of fine matching lace, lined in flesh color ninon. Moderately full 4-gore skirt. All around peplum, softly draped in front. Zipper down back. Dry clean. *Juniors' sizes 9, 11, 13, 15, 17; see size chart page 130. Also misses' sizes 10, 12, 14, 16, 18; see size chart on page 130. State size.* Shpg. wt. 1 lb. 8 oz.
031 E 8203—Black   031 E 8204—Dusty pink
031 E 8205—Aqua blue........... Each $11.98

New backswept skirt with pointed back yoke and rippling fullness . . . graceful and sophisticated. Triple tiered scalloped collar; slim skirt front with softly draped peg top. Zipper down the back; fabric belt. Dry clean. *Juniors' sizes 9, 11, 13, 15, 17; see size chart on page 130. Also misses' sizes 10, 12, 14, 16, 18; see size chart on page 131. Please state correct size.* Shpg. wt. 1 lb. 8 oz.
031 E 8206—Black   031 E 8207—Medium gray
031 E 8208—Navy blue........... Each $10.98

Catalog numbers beginning with "0" are shipped from Philadelphia or Kansas City. Please order and pay postage from Sears nearest mail order house. Use Sears convenient Easy Terms . . . see inside back cover.

THE 6 KERRYBROOKES
shown on these 2 pages are expertly cut and tailored, carefully and evenly stitched,
MADE BETTER 8 WAYS.............

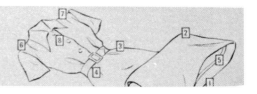

$12.98 Rayon crepe
$10.98 Rayon sheer

$13.49 Rayon crepe
$11.49 Rayon sheer Misses' sizes only

$10.49

EXTRA FINE QUALITY RAYON CREPE . . that looks and feels and drapes like

expensive silk . . same styles and prints in easy-to-wash sheer rayon crepe

New backswept skirt, draped peplum . . flattering from every angle. Beautiful pink and white flower print on dark backgrounds. *Misses' sizes* 10, 12, 14, 16, 18, 20; *also Juniors' sizes* 9, 11, 13, 15, 17. Check measurements with size charts on pages 142 and 143. *State correct size.* Shpg. wt. 1 lb. 8 oz.

In extra fine quality rayon crepe . . dry clean
031E9139–Black   031E9140–Navy blue
031E9141–Dark brown   Each........$12.98
In cool rayon sheer crepe . . hand wash separately
031E9142–Black   031E9143–Navy blue
031E9144–Dark brown   Each........$10.98

The new square neckline, softly draped . . full skirt in front and back. Bright multicolor bouquet print on dark or medium grounds. A dress that's equal to the most special occasions. Patent-like plastic belt. *Misses' sizes* 12, 14, 16, 18, 20; see size chart, page 143. *State size.* Shpg. wt. 1 lb. 8 oz.

In extra fine quality rayon crepe . . dry clean
031E9133–Black   031E9134–Turquoise blue
031E9135–Medium brown   Each...$13.49
In cool rayon sheer crepe . . hand wash separately
031E9136–Navy blue   031E9137–Medium green
031E9138–Medium gray Each..........$11.49

Catalog numbers beginning with "0" are shipped from Philadelphia or Kansas City. Order and pay postage from Sears nearest mail order house. Use Sears Easy Terms . . full information on inside back cover.

CRISP RAYON TAFFETA expertly

tailored the Kerrybrooke way

Two-piece outfit in sophisticated black with white plaid . . wonderfully flattering, extremely versatile. The front-flaring peplum fits smoothly in back. The 6-gore skirt is beautifully cut, looks smart with other blouses. Sparkling gold-color metal buttons down the jacket front and on the cuff pockets. Black patent-like plastic belt. Fine quality rayon taffeta; dry clean. *Misses' sizes* 10, 12, 14, 16, 18, 20; *also Juniors' sizes* 9, 11, 13, 15, 17. See size charts on pages 142 and 143. Please check your measurements (see page 123). *State your correct size.* Shpg. wt. 1 lb. 12 oz.
031 E 9145—Black and white plaid taffeta top, plain black taffeta skirt................$10.49

1. 2-inch skirt hems	5. Hems are carefully blind stitched, seams are pinked
2. ⅞-in. sideseams	6. Waist, shoulders, yokes are taped or double stitched
3. Zipper plackets	7. Good shoulder pads . . neatly tacked, easy to detach
4. Reinforced belts	8. Buttonholes are closely stitched, evenly spaced

Kerrybrooke
THE **RIGHT** WAY TO SAY
FASHIONS

JUNIORS' SIZES

BEAUTIFUL RAYON CREPE

finely ribbed, silk-like texture
.. same style in rayon alpaca

$14.98 $12.98
Our best rayon crepe   Rayon Alpaca

Two-piece and terrific .. taffeta-lined peplum, tab collar with handsome gold-color ornament. Dry clean. *Sizes 9, 11, 13, 15, 17; see size scale, page 189. Please state size.* Shipping weight 1 pound 12 ounces.

In our most beautiful rayon crepe
031 D 8015—Black...........$14.98
031 D 8016—Purple wine...... 14.98
031 D 8017—Deep blue....... 14.98
In our best quality rayon alpaca
031 D 8018—Black...........$12.98
031 D 8019—Sapphire blue. ... 12.98
031 D 8020—Cocoa brown..... 12.98

THE PETTICOAT DRESS

is flirtatious and romantic
in rustling rayon taffeta

$11.98

Smooth princess silhouette with a 120-inch sweep of skirt accented by a bright woven plaid ruffle of rayon taffeta. Fabric binding at the neckline ties in a bow to match the band around the skirt. Zipper down back. Dry clean. *Sizes 9, 11, 13, 15. Please state size.* Shpg. wt. 1 lb. 8 oz.
031 D 8021—Black...........$11.98
031 D 8022—Dark brown...... 11.98

IMPORTANT LITTLE SUIT

that's always on the go ..
crisp black rayon faille

$13.98

Brief fitted jacket .. 8-gore, 92-inch skirt .. a suit that knows no season, looks smart with a blouse or without. The scallops go all around the cape collar and the bottom of the jacket. Plastic and gold-color metal buttons. Unlined jacket. Dry clean. *Sizes 9, 11, 13, 15, 17; scale, page 189. State size.* Shpg. wt. 1 lb. 12 oz.
031 D 8025—Black.........$13.98

SWISHY RAYON TAFFETA

in black with silvery-white
checks .. 100-inch bias skirt

$8.98

You'll love the slimness of the waist, the sweep of the skirt, the rustle of the tissue-crisp taffeta. Rhinestone and jet like buttons. Smooth fitting midriff of black taffeta. 1-inch taped hem. Dry clean. *Sizes 9, 11, 13, 15, 17; size scale, page 189. State size.* Shpg. wt. 1 lb. 8 oz.
031 D 8027—Black rayon taffeta with silvery-white checks.........$8.98

Catalog numbers beginning with "O" are shipped from Philadelphia or Kansas City. Order and pay postage from Sears nearest mail order house. You can order anything in this catalog on Sears Easy Terms. See inside back cover.

Please check your measurements with the size scale on page 189. The same size will fit you whether you buy a low priced dress or our best quality.

THE 8 KERRYBROOKES
shown on these pages are
expertly cut and tailored..
carefully, evenly stitched,
MADE BETTER 8 WAYS

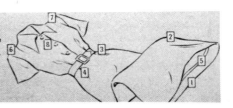

D $5.54

C $5.54

A $4.84   B $5.84   C $5.54

E $5.84

A Polka Dot Poplin with peplum

Cotton with a new fall look. Fine poplin with a collar that gives the new rounded shoulders, divided front peplum, white piping, contrasting bow and buttons. Buttons to waist in back. Artificial leather belt. Skirt flares with a swirly look. Wash separately. *Sizes 9, 11, 13, 15; scale, opposite page. State size.* Shpg. wt. 1 lb. 3 oz.
027 D 7030 — Navy blue and white. $4.84
027 D 7031 — Red and white. 4.84

B Two-piece Gingham ballerina suit

A ballerina flare in the stunning woven plaid gingham skirt topped by a ballerina jacket in solid color cotton trimmed with plaid. Its waist nips in, its peplum ripples. Plaid-covered buttons. Washable. *Sizes 9, 11, 13, 15; size scale on opposite page. State size.* Shpg. wt. 1 lb. 5 oz.
027 D 7028 — Blue plaid with blue. $5.84
027 D 7029 — Yellow plaid with black. $5.84

C Sanforized Chambray shirtwaist dress

The long sleeves are news, the matching stripes - and - solid combination is news . . . quality is typically Kerrybrooke. Sanforized chambray (won't shrink more than 1%). Gold color buttons, wide artificial leather belt, zipper placket at side. Washable. *Sizes 9, 11, 13, 15; scale, opposite page. State size.* Shpg. wt. 1 lb. 6 oz.
027 D 7020 — Light navy blue
027 D 7021 — Light brown
Each. $5.54

D Woven Rainbow Plaid Gingham with flirty ruffles

Ruffled hipline with white cotton embroidery at sleeves. Skirt gathered all around. Buttons in back. Washable. Sizes 9, 11, 13, 15; scale, opposite page. Shpg. wt. 1 lb. 2 oz.
027 D 7025 — Rainbow plaid. *State size.* $5.54

E Bright Navy on a curve with whirling red petticoat frill

Flashing red cotton print accents the new look in navy cotton with linen-like finish. Buttons in back. Wash separately. *Sizes 9, 11, 13, 15; scale, opposite page.* State size. Shpg. wt. 1 lb.
027 D 7022 — Bright navy blue with red . . $5.84

Catalog numbers beginning with "0" are shipped from Kansas City or Philadelphia. Order and pay postage from your nearest Sears mail order house.

FOR JUNIORS

A $5.84

B $3.94

C $5.46

D
Saucy
Back Talk
in a dress up
cotton
$5.77

134 .. SEARS-ROEBUCK PCBKMNAMG

JUNIOR COTTONS SPARKED WITH EXCITEMENT .. gay run styles ..

Kerrybrooke quality in fine fabrics .. all wonderfully tubbable

A SANFORIZED WITH DOUBLE PEPLUM that flounces all around the jacket of this colorfully striped two-piecer. It's made of washable woven chambray that won't shrink more than 1%. Peter Pan collar, turn-back cuffs, double tie-back sash, deep horizontally striped yoke make a big-hit combination of softness and sophistication. Gored skirt, zip placket. *Sizes 9, 11, 13, 15. See size chart on opposite page. Please state size.* Shipping weight 1 lb. 3 oz.
027E7042–Brown background $5.84
027E7043–Blue background.. 5.84

B SWISS MISS DREAM DRESS of Sanforized broadcloth (max. fab. shrink. 1%) makes you look as pretty as an old fashioned portrait. Blouse effect of white dotted swiss, embroidery trim. Self lacing criss-crosses through white plastic eyelets to waist. Skirt gathered all around. No tuck-in problem; it's one-piece. And so low-priced, too! Washable. *Sizes 9, 11, 13, 15. Size chart, opposite page. State size.*
027 E 7047—Yellow........$3.94
027 E 7048—Blue.......... 3.94
027 E 7049—Pink.......... 3.94

D SAUCY BACK TALK in broadcloth and plaid gingham makes this the junior dress sensation of the year. They'll say that YOU are something special, too, when you show off its breathtaking ruffles, its deep-necked gingham bodice, its big tie-back sash, its softly gathered broadcloth skirt. Washable. *Sizes 9, 11, 13, 15. Size chart, opposite page. State size.* Shipping weight 1 lb. 3 oz.
027 E 7040—Yellow and black................................$5.77
027 E 7041—Red and blue.................................... 5.77

C SANFORIZED WOVEN SEERSUCKER SUIT has lots of attention-winning details yet needs very little attention from you to keep it neat. Washes beautifully, needs no ironing. Jacket has 2 smart slits at waist in front; ties snugly in back, showing up inverted box pleat. Jaunty cap sleeves are slit to shoulder. Gored skirt, snap placket. Washable; maximum fab. shrink. 1%. *Sizes 9, 11, 13, 15, 17. Size chart on opposite page. Please state size.* Shpg. wt. 1 lb. 5 oz.
027 E 7044—Brown........$5.46
027 E 7045—Aqua green.... 5.46

Catalog numbers beginning with "0" are shipped from Kansas City or Philadelphia. Order and pay postage only from your Sears nearest mail order house. Pay for your complete spring and summer outfit on Sears Easy Terms. See inside back cover for complete details.

[A] $3.98
Sheer
Gingham

[B] $3.98
80-sq. Percale

[C] $7.95
Rayon Taffeta

[D] $5.98
Rayon Taffeta

HONEYLANE
THE RIGHT WAY
TO SAY
GIRLS' WEAR

DRESSY-LOOKING WASHABLE COTTONS with those

lovable wide sweeping skirts and feminine frills

that you find on more expensive dresses $3.98 Each

[A] CHECKED SHEER TISSUE GINGHAM has square ruffled yoke of white permanent finish organdy and medallion applique. Tiered dirndl skirt; tie-back sash. Washable. *Sizes 7, 8, 10, 12, 14; see size chart, page 48. State size.* Shpg. wt. 14 oz.
077 E 2110—Green and white check
077 E 2111—Red and white check
Each.......................$3.98

[B] VESTEE-EFFECT black bodice joins aqua plaid in washable 80-square percale. Cotton eyelet on bodice front and black petticoat flounce. Button back to waist. Tie-back sash. *Sizes 7, 8, 10, 12, 14; see size chart on page 48. State size.* Shpg. wt. 1 lb. 1 oz.
077 E 2112—Aqua blue plaid with black.......................$3.98

VERSATILE RAYONS for daytime wear or parties

[C] PRETTY PARTY DRESS in lustrous rayon taffeta. Four-tier ruffle skirt and self fold yoke with bow. Elastic ruffle edge sleeves. Dressy tie-back sash. Dry clean. *Sizes 7, 8, 10, 12, 14; see chart on page 48. State size.* Shpg. wt. 1 lb. 2 oz.
077 E 2118—Blue   077 E 2120—Pink
077 E 2119—White Each.....$7.95

[E] MULTICOLOR STRIPED SHIRRED RUFFLE sweeps around front and up back into provocative bustle. Full skirt. Bertha collar. Back buttons to waist. Spun rayon. Dry clean. *Sizes 7, 8, 10, 12, 14; see chart, page 48. State size.* Shipping weight 1 lb. 2 oz.
077 E 2113—Copen blue.....$3.98
077 E 2114—Rose...........3.98

[D] MULTICOLOR PLAID RAYON TAFFETA with crisp, cool-frosting white cotton embroidered eyelet ruffle on yoke and "peek-a-boo" petticoat ruffle. Circular skirt; tie-back sash. Back buttons to waist. Dry clean. *Sizes 7, 8, 10, 12, 14; see chart, page 48. State size.* Shpg. wt. 15 oz.
077 E 2115—Multicolor plaid..$5.98

[F] PASTEL RAYON FAILLE. Demure ruffled white cotton embroidered eyelet for front insert and puff sleeves. Bow at neck; self covered belt. Full shirred skirt. Back opening. Dry clean. *Sizes 7, 8, 10, 12, 14; see chart, page 48. State size.* Shpg. wt. 1 lb. 2 oz.
077 E 2116—Yellow.........$5.98
077 E 2117—Aqua blue 5.98

Numbers beginning with "0" shipped from Chicago, Philadelphia, or Atlanta. Order and pay postage from Sears nearest mail order house. See inside back cover for Sears Easy Terms.

[E] $3.98
Spun Rayon

[F] $5.98
Rayon Faille

ADORABLE RAYONS

with novel front and back treatments

for eye appeal from all angles

PCBAMG *PAGE 49 .. GIRLS' WEAR*

FOR MISSES

[A] $4.97

[B] $5.58

[C] $3.94

[D] $7.84

[E] $2.97

COLORFUL COTTON PLAY CLOTHES . . . they're Kerrybrooke quality and fun to wear

Each one is an important new fashion, and you can count on them to wash beautifully

[A] PRINTED PLAYSUIT with skirt to match in fine, crisp colorful cotton. Sunback playsuit with white "cuff" and ruffle at top, buttons in back. Stitched pleats in front. Button-front skirt with gathers all around has one pocket trimmed like the top. The whole smart washable outfit at a low price! *Sizes 10, 12, 14, 16, 18; Please state size.* Shpg. wt. 1 lb. 2 oz.
07 E 652—Aqua blue ground
07 E 653—Rose background
Each outfit.........$4.97

[B] SANFORIZED 80-SQ. COTTON shirred midriff playsuit in one of the new calico prints. Ruffled bra top with elastic at midriff (ties in back). Matching shorts button in back. Ruffled skirt slips over the head, with deep rows of firm elastic shirring to make it fit your waistline. Washable (max. fab. shrinkage 1%). *Sizes 10, 12, 14, 16, 18. Please state size.* Shpg. wt. 1 lb. 2 oz.
07 E 655—Red print. .$5.58
07 E 656—Yellow print 5.58
07 E 657—Black print. 5.58

[C] SANFORIZED DENIM outfit shows how smart and feminine this sturdy cotton can be. 4-gore swing skirt has white ric-rac bands, zip placket. Cap sleeved top has elastic shirring at bare midriff. Wash separately. (Max. fab. shrink. 1%.) *Sizes 12, 14, 16, 18. State size.* Shpg. wt. 15 oz.
07 E 658—Red......$3.94
07 E 659—Light blue. . 3.94
07 E 660—Gray...... 3.94
Skirt only. Shpg. wt. 11 oz.
07 E 2594—Red......$2.94
07 E 2595—Light blue 2.94

[D] SANFORIZED DENIM slack suit in the ranch style fashion that smart Westerners made famous. Tuck-in shirt top can be worn jacket style. Trimmed with rayon soutache braid, simulated pockets. Slacks have zipper at back. 2 pockets. (Max.fab.shrink. 1%.) Wash separately. *Sizes 12, 14, 16, 18. Please state size.* Shipping weight 1 lb. 12 oz.
07 E 882—Red with white
07 E 883—Lt. blue, white
07 E 884—Gold with black
Each outfit.........$7.84

SHIRRED TOP 2-piece sun dress in gay cotton $2.97

[E] MULTICOLOR STRIPED cotton, in beautiful colors combined with solid color cotton. The top is completely shirred all around with elastic, fits like your skin. Ruffle at top and below waistline. A narrow halter of self fabric ties at back of neck. Solid color skirt gathered all around. Washable. *Sizes 10, 12, 14, 16. Please state correct size.* Outfit shipping weight 10 ounces.
07 E 661—Medium green with stripes.........................$2.97
07 E 662—Yellow with stripes................................. 2.97
07 E 663—Black with stripes.................................. 2.97

Size Chart for Misses' Sportswear

Order size:..	10	12	14	16	18	20
If hips are...	34	35	36½	38	39½	41 in.
If waist is....	24	25½	27	28½	30	32 in.
If bust is....	31	32½	34	35½	37	39 in.

Whether you buy our low priced merchandise or our best quality the same size will fit you. Measure carefully, be sure to order your correct size. See measuring instructions on page 123. Use Easy Terms, for details see inside back cover.

Catalog numbers beginning with "0" are shipped from Philadelphia or Kansas City. Order and pay postage from Sears nearest mail order house. All other numbers are shipped directly from nearest mail order house.

Pick **BRIGHT, COLORFUL** leather play shoes for sun-filled hours

Easy-comfort platforms . . sizes for girls of any age

$4.98 ANY PAIR

N Play-minded wedgie. California-style platform, wedge heel. Adjustable instep strap, air-conditioned vamp. Searo-sole (rubber composition).
• C (medium) women's, misses' sizes 4, 4½, 5, 5½, 6, 6½, 7, 7½, 8½, 9. *State size.* Shpg. wt. 1 lb. 2 oz.
54 E 7297—Red smooth leather
54 E 7298—White smooth leather
54 E 7296—Black patent leather............Pair $4.98

R Leather tie for your busy summer schedule. Open toe, closed back. California-style platform, wedge heel. Searo-sole (rubber composition).
• B (narrow) women's, misses' 4½, 5, 5½, 6, 6½, 7, 7½, 8, 8½, 9, 9½, 10. *State size.* Shpg. wt. 1 lb. 2 oz.
54 E 7352—Black smooth leather
54 E 7354—White smooth leather
54 E 7353—Brown smooth leather...............Pair $4.98

P Smoothie Tie. Covered toe and back. California-cushion platform, wedge heel. Searo-sole (rubber composition).
• C (medium) women's, misses' sizes 4, 4½, 5, 5½, 6, 6½, 7, 7½, 8, 8½, 9. *State size.* Shpg. wt. 1 lb. 2 oz.
54 E 7928—White smooth leather
54 E 7925—Black smooth leather
54 E 7926—Brown smooth leather
54 E 7927—Red smooth leather...................Pair $4.98

T Fine company for your cool cottons, your pretty sheers. Pool-cool bracelet sandal, raised high above hot-pavements on a flexible California-style platform. Your favorite wedge heel, leather sole.
• B (narrow) women's, misses' sizes 4, 4½, 5, 5½, 6, 6½, 7, 7½, 8, 8½, 9. *State size.* Shpg. wt. 1 lb. 2 oz.
54 E 7328—Red smooth leather
54 E 7329—White smooth leather...............Pair $4.98

V Bracelet Siren. Slenderizing diagonal straps, foot-shortening bow. California-type platform, wedge heel. Searo-sole (rubber composition).
• C (medium) women's, misses' sizes 5, 5½, 6, 6½, 7, 7½, 8. *State size.* Shpg. wt. 1 lb. 2 oz.
54 E 7464—Red suede leather
54 E 7444—Black suede leather
54 E 7484—White suede leather..............Pair $4.98

X Haiti-inspired sandal. Sisal (raffia-like weave) upper and sole. 3-inch wedge heel. Wear it for all summer activities; choose a bag to match.
• B (narrow) width in women's and misses' sizes 4½, 5, 5½, 6, 6½, 7, 7½, 8. *Please state size.* Shipping weight 1 pound 2 ounces.
05 E 8074M—Red sisal, natural tan trim
05 E 8075M—Natural tan, brown trim
05 E 8073M—Black sisal, gold color trim........Pair $4.98

W Summer standby. U-throated leather tie; right for all daytime activities. California-style ½-inch platform; wedge heel, leather sole.
• C (medium) 4½, 5, 5½, 6, 6½, 7, 7½, 8, 8½, 9, 9½, 10. *State size.* Shpg. wt. 1 lb. 2 oz.
54 E 7341—White leather
54 E 7340—Black leather
54 E 7300—Brown leather...................Pair $4.98

Y Sisal (raffia-weave) shoulder bag. About 12x 7¼-in. Shpg. wt. 1 lb. 2 oz. 20% Fed. Tax included.
05 E 1780ME—Red and natural tan sisal...................$3.53
05 E 1781ME—Natural tan with brown sisal.............$3.53
05 E 1782ME—Black, gold... 3.53

Kerrybrooke
THE **RIGHT** WAY
TO SAY
WOMEN'S SHOES

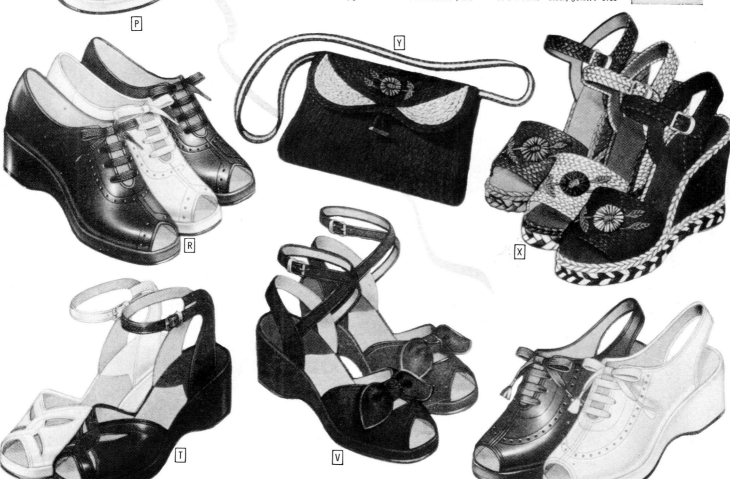

Don't take a chance on your shoe size. Measure your feet before ordering. See Sears 4-point measuring plan, page 1173

Now.. a
SPECIAL LOW PRICE
for America's favorite
Western sport shirt

- Sanforized novelty print design
- 2-way open-or-close collar
- In-or-out sport bottom

WAS $1.94 $1.55 Each   3 for $4.50

Fraternity Prep MADE OF A PACIFIC FABRIC SANFORIZED SHRUNK

For extra thrift, buy 3 and save even more!

We were just swamped with orders for this smart novelty shirt! So we bought more—plenty more—to get a sensationally low price. Now we can offer the same shirt made of fine Pacific cotton fabric at over 20% below the original price! It's a honey of a pattern—"Coca-Cola"* bottles and crowns in sparkling color "roped" by twirling lariats. Cool, comfortable short sleeve style with top quality Fraternity Prep workmanship. 2-way collar may be worn open or closed. Square-cut bottom—good looking in or out. Sanforized to keep its fit—shrinkage not over 1%. Clear, fast-to-washing colors. Double stitched. *Save more—buy 3!* Shipping weight ea. 8 oz.
  State size 8, 10, 12, 14, 16, 18. Size chart opposite page.
43 E 3300—Blue
43 E 3301—Tan
43 E 3302—Maize...........$1.55 each   3 for $4.50
*"Coca-Cola" is the registered trademark which distinguishes the product of The Coca-Cola Company.

Roy Rogers Trigger

A Wool felt rodeo hat $1.98

B Rayon scarf with slide $1.15

C 2-tone Western style Sanforized poplin shirt $2.87

See page 106 for Roy Rogers denim dungarees to complete your outfit

D Better quality shirt knit of blended yarns 69c

E Sanforized broadcloth 2-piece pajamas $2.59

F Colorful sweatshirt with thick inside fleecing 97c

G Trigger pistol and leather holster set $2.79

H Western style belt of embossed steerhide 94c

Other Western style belts on page 96

J Embossed saddle leather boots $9.85

Described on opposite page. Add Roy Rogers accessories to your Easy Terms .. details on inside back cover

SWIMWEAR styled in the California manner

. . choose matched beach set or trunks alone

Jr. sizes 4 to 10

[A] 4-Color Print Set. $1.10 Trunks. Sanforized, vat-dyed cotton twill—shrinkage 1%. Trunks have elastic drawstring waist and full cotton support. Matching 1-pocket shirt. An ideal beach and swim twosome.

State size 4, 6, 8, 10. See chart. Shipping wt. for the set 14 oz.
43 E 2830—Set, blue combination
43 E 2831—Set, tan comb... ..$2.98

Trunks Separately. Shipping wt. 7 oz. *Sizes* above. *State size.*
43 E 2822—Trunks, blue comb.
43 E 2823—Trunks, tan comb.. $1.10

[B] Boxer Style Shorts 98c for that trim, neat look on the beach. Sturdy, durable cotton twill in bright vat-dyed colors. Sanforized—won't shrink over 1%. Elastic waistband with drawstring; cotton support.

State size 4, 6, 8, 10. See size chart below. Shpg. wt. 7 oz.
43 E 2814—Tan
43 E 2816—Powder blue......98c

[C] Part Wool Trunks 98c in popular stretchy rib knit stitch that fits the body snugly and smoothly. Made of 40% new wool, 60% long-wearing cotton. Strongly stitched seams throughout. White web belt with rust-proof metal slide buckle.

State size 4, 6, 8, 10. See size chart below. Shpg. wt. 5 oz.
43 E 2804—Navy blue
43 E 2805—Maroon.........98c

Boys' sizes 8 to 18

[D] 4-Color Swim Set. $1.59 Trunks. Well made of Sanforized, vat-dyed cotton twill—shrinkage 1%. Elastic drawstring trunks with handy flap pocket and sturdy built-in cotton support. Matching 1-pocket shirt.

State size 10, 12, 14, 16, 18. See chart. Shpg. wt. for set 15 oz.
43 E 2928—Set, blue combination
43 E 2929—Set, tan comb. .$3.98

Trunks Separately. Shipping weight 8 oz. *Sizes* above. *State size.*
43 E 2911—Trunks, blue comb.
43 E 2912—Trunks, tan comb.. $1.59

[E] Boxer Shorts—can $1.59 also double as camp shorts. Carefully made of Sanforized cotton twill—shrinkage 1%. Vat-dyed colors. All-around elastic waist with drawstring; full cotton support. Flap pocket.

State size 10, 12, 14, 16, 18. See chart below. Shpg. wt. 7 oz.
43 E 2920—Tan
43 E 2922—Blue...........$1.59

[F] 100% Worsted $1.59 **Trunks**—give good service year after year. Knit of twisted wool worsted yarns in snug-fitting rib stitch. Comfortable built-in support of sturdy cotton. All around elastic waist for trim fit. Button flap pocket.

State size 8, 10, 12, 14, 16. See chart below. Shpg. wt. 7 oz.
43 E 2913—Royal blue
43 E 2914—Maroon.......$1.59

[A] 2-pc. set $2.98 Trunks alone $1.10

[D] 2-pc. set $3.98 Trunks alone $1.59

[B] 98c

[C] 98c

[E] $1.59

[F] $1.59

$1.89 $1.89 $1.39

Last Fall Price was $1.29   NOW 98c

WALT DISNEY'S collection of cartoon characters

All your favorites . . including Mickey Mouse, Donald Duck, Pluto and others in bright colors on sturdy, washable cotton playwear

$1.55 each

TOOTSIE ROLL SHIRT . . . only at Sears

- The season's newest, smartest shirt of mercerized, Sanforized cotton broadcloth in vat-dyed colors
- Short-sleeve classic style . . girls' all-time favorite

HERCULES
THE *RIGHT* WAY
TO SAY
WORK CLOTHING

A Was $4.89
$4.69   2 for
Each $9.19

B Was $4.89
$4.69   2 for
Each $9.19

Shopcoat
$3.98   2 for
Each $7.79

C Was $4.89
$4.69   2 for
Each $9.19

D Was $4.89
$4.69   2 for
Each $9.19

Shopcoat
$3.98   2 for
Each $7.79

E Was $4.89
$4.49   2 for
Each $8.79

F Was $4.89
$4.69   2 for
Each $9.19

G Last Fall Price Was
$5.45
$4.69 each
2 for $9.19

Shopcoat
$3.98   2 for
Each $7.79

H Was $4.48
$4.29   2 for
Each $8.39

Shopcoat
$3.39   2 for
Each $6.59

374 .. SEARS, ROEBUCK AND CO. ALL

Fashion Tailored
THE RIGHT WAY
TO SAY
MEN'S
CLOTHING

[A]
Same Quality
was $14.95
$12.95

[B] **$9.75**   [C] **$8.69**

LEISURE COATS for carefree hours ..
designed for complete ease of action
with the tailoring you expect in suits

[A] **Handsome ranch-style** .. masculine as a brier   **$12⁹⁵**
pipe, good-looking as a hand-tooled saddle.
100% virgin wool .. tough and rugged, yet luxuriously soft.
Four rodeo-style pockets; lower pockets reinforced with genuine
leather. Careful FASHION TAILORED workmanship. Padded
shoulders. Full rayon lining. Shpg. wt. 3 lbs. 2 oz.
Even sizes 34-46-in. chest. Shipped from Chicago; see below.
055 K 8275—Gray and maroon combination
055 K 8276—Palomino (tan) and brown combination.....$12.95

[B] **All-rayon gabardine** in rich, deep solid colors.   **$9⁷⁵**
A crease-resistant, extra-tough fabric in a style
as modern as television! Smart two-button jacket-style cuffs;
two patch pockets. Padded shoulders give better fit and a husky,
athletic look. Expertly FASHION TAILORED throughout. Unlined
.. all seams carefully finished. Shpg. wt. 1 lb. 10 oz.
Even sizes 34-46-in. chest. Shipped from Philadelphia; see below.
45 K 8266—Cocoa brown   45 K 8268—Maroon
45 K 8270—Gray....................................$9.75

[C] **Our lowest-priced leisure coat** .. 100% wool.   **$8⁶⁹**
A good-looking model that gives you a lot for
your money .. in fabric, in workmanship, in appearance. Rich,
suede-like all virgin wool solid color front. 100% virgin wool
collar, sleeves, and back in lively glen plaid pattern. FASHION
TAILORED to fit and look right. Two patch pockets. Rayon lined
yoke; rayon piped sleeve seams. Shpg. wt. 2 lbs. 11 oz.
Even sizes 34-46-in. chest. Shipped from Philadelphia; see below.
45 K 8263—Blue   45 K 8261—Tan..........$8.69

Our 'San Fernando' model   **$15⁹⁵**
in rich, all-rayon gabardine

Top choice for comfort and style. Smooth all-rayon
gabardine .. crease-resistant, long-wearing. Cut for
action with fullness and side gussets in back. Front
knife pleats. 3-pc. belt, stitched in back; side pieces
detachable. Saddle-bag pockets. Padded shoulders.
Full rayon lined. Shpg. wt. 2 lbs. 12 oz. See at right.
Even sizes 34-46-in. chest. Shipped from Chicago.
055 K 8272—Gray-green   055 K 8273—Gray-blue
055 K 8274—Maroon......................$15.95

476 .. SEARS, ROEBUCK AND CO. P

PERFECT FIT GUARANTEED

HOW TO ORDER: *State chest
measurement taken over vest.*
For all Leisure Jackets, *order
and pay postage from your
nearest Sears mail order house,
regardless of shipping point.*
Use Sears Easy Terms when
you buy . . . see inside back
cover for complete details.

Our new 'Santa Cruz' style   **$14⁹⁵**
in fine pinwale corduroy

The season's most popular jacket .. styled and made in
California, the sport style center of the world. Designed
for your casual moods, yet smart enough for all informal
occasions. Narrow pinwale corduroy has a soft, velvet-
like finish but takes "knocking about" in stride. Shirred
yoke, front and back. Padded shoulders; saddle-bag
pockets; removable tie belt. Full rayon lining. Really
looks like dollars more! Shpg. wt. 2 lbs. 6 oz. See at left.
Even sizes 34-46-in. chest. Shipped from Chicago.
055 K 8277—Maroon   055 K 8278—Green
055 K 8279—Gray....................$14.95

[B] Narrow Wale Corduroy **$7.96** **$8.96**
Misses'   Women's

[C] Sanforized Cotton **$4.96** **$5.64**
Misses'   Women's

[D] Dotted Spun Rayon **$4.96** **$5.56**
Misses'   Women's

[A]
100% Wool
Flannel
$8.96
Misses'
$9.96
Women's

All-Time Classic

PRICES ARE DOWN
Famous Kerrybrooke Robe
in 4 superior fabrics

- **Sears rigid specifications** assure fine workmanship and good fit
- **Generous overlap** with wide facings
- **Full length seams** double stitched
- **Shoulder pads** self-fabric covered
- **Trimming** .. smart piping and tassels
- **Belt loops** firmly sewed to stay on
- **Collar** contour shaped for smart fit

[A] **WOOL FLANNEL $8.96** misses' sizes
Beautiful warm wool flannel in glowing colors at our lowest price in years. White rayon piping and tassels. Armholes neatly overcast. Big pocket. Dry clean. Shpg. wt. 2 lbs. 6 oz. *State size.* Size charts, page 163. *Misses' sizes* 12, 14, 16, 18, 20.
027 K 7795—Royal blue...........$8.96
027 K 7796—Dark red............ 8.96
027 K 7797—Navy blue............ 8.96
Women's sizes 38, 40, 42, 44.
027 K 7800—Royal blue...........$9.96
027 K 7801—Wine red............ 9.96
027 K 7802—Navy blue............ 9.96

[B] **CORDUROY $7.96** misses' sizes
Warm, durable velvet-like cotton now lower priced. White piping and tassels. Overlock finish at armholes. Big pocket. Dry clean. Shpg. wt. 2 lbs. 4 oz. *State size.* Size charts on page 163.
Misses' sizes 12, 14, 16, 18, 20.
027 K 7805—Royal blue...........$7.96
027 K 7806—Bright red............ 7.96
Women's sizes 38, 40, 42, 44.
027 K 7810—Royal blue...........$8.96
027 K 7811—Bright red............ 8.96

[C] **SANFORIZED $4.96** misses' sizes
Cord-striped in white, tailored superbly, washable cotton (max. fab. shrink. 1%). Piping and tassels are bright red. *State size.* Size chart on page 163.
Misses' sizes 12, 14, 16, 18, 20.
027K7700–Med. red   027K7702–Med. green
027K7701–Med. blue   027K7703–Med. brown
Shpg. wt. 1 lb. 4 oz..........Each $4.96
Women's sizes 38, 40, 42, 44.
027K7705–Med. red   027K7707–Med. green
027K7706–Med. blue   027K7708–Med. brown
Shpg. wt. 1 lb. 4 oz..........Each $5.64

[D] **SPUN RAYON $4.96** misses' sizes
A real budget-priced value. Fabric is crease-resistant, ideal for home, travel or dormitory. White dots on colorful background. White rayon piping and tassels. Hand wash separately. Shipping weight 1 lb. 10 oz. *State size.* Size chart on page 163.
Misses' sizes 12, 14, 16, 18, 20.
027K7815–Navy blue   027K7816–Deep red
027K7817–Aqua green   Each........$4.96
Women's sizes 38, 40, 42, 44.
027K7820–Navy blue   027K7821–Deep red
027K7822–Aqua green   Each........$5.56

Numbers beginning "0" shipped from Philadelphia or Kansas City. Order, pay postage from Sears nearest mail order house.

Knit Nylon
**LINGERIE YOU'LL
TREASURE FOR YEARS**
DESCRIBED ON OPPOSITE PAGE

A $6.89

B $4.89

C $8.89

D $7.89

G $8.89

F $4.49

E $5.49

H $6.89

Charmode
THE RIGHT WAY
TO SAY
**WOMEN'S
INTIMATE
APPAREL**

330 . SEARS ROEBUCK AND CO. CP

Easy Terms inside back cover

M $7.95

N $6.85

P $6.85

T $7.35

$6.85 L
Better
Quality

$5.50
Good
Quality

R $5.85

GOLD BOND CASUALS . . Easy-on-the-eye with their
bold lines . . Wear anyplace, anytime; with blue-jeans or suits

Any 2
$1.44 ties
on this page
$2⁷⁴

S $1.44   T 94c   U $1.44   V 94c   W $1.44   X $1.44   Y 94c   Z $1.44

AA
94c

PILGRIM CELANESE* RAYON TIES give you distinctive patterns in a riot of brilliant colors

SPORTSWEAR

4-season combinations .. put you
at your casual best, year 'round

Fashion
Tailored

THE RIGHT WAY
TO SAY

MEN'S
CLOTHING

A
Coat
$17.50

C
Coat
$14.95

E
Coat
$17.95

G
Coat
$18.95

D
Slacks
$4.98

F
Slacks
$9.94

B
Slacks
$7.90

H
Slacks
$13.95

C D 2-piece Outfit
$19 50 Cash $2.00 DOWN

E F 2-piece Outfit
$27 40 Cash $3.00 DOWN

A B 2-piece Outfit
$24 95 Cash $2.50 DOWN

G H 2-piece Outfit
$32 40 Cash $3.50 DOWN

Descriptions on opposite page .. Easy Terms details inside back cover

NEW AWARD COAT SWEATER

Heavy, warm outdoor weight . .
all fine new wool worsted

$4.98

• Grand for school, sports wear.
• Tops in warmth . . knit of the heaviest 2-ply worsted yarns.
• 5-inch felt letter included . . your choice of gold or white.

The handsome award sweater every boy wants for showing off his school or club letter. Firmly knitted of virgin wool that keeps its spring . . holds its shape. Wonderfully warm. Takes plenty of rugged wear, because it's knit of tightly twisted, strong new wool yarns. Neck and shoulder seams taped to assure proper fit; will not sag. Tubular trim at collar, front, and two lower set-in pockets.

Heavy, continuous ribbed cuffs. Wide turn-up hemmed bottom. Your choice of a white or gold colored 5-inch felt letter included at no extra charge. Letter is easy to press on. Hand wash separately.

State color kelly green, royal blue, maroon, jockey red, white. *State initial letter wanted, and initial color gold or white. State size* 10, 12, 14, 16, 18. See size chart on opposite page. Measure . . to be sure.

43 KR 2553—Shpg. wt. 1 lb. . $4.98

Roy Rogers

Rodeo Pants

• colorful 2-tone
• "cowboy" legs
• Western-pockets
• "Jeweled" trim

$4.49 Pants

Boxer-style
$2.39

$4.49

Yippee! Your pal Roy corralled 'em just for you . . . Rodeo-style pants. Sold by mail by Sears only! Heavy cotton cavalry twill, with narrow rider-style legs. Sanforized and vat-dyed. 2 "jewel" trim front pockets. 1 back pocket. No belt.
State size 4, 6, 8, 10, 12. See size chart, facing page. Shipping wt. 1 lb. 7 oz.
40K4001—Gray, green trim.
40K4002—Tan, brown trim Roy Rogers Pants $4.49

Rugged part wool longies at a price you'll find hard to match for this quality. Tightly-woven fabric contains 40% wool, 40% rayon, 20% nylon. All-around elastic waist for snug fit. 2 pockets, serged seams, fly opening. *State size* 4, 6, 8, 10. See size chart, facing page. Shipping wt. 1 lb. 5 oz.
40K3989—Med. blue $2.39

CLOTH FRONT COAT SWEATERS

CHECKED WOOL CLOTH **$1.94** FRONT, WITH ZIPPER. Attractive checked front of all wool cloth, closely woven for longer wear. Lightly brushed panel-rib cotton back and sleeves are sturdy, allow plenty of s-t-r-e-t-c-h. Full length, easy-sliding zipper. Shoulders are set-in for smooth fit. Tightly ribbed cuffs and bottom. Ribbed trim at two lower set-in pockets. Lots of warmth and wear for such a thrifty price. Grand for school, sports. Hand wash separately. *State size* 8, 10, 12, 14, 16. See size chart on opposite page. Shpg. wt. 14 oz.
43K2511—Luggage brown combination
43K2510—Blue combination. $1.94

WESTERN-STYLED **$2.98** WOOL FRONT, BUTTON COAT. Vigorous, exciting Western design with lots of snap 'n' dash! Tailored just like jackets cowboys wear for dress-up! 2-tone front of all wool suede cloth —soft-textured, yet rugged. Sturdy back and sleeves are lightly brushed ray-fleece (rayon-cotton mix) in firm panel rib knit. Smart whipstitching at front panels and set-in pockets. Ribbed cuffs, bottom. Comfortable . . . cut roomy for active boys. Hand wash separately. *State size* 8, 10, 12, 14, 16, 18. Size chart on opposite page. Shipping weight 15 ounces.
43 K 2550—Blue combination
43 K 2551—Maroon and gray $2.98

Roy Rogers
VIRGIN WOOL PULLOVER

$3.77

Heavy outdoor weight . . cozy-warm! Sizes 4 to 12

Exceptionally warm, rugged Roy Rogers sweater he can be mighty proud of! Jacquard-knit design of Roy Rogers on prancing Trigger, on both front and back. Closely knit of finest, springiest worsted yarns which have been tightly twisted for extra strength. Keeps its shape through lots of hard rough 'n' tumble wear. Attractive Western-style shoulders and sleeves. Tightly ribbed cuffs and bottom fit snugly, keep him well protected from the cold. Hand wash separately. *State size* 4, 6, 8, 10, 12. Size chart at right above.
43 K 2266—Gray and maroon combination
43 K 2267—Pine green combination
43 K 2268—Rust combination. Shipping weight 10 oz. $3.77

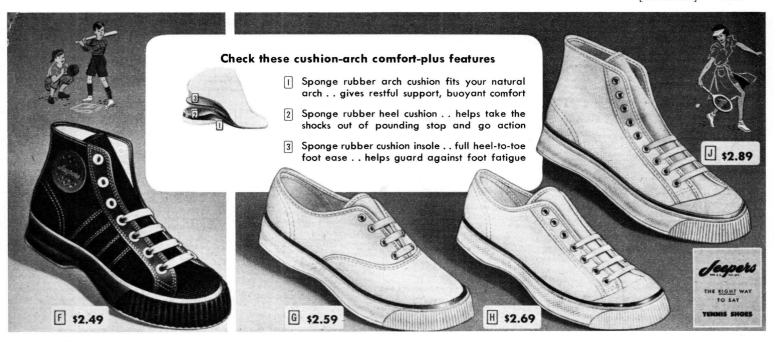

Check these cushion-arch comfort-plus features

1. Sponge rubber arch cushion fits your natural arch . . gives restful support, buoyant comfort
2. Sponge rubber heel cushion . . helps take the shocks out of pounding stop and go action
3. Sponge rubber cushion insole . . full heel-to-toe foot ease . . helps guard against foot fatigue

F $2.49

G $2.59

H $2.69

J $2.89

Jeepers
THE RIGHT WAY TO SAY
TENNIS SHOES

STURDY FOR SMALL BOYS

Cushion-arch heel-to-toe ease

F A sport champion. Takes toughest wear, gives lasting comfort. Wear-resisting black canvas. Durable spot cut, molded-type rubber sole; deep cleated for sure footed action. Shape-retaining counter, webbing backstay. Rubber foxing, toe guard.
- Small boys' sizes 11, 11½, 12, 12½, 13, 13½, 1, 1½, 2. Wide width. *See how to order high shoes below. Please state size.* Shpg. wt. 1 lb. 14 oz.
76 K 9562—Black. . . . . Pair $2.49

WOMEN'S, MISSES' CUSHION-ARCH JEEPERS

Shock-absorbing triple cushions, amazingly comfortable, a new thrill for play hours; extra durable

G Plain Toe Oxford. Cushion-arch built-in features give you playing ease supreme. Durable, porous white canvas; easy fitting. White rubber foxing, blue trim. White rubber toe guard reinforcement. Non-marking genuine crepe rubber sole.
- Women's, misses' 3½, 4, 4½, 5, 5½, 6, 6½, 7, 7½, 8, 8½, 9. Wide width. *How to order oxfords below. State size.* Shpg. wt. 1 lb. 14 oz.
76 K 9543—White. . . . . Pair $2.59

H Lace-to-toe Oxford. Snug, easy-to-adjust fit plus Cushion-arch Jeepers triple-cushion comfort. Helps you get more fun out of active sports. Strong white canvas. White rubber foxing, toe guard; blue trim. Non-mark crepe rubber sole.
- Women's, misses' 3½, 4, 4½, 5, 5½, 6, 6½, 7, 7½, 8, 8½, 9. Wide width. *How to order oxfords below. State size.* Shpg. wt. 1 lb. 14 oz.
76 K 9546—White. . . . . Pair $2.69

J Our Finest Cushion-arch Shoe Snug-fitting lace-to-toe style combined with firm ankle support and grand Cushion-arch shock-softening ease. Sturdy white canvas; white rubber foxing, blue trim. White toe guard. Non-mark crepe rubber sole.
- Women's, misses' 3½, 4, 4½, 5, 5½, 6, 6½, 7, 7½, 8, 8½, 9. Wide width. *How to order high shoes below. Please state size.* Shpg. wt. 2 lbs.
76 K 9557—White. . . . . Pair $2.89

K $1.69 8 to 10½

L $1.89 12½ to 3

M $1.69 8 to 12

N $2.29

EASY-ACTION JEEPERS

For small boys, children

K Brown canvas, brown sole, foxing or black canvas, gray sole, foxing. Non-skid rubber sole. No cushion-arch.
- Small boys' 11, 11½, 12, 12½, 13, 13½, 1, 1½, 2. Wide width. *How to order high shoes below. Please state size.* Shpg. wt. 1 lb. 10 oz.
76 K 9549—Brown. . . . . Pair $1.79
76 K 9553—Black. . . . . Pair 1.79
- Children's 8, 8½, 9, 9½, 10, 10½. Wide width. *How to order high shoes below. Please state size.* Shpg. wt. 1 lb. 5 oz.
76 K 9550—Brown. . . . . Pair $1.69
76 K 9554—Black. . . . . Pair 1.69

SURE-FOOTED JEEPERS . . for women, misses, girls and children

Lightweight, yet built for action . . sturdy canvas uppers, durable rubber soles

L Action-loving, right for gym classes, indoor and outdoor sports. White rubber foxing, protective toe guard. Lace-to-toe for snug fit. White canvas. Non-mark rubber sole. No cushion-arch *See how to order high shoes below.*
- Women's, misses' 3½, 4, 4½, 5, 5½, 6, 6½, 7, 7½, 8, 8½, 9, 9½, 10. Wide width. *State size.* Shpg. wt. 1 lb. 12 oz.
76 K 9539—White. . . . . Pair $1.98
- Girls' 12½, 13, 13½, 1, 1½, 2, 2½, 3. *Please state size.* Shpg. wt. 1 lb. 7 oz.
76 K 9540—White. . . . . Pair $1.89

M Durable, easy-fitting white canvas oxford. White rubber foxing, toe-guard reinforcement. Strong non-marking rubber sole. No cushion-arch features. *See how to order oxfords below.*
- Women's, misses' 3½, 4, 4½, 5, 5½, 6, 6½, 7, 7½, 8, 8½, 9. Wide width. *State size.* Shpg. wt. 1 lb. 11 oz.
76 K 9529—White. . . . . Pair $1.89
- Girls' sizes 12½, 13, 13½, 1, 1½, 2, 2½, 3. Wide width. *Please state size.* Shpg. wt. 1 lb. 5 oz.
76 K 9530—White. . . . . Pair $1.79
- Children's 8, 8½, 9, 9½, 10, 10½, 11, 11½, 12. Wide width. *Please state size.* Shpg. wt. 1 lb. 2 oz.
76 K 9531—White. . . . . Pair $1.69

N 3-eyelet Oxford . . . one of the most practical styles you could want! Trim 'n' tidy of woven cotton you can clean with soap and water. White rubber sole, ⅞-in. molded rubber heel. *Order same size as your shoe.*
- C (medium) women's, misses' 4, 4½, 5, 5½, 6, 6½, 7, 7½, 8, 8½, 9. *Please state size.* Shipping weight 1 lb.
76 K 9580—Brown, white trim . . . Pair $2.29
76 K 9579—Blue, white trim . . . . Pair 2.29
76 K 9578—All white . . . . Pair 2.29

How to Order High Shoes: If you wear A width or narrower shoes, order your Jeeper a half size smaller. (*Example:* for size 6 shoe, order Jeeper size 5½). For B width or wider shoes order Jeeper the same size as your regular shoe.

How to Order Oxfords: All except 76K9580, 76K9579 and 76K9578. For B width or narrower shoes, order Jeeper half size smaller (*Example:* size 6, order size 5½). If you wear C width or wider shoe, order your Jeeper same size as your regular shoe.

It's practical, convenient to order on Sears Easy Terms; see inside back cover for details

$7.98
Juniors' sizes
only

$9.98
Juniors' and
Misses' sizes

Complete outfit **ONLY** $9.98 Juniors' and Misses' sizes

NEW PETIT-POINT PRINT

hand screened on our finest
quality rayon romaine crepe

Soft shirring and bustles do marvelous
things for a Junior figure. Duco printed
design resembles fine needlepoint embroidery . . . fuchsia pink and white bow
knots on navy, sapphire blue and white
on black. Zipper down back. Dry clean.
Juniors' sizes 9, 11, 13, 15, 17; see size
chart, page 163. *Measure; state size.* Shpg.
wt. 1 lb. 8 oz.
031 K 9009—Navy blue ground.... $7.98
031 K 9010—Black ground......... 7.98

Measure .. to be sure; see page 163. Numbers beginning with "0" are shipped from Philadelphia or Kansas City. Order, and pay postage from Sears nearest mail order house.
Everything in Sears catalog is available on Easy Terms. See inside back cover.

EMPIRE MIDRIFF DRESS

in our most beautiful rayon
crepe that looks like silk

This is the new Empire style that gives
you an extremely flattering bustline and
a wonderfully slim looking waist. Midriff band, full skirt all around. Soft, finely
ribbed rayon crepe; dry clean. *Sizes* 9, 11,
13, 15, 17; *also sizes* 10, 12, 14, 16, 18.
Please state size. Shipping weight
1 lb. 8 oz.
031 K 9012—Black................$9.98
031 K 9013—Lime green........... 9.98
031 K 9014—Sapphire blue......... 9.98

DRESS AND JACKET ENSEMBLE

in moire-patterned rayon faille

Practically a whole dress-up wardrobe at one
sensible Sears price. The dress has a rayon
crepe top with a sequin collar, a 4-gore bias
skirt. The collarless jacket has fabric buttons
and bows, all-around peplum. Black with
white top, silver-color sequins; brown with
aqua top, aqua sequins; green with pink top,
pink sequins. Dry clean. *Sizes* 9, 11, 13, 15, 17;
also sizes 10, 12, 14, 16, 18. See size charts,
page 163. *State size.* Shpg. wt. 1 lb. 8 oz.
031 K 9015—Black with white top......$9.98
031 K 9016—Dark brown with aqua blue. 9.98
031 K 9017—Dark green with light pink. 9.98

1. 2-inch skirt hems
2. Wide sideseams
3. Zipper plackets
4. Reinforced belts

5. Hems are carefully blind stitched, seams are pinked
6. Waist, shoulders, yokes are taped or double-stitched
7. Good shoulder pads .. neatly tacked, easy to detach
8. Buttonholes are closely stitched, evenly spaced

$8.98
Juniors' sizes only

$7.98
Juniors' sizes only

$5.98
Juniors' and
Misses' sizes

$6.98
Juniors' and
Misses' sizes

MENSWEAR SUITING

woven pinchecks in crisp, crease-resistant
rayon .. looks and tailors like worsted sharkskin

PLAID GINGHAM..WASHFAST, PRE-SHRUNK

Dark, handsome colors
for year 'round wear

Black top of butcher
rayon; cotton skirt

New contrast color suitdress to
wear with or without a blouse.
Brief, nipped-in jacket accented
with darker color rayon gabardine
undercollar, pocket flaps and buttons. Slim 6-gore skirt. Dry clean.
Juniors' sizes 9, 11, 13, 15, 17 only.
See page 163. *Measure; state your
correct size.* Shpg. wt. 1 lb. 12 oz.
031 K 9106—Med. gray with black
031 K 9107—Med. brown with dark
brown. Each..............$8.98

Coachman dress with shining
metal buttons, overcollar and cuffs
of crisp white pique. 4-gore bias
skirt has side pleat and gathers
in front. Back bodice dips to a
V. Remove overcollar and cuffs;
hand wash dress separately. Silver-color buttons on gray; gold-
color on brown. *Sizes 9, 11, 13, 15.
State size.* Shpg. wt. 1 lb. 8 oz.
031 K 9109—Medium gray.. .$7.98
031 K 9110—Medium brown. 7.98

Beautiful multicolor plaid with
a sophisticated bustle back and
the long basque bodice that does
such nice things for your figure.
Won't shrink more than 1%.
*Juniors' sizes 9, 11, 13, 15, 17; also
Misses' sizes 10, 12, 14, 16, 18.
State size.* Shpg. wt. 1 lb. 8 oz.
031 K 9112—Colorful violet plaid
031 K 9113—Colorful brown plaid
031 K 9114—Colorful green plaid
Each.................$5.98

Choice of three multicolor cotton
plaids .. 4-gore skirt, won't shrink
more than 2½%. Black butcher
rayon jacket, hand wash separately. Waistline dips in back, triple
peplum goes all around. *Sizes 9,
11, 13, 15, 17; also sizes 10,12, 14, 16,
18. State size.* Shpg. wt. 1 lb. 12 oz.
031 K 9115—Black with red plaid
031 K 9116—Black with green plaid
031 K 9117—Black with royal blue
plaid................Each $6.98

Numbers beginning with "0" are shipped from Philadelphia or Kansas City. Order and pay postage from Sears nearest mail order house.

Measure to be sure

Measure your bust, waist and hips every time you order.
See page 163 for instructions and size charts. Be sure
the style you want comes in your size. Order same size
whether you buy a low priced dress or our best quality.

174 .. SEARS, ROEBUCK AND CO. CPBKASLAG

THE 8 KERRYBROOKES
shown on these two pages are expertly
cut, finished with fine dressmaker details
MADE BETTER 8 WAYS..........

Fashions that feminine America loves
Gay Ballerinas, sweet Baby Dolls
Sears money-saving prices

Also red or green
T $2.88

In suede or patent
P $2.88

R $2.88

N $2.88
Also in red, green

Y $2.88

Also black red, green
X $3.88

W $3.88
Also red or green

V $3.88
Also in brown

Kerrybrooke
THE RIGHT WAY TO SAY
TEEN AGE SHOES

N Red, green, or black. Youthful ballerina. Concealed wedge for greater comfort. Rayon faille collar binding; draw string bow. Panolene (composition) sole. Three colors.
• B (narrow) sizes 3½, 4, 4½, 5, 5½, 6, 6½, 7, 7½, 8, 8½, 9, 9½, 10. *Please state size.* Shpg. wt. 1 lb. 2 oz.
54 K 7248—Black leather.........Pair $2.88
54 K 7247—Black suede..........Pair 2.88
54 K 7591—Red leather..........Pair 2.88
54 K 7592—Green leather.........Pair 2.88

V Suede or leather. Fashion's darling in a charming anklet for round-the-clock wear. Narrow straps cross in front to make your foot look slender. Low-cut V-line throat, pointed back, wedge heel, Searo-sole.
• B (narrow) sizes 4, 4½, 5, 5½, 6, 6½, 7, 7½, 8, 8½, 9, 9½, 10. *Please state size.* Shipping weight 1 lb. 2 oz.
54 K 7600—Black suede..........Pair $3.88
54 K 7620—Black leather.........Pair 3.88
54 K 7621—Brown leather........Pair 3.88

P Merry ballerina, scooped low at the sides. Rayon faille band runs around the collar to meet a coquettish bow perched at the top of the quaint peaked back. Concealed wedge for underfoot comfort . . . Searo-sole and heel lift.
• B (narrow) in sizes 4, 4½, 5, 5½, 6, 6½, 7, 7½, 8, 8½, 9. *Please state size.* Shipping weight 1 lb. 2 oz.
54 K 7610—Black suede..........Pair $2.88
54 K 7633—Black patent.........Pair 2.88

W Baby doll pump; black patent or suede, bright green or red leather. Slender straps, lateral and diagonal cross the open vamp. Low wedge heel, strong Searo-sole.
• C (medium) in sizes 3½, 4, 4½, 5, 5½, 6, 6½, 7, 7½, 8, 8½, 9. *Please state size.* Shpg. wt. 1 lb. 2 oz.
54 K 7585—Black patent.........Pair $3.88
54 K 7580—Black suede..........Pair 3.88
54 K 7587—Green leather........Pair 3.88
54 K 7586—Red leather..........Pair 3.88

R Party-going ballerina dressed up with rayon ribbon lacing, a perky bow at the side. The scalloped collar is bound with rayon faille. Concealed wedge to raise your foot for greater walking comfort. Soft black suede with Searo-sole and heel lift. You'll love it with feminine party clothes.
• B (narrow) width in sizes 4, 4½, 5, 5½, 6, 6½, 7, 7½, 8, 8½ and 9. *Please state size.* Shpg. wt. 1 lb. 2 oz.
54 K 7609—Black suede..........Pair $2.88

X Brown, black, red, or green. Impish baby doll pump. Pointed back topped with a perky leather loop. Ridged moc vamp, low wedge heel, Searo-sole (rubber composition).
• B (narrow) sizes 4, 4½, 5, 5½, 6, 6½, 7, 7½, 8, 8½, 9, 9½, 10. *Please state size.* Shipping weight 1 lb. 2 oz.
54 K 7602—Brown leather........Pair $3.88
54 K 7601—Black suede..........Pair 3.88
54 K 7603—Red leather..........Pair 3.88
54 K 7604—Green leather........Pair 3.88

T Ballerina beauty for daytime or evening. Flattering V-line vamp; slender straps cross your instep, buckle at the side. Inside wedge for comfort, Searo-sole, heel lift.
• B (narrow) sizes 3½, 4, 4½, 5, 5½, 6, 6½, 7, 7½, 8, 8½, 9, 10. *State size.* Shpg. wt. 1 lb. 2 oz.
54 K 7605—Black suede..........Pair $2.88
54 K 7606—Black leather.........Pair 2.88
54 K 7607—Red leather..........Pair 2.88
54 K 7608—Green leather........Pair 2.88

Y Baby doll pump of Norzon wonder fabric looks like suede, feels like suede, soap and water washable. Low wedge heel, Searo-sole.
• C (med.) 4, 4½, 5, 5½, 6, 6½, 7, 7½, 8, 8½, 9. *State size.* Shpg. wt. 1 lb. 2 oz.
54 K 7539—Black Norzon........Pair $2.88

We invite you to examine *without charge*, Volume 1 of the American Peoples Encyclopedia. See pages 916 and 917 for complete details.

For smart shoes, shop from the wide variety illustrated here . . . For Easy Terms see inside back cover